OUT OF THE SHADOWS

Other books by Dr David Clarke and Andy Roberts

Phantoms in the Sky: UFO's a Modern Myth?
The UFOs that Never Were (with Jenny Randles)

OUT OF THE SHADOWS

UFOs, The Establishment and
The Official Cover Up

DR DAVID CLARKE AND ANDY ROBERTS

PIATKUS

Copyright © 2002 by Dr David Clarke and Andy Roberts

First published in 2002 by
Judy Piatkus (Publishers) Limited
5 Windmill Street
London W1T 2JA

e-mail: info@piatkus.co.uk

The moral right of the author has been asserted

A catalogue record for this book is
available from the British Library

ISBN 0 7499 2290 7

Text design Jerry Goldie Graphic Design
Edited by Lizzie Hutchins

This book has been printed on paper manufactured
with respect for the environment using wood from
managed sustainable resources

Printed and bound in Great Britain by Mackays Ltd, Chatham

Contents

Acknowledgements

Numerous organisations and individuals have assisted us in the research and writing of this book. We wish to thank everyone who has contributed documents, material, memories, advice or interviews and also our agent, Chelsey Fox, and the editorial staff at Piatkus for their faith in the project.

Friends, colleagues and fellow researchers we wish to thank individually include: Nick Redfern, Jenny Randles, James Easton, Ian Ridpath, Paul Fuller, the late Ralph Noyes, Nick Pope, Clas Svahn and Anders Liljegren, Joel Carpenter, Jan Aldrich, Bill Chalker, John Heptonstall, Richard Hall, Gary Anthony, Rod Howarth, Martin Shough, Mike Wootten, Martin Bowman, Clive Williams, Duncan Curtis, Steve Payne and Talbot K. Green.

Thank you to the public institutions, libraries, archives and organisations whose staff have assisted our research, in particular the staff of DAS4 at the Ministry of Defence and the Departmental Record Office (MoD), Andrew Brown at the Home Office, Alan Haywood and the Churchill Archives Centre (University of Cambridge), the Public Record Office, the British Library Newspaper Library, the Imperial War Museum, the RAF Museum, the Trustees of The Broadlands archive (University of Southampton), the Meteorological Office archive (Bracknell), the RAF Personnel Management Agency, the RAF Air Warfare Radar Museum (RAF Neatishead), the RAF Air Historical Branch (Bentley Priory), the American Philosophical Society and the University of Colorado.

Acknowledgement is due to the numerous serving and retired MoD and RAF personnel who have granted interviews or contributed their stories or memories to our ongoing research. In particular we wish to thank John Brady, Dave Chambers, Ivan Logan, Ian Fraser-Ker, Grahame Scofield, Les Arthur and Chris Hann of 23 Squadron, Geoffrey Smythe and Terry Johnson of 25 Squadron, Wing Commander Myles Formby and Juliet Formby, F. H. C. Wimbledon, the late Sir Peter Horsley, Air Commodore M. J. E. Swiney OBE, Sir Edward Fennessy CBE, Group Captain William Kent, A. Bardsley, Roy Bullers, Peter Cribb, Group Captain Harold Collins, Gerry Raffe, Alex Cassie, G. Burgess, David Roberts, Wing Commanders Stanley J. Hubbard and Frank Jolliffe, Squadron Leader D. J. Coumbe and the late Wing Commander R. G. 'Tim' Woodman.

We wish to thank the Trustees of The Broadlands Archive for permission to quote from Lord Mountbatten's papers.

We owe a pint to Paul Fuller and Steve Payne for proofreading the manuscript and both of us thank Carolyn for her constant encouragement, enthusiasm and attention to detail. Andy Roberts thanks Maxine Linford for the changes.

UFOs: A Saucerful of Secrets

Everyone in the English-speaking world has an instant understanding of the terms 'flying saucer' and 'unidentified flying object' (UFO). In use for more than 50 years, they are loaded with significance; they conjure up a myriad of images in the mind's eye. From the rocket ships of early science fiction to the late 20th-century terror of abduction, UFOs offer the promise of worlds inhabited by creatures far in advance of humankind. Creatures who come from so far to be so near. Aliens.

Belief in aliens has grown to the point where hundreds of thousands of people believe that the Earth is being visited by beings from space. This belief has been reinforced by the numerous books, films and television programmes that have documented in great detail the stories of those who claim contact with UFOs and their occupants. These experiences encompass everything from sightings of unexplained lights in the sky to full-blown 'close encounters of the third kind', while more sinister yet are the experiences of those who claim they have been visited by aliens, often since childhood, and 'abducted' for as yet unfathomable reasons.

If just one of these amazing stories is true then the world is facing the greatest crisis in history. Evidence that mankind is not alone in the universe would precipitate huge global changes. Religion, politics and social order could be swept away by the arrival of saviours or, worse, the fear of aggressors from other worlds. As with all threats from the outside, people look to their governments for knowledge and protection. Yet world governments have been slow to acknowledge any investigation of the UFO enigma. Since the first flying saucer reports in 1947, British governments have followed in the footsteps of their American allies and repeatedly denied any interest in the subject. In public at least, military experts have poured scorn upon reports of sightings and justified their indifference by claiming that UFOs are of 'no defence significance'.

Until recent years it has been practically impossible to investigate the British Ministry of Defence's (MOD) knowledge of the subject. Unlike the USA, Britain has not had a Freedom of Information Act (FOIA). As a result, public access to official files has been severely hampered. Public records have remained closed to scrutiny for 30 years after the last action taken on the file and even under this '30-year rule' many thousands of defence files from the early years of the Cold War are still being withheld because of their 'sensitive' content. Some files are withheld for over 50, 75 or even 100 years. It is not surprising, given this culture of secrecy, that a popular belief in a high-level 'cover up' of UFO secrets has developed.

Despite these obstacles, over the past two decades hundreds of files produced by branches of the MoD, the Royal Air Force (RAF) and other government departments have been released to the Public Record Office (PRO), and more become available every year. In writing this book we have drawn heavily upon the contents of these files as primary evidence to reconstruct the secret history of official UFO investigations in Britain. These have been supplemented by the contents of more recent documents which remain 'closed' under the existing rules for 30 years. Drawing upon our experience as researchers we have also been able to gain access to many formerly 'secret' files under a new policy of openness that is preceding the introduction of a British FOIA.

Official documents are open to many different interpretations, however, and can only provide a small part of the real story. They have to be placed in context by oral history, by the evidence of those who participated directly in the events. So the paper trail led us to high-ranking politicians, defence officials and scientists who had been involved in official studies of UFOs, studies whose very existence had been long denied. With very few exceptions, those we approached were happy to discuss 'on the record' their role in official investigations, other than where this impacted upon official secrets. Throughout this book we have been careful to use the real names of those who have provided testimony, and their identity and credentials can be independently verified.

We were also able to record the evidence of many military personnel who participated in dramatic UFO incidents that remained 'official secrets' for more than half a century. Many of those we interviewed were speaking openly for the first time of their experiences. Some were pilots or navigators of fighter aircraft that were scrambled to investigate 'unidentified' objects. Some had become convinced of the reality of UFOs after witnessing aerial phenomena while on duty. Some had fallen foul of the official policy of denial, finding their stories dismissed, filed away, 'destroyed' or deemed of 'no historical interest'.

Our enquiries satisfied us that contrary to official denials, during the Cold War at least, UFOs were very much of interest to the MoD and to all members of the NATO alliance. We found plenty of evidence of British government investigations of 'aerial phenomena' dating back to the closing years of World War II.[1] At a time of high international tension, elusive phenomena that were able to penetrate the most advanced air defences were of concern to the highest levels of government.

For a time in the 1950s household names in the British Establishment expressed their personal belief in the existence of UFOs and some believed they really were flying saucers from outer space. Intelligence studies of sightings were ordered by the MoD and their American counterparts, and when sensational media reports led to questions in Parliament, even pragmatic politicians were forced to take an interest.

These concerns were amplified at the height of the Cold War by the fear that 'unidentified flying objects', as the military preferred to call them, could as easily be Russian missiles as visitors from another world. It was as a direct result of this tide of paranoia that British official investigations of UFOs were drawn under the all-inclusive umbrella of the Official Secrets Act (OSA), with severe penalties for those who leaked information 'harmful to national security'. This of course simply added to the suspicions of those who believed there was a conspiracy to hide 'the truth' from the public.

The fact that belief in magical visitors from outer space emerged during the Cold War, a time when the future of the civilised world was under the continual threat of mutually assured destruction, says a great deal about how official history and the 'hidden history' of belief go hand in hand. Belief in ghosts, fairies, angels and now UFOs and aliens lies at the heart of human mythic imagination and can reveal much about the age we are living in and our hopes and fears for the world. Most areas of social and political history have already been documented, yet the UFO enigma remains one of the few areas of popular culture untouched by academics of any discipline. It is therefore as social historians and folklorists, rather than UFOlogists, that we have approached the greatest mystery of the 20th century.

Today historians on both sides of the Atlantic have access to many thousands of formerly 'Top Secret' documents that clearly demonstrate how world governments, specifically those of the USA and Britain, monitored UFO reports for their defence and intelligence content. This level of interest has led a growing number of people to believe that world governments are concealing UFO evidence from their citizens. This is the 'cover up' so ably articulated by TV shows such as *The X-Files* and *Dark Skies*. Proponents of this conspiracy theory claim that governments fear mass panic if the truth about the alien presence is revealed and have chosen instead to adopt a policy of silence. They point to the mass hysteria that, it was claimed, gripped the USA following Orson Welles' infamous *War of the Worlds* radio broadcast in October 1938, when hundreds of people became convinced that Martians were attacking New York.[2] Extreme variants of the conspiracy have it that some governments are in possession of crashed UFOs and alien cadavers, or in direct communication with aliens themselves, either working with or for them on some as yet undisclosed agenda. This would truly be the ultimate secret of the ages!

If any long-term coherent cover up of UFO information does exist, however, then it must operate at all levels of government and the media. It must encompass all the relevant written materials, from the briefest hand-written note in government files to entries in squadron log books to letters in the personal papers of members of the Establishment. Hundreds of politicians, service personnel, police officers, clerks and officials, over half a century, would be required to excise any reference to the reality of UFOs from official documents and the media. The number of people who would have taken part in this cover up would be vast, yet not one person has broken ranks to 'blow the whistle' on the greatest story ever told. Meantime, millions of dollars are being spent every day on space probes and radio telescopes that are searching for evidence of alien life. Would there be any reason for a conspiracy of silence if that evidence already existed?

At the other end of the spectrum of belief from the conspiracy theorists are the rationalists who are sceptical about UFOs and the debunkers who feel that as there is no proof of their existence they are not worthy of further study. From either point of view, though, a visitor from outer space would be the greatest event in human history.

Certainly the idea of deep government knowledge of UFOs continues within popular folklore. Those who adhere to this theory frequently point to the press as being complicit in the cover up. Journalists are often accused of being 'disingenuous' when they fail to give column inches to the latest wild theory or fantastic sighting, or it is alleged that the government has slapped a D Notice on information relating to UFOs to prevent publication. However, the idea that journalists, in particular, would be party to any cover up of UFO activity is ludicrous. Nothing motivates journalists more than the suggestion that information of any kind is being withheld. The very act of trying to prevent information about UFOs from being published would be reason enough for journalists to expose it.

The work of one award-winning journalist, Paul Lashmar, helps us to place the official secrecy surrounding UFOs into its correct historical context. Lashmar has made a detailed study of the role of the RAF in a programme of American spy flights over Russia that began at the end of World War II and reached a peak in the mid-1950s.[3] Although the RAF's deep involvement in hundreds of intruder missions into Soviet airspace was authorised by Winston Churchill, these facts remained 'Above Top Secret' long after the ending of the Cold War, with outright denial meeting every request for information. When Lashmar asked for copies of intelli-gence files relating to spy flights from British airfields he was told there was 'no trace of withheld records on overflights ... and it must be assumed that they have not been preserved'. Yet when pressure was brought to bear, these 'non-existent' files were suddenly 'found'. Ironically, when the journalist interviewed CIA historian Don Welzenbach, who had written the agency's own history of the spy flights, he was informed that his book was being withheld because 'a certain foreign country ... would not admit that they had participated in the programme... That country is Britain.'[4] What are the secrets that the British MoD still wishes to conceal, at a time when the USA and Russia are happy to come clean about their respective parts in this undeclared conflict? Is this an example of secrecy for the sake of secrecy, a tradition that has characterised the British Establishment for centuries, or evidence of a conspiracy more earth-shaking than the concealment of alien visitations?

Lashmar's search for Cold War spy-plane flight details in many ways mirrors our own search for the truth behind British intelligence's role in monitoring UFO reports. We too have been told certain documents never existed or have been destroyed in line with procedure, yet have found that with persistence and asking the correct questions the files have been mysteriously located and made available to us, often far in advance of their official release to the PRO. Is this evidence of a concerted attempt to hide the truth about UFOs from the public? Or simply the lumbering machinery of government administration at work?

By pursuing the British government's interest in UFOs to its source, this book aims to answer these questions and place the unfolding mystery within its historical context. We have followed the paper trail from 1942 to 2002 and searched diligently for traces of UFO secrets both in government archives and the memories of those who served their country in peace and war. Where we have found evidence of concealment, we have suggested reasons why secrecy was necessary. Rather than rely on what has been published in the past we have reinvestigated many 'classic' sightings from the dawn of the contemporary UFO age and sought out original witnesses and primary documentation. The answers may not be what you expect. But the facts that we have unearthed about government involvement in the study of UFOs are a valid part of history, of a 'hidden history' which has been concealed for so long because it exposes government impotence in the face of an unsolved mystery. Whether or not that mystery is indicative of a government cover up of the existence of alien spacecraft we will leave you to decide.

The real story of the MoD's involvement with UFOs begins in World War II. Not in a smoke-filled oak-panelled room in Whitehall, but in the cramped confines of the rear-gun turret of a Lancaster bomber.

Chapter 1

WHERE THERE'S FOO, THERE'S FIRE

'Soon after leaving the target our rear-gunner reported he could see two orange-coloured lights following us.'

Bernard Dye, mid-upper gunner, RAF[1]

Until the late 1930s flying had been the pursuit of the élite, available only to the wealthy or members of the RAF. The advent of World War II suddenly saw thousands of aircraft being flown daily, clocking up millions of hours of air time. It was only natural that with this increase in air traffic any unusual aerial phenomena would be experienced and reported with greater frequency.

In the UK both Bomber and Fighter Command were crewed entirely by volunteers who risked death flying mission after mission over enemy-held territory. Losses from enemy fighters and anti-aircraft batteries were appalling, with the average life expectancy being a matter of months. Pilots and aircrews were in a constant state of anxious awareness. Their lives depended on being able to spot enemy aircraft successfully or to judge correctly the height and type of anti-aircraft ordnance used against them. Each airman had to be on full alert, eyes scanning the skies for potential trouble. Experience was gained quickly and aircrews prided themselves on their observational abilities, confident they could identify and deal with anything the enemy could throw at them.

Foo-fighters

In 1942 reports began to circulate at RAF stations of unusually shaped lights and craft which came from nowhere to stalk bombers and fighters

								(1)	(2)	(3)	(4)	(5)
				YD –			TOTALS BROUGHT FORWARD	54·40	702·15	3·00	89·25	2·3
	1	BEAUFIGHTER	O	SELF	F/s Izowsky	NAVAL CO-OP. on CRUISERS						
	1	BEAUFIGHTER	O	SELF	F/s Izowsky	TORPEDO ATTACKS ON CRUISERS						
	2	BEAUFIGHTER	O	SELF	F/s Izowsky	SCRAMBLE on BARI						
	2	BEAUFIGHTER	O	SELF	F/s Izowsky	NAPLES PATROL	Got there at end of raid, 9.C.I. no help.				
	4	BEAUFIGHTER	O	SELF	F/s Izowsky	N.F.T.	Army throwing out quite a barrage on the				
	5	BEAUFIGHTER	O	SELF	F/s Izowsky	To POMIGLIANO	Naples Ha! Letting under Vesuvius!				
	5	BEAUFIGHTER	O	SELF	F/s Izowsky	NAPLES PATROL	Nothing happening at all.				
	6	BEAUFIGHTER	O	SELF	F/s Izowsky	N.F.T.						
	7	BEAUFIGHTER	O	SELF	F/s Izowsky	To GROTTAGLIE						
	8	BEAUFIGHTER	O	SELF	F/s Izowsky	N.F.T.						
	8	BEAUFIGHTER	O	SELF	F/s Izowsky	BARI PATROL	Scratch& about at O: ax'z Scr				
	9	BEAUFIGHTER	O	SELF	F/s Izowsky	To POMIGLIANO						
	9	BEAUFIGHTER	O	SELF	F/s Izowsky	NAPLES PATROL	weather foul. lightning rain etc.				
	9	BEAUFIGHTER	O	SELF	F/s Izowsky	NAPLES PATROL	Better weather but had k patrol at				
	10	BEAUFIGHTER	O	SELF	F/s Izowsky	N.F.T.						
	11	BEAUFIGHTER	O	SELF	F/s Izowsky	To GROTTAGLIE						
	12	BEAUFIGHTER	O	SELF	F/s Izowsky	N.F.T.						
	12	BEAUFIGHTER	O	SELF	F/s Izowsky	BARI – BRINDISI PATROL	S.F.A.				
	13	BEAUFIGHTER	O	SELF	M/k Izowsky	To POMIGLIANO						
	14	BEAUFIGHTER	O	SELF	F/s Izowsky	N.F.T.						
	14	BEAUFIGHTER	O	SELF	F/s Izowsky	NAPLES PATROL	"Screaming Dog-fight with the light"				
	15	BEAUFIGHTER	O	SELF	F/s Izowsky	To GROTTAGLIE						
	16	BEAUFIGHTER	O	SELF	F/s Izowsky	N.F.T.						
					GRAND TOTAL [Cols. (1) to (10)]	1249 hrs. 30 Mins.	TOTALS CARRIED FORWARD	54·40	702·15	3·00	89·25	2·3

Figure 1: **Flying log-book entry by Squadron Leader P. Wells, 14 December 1943: 'Screaming dogfight with "the light"'** (Copyright: P. Wells)

alike. These aerial phenomena have gone down in UFO history as 'foo-fighters', a term given to them by an unknown American airman in late 1943. No one is certain where the name came from and it may have originated in a popular 1940s cartoon strip featuring the character Smokey Stover, whose nonsensical catchphrase was 'Where there's foo, there's fire.' Alternatively 'foo' may have derived from the French word for 'fire', *feu*, as the foo-fighters were often described as being like a fireball.[2]

Whatever its origin, 'foo-fighter' was a term specific to the American forces. 'The light' or 'the thing' were the two most common terms in use in RAF squadrons from 1942 onwards. A contemporary example comes from 14 December 1943, when Squadron Leader P. Wells wrote in his flight log of a 'screaming dogfight with "the light" ' (*see* Figure 1). Wells said, 'Foo-fighters is a new name to me. We always called them "the light" in the squadrons in which I served in 1943–44.'[3]

Other aircrews rationalised their sightings as evidence of new jets or 'rockets' and referred to them in those terms in flight logs or at debrief-ings. They were more than a little fearful that new enemy aircraft or weaponry had been developed which could easily outpace their lumbering bombers or outgun the fastest fighter planes.

Research into foo-fighters has been largely confined to the USA, where numerous first-hand accounts of the phenomena have been discovered. However, researchers have had little success in determining the US government's attitude towards the foo-fighters. Rumours of a secret study abound, but there is little evidence to suggest one took place. In fact there is compelling evidence to the contrary.

Writing about foo-fighters in a CIA document, historian Gerald Haines noted,

> 'Fearing they might be Japanese or German secret weapons, OSS investigated but could find no concrete evidence of enemy weapons and often filed such reports in the "crackpot" category.'[4]

The Office of Strategic Services (OSS), a forerunner of the CIA, headed by General William J. Donovan. Author Warren Smith unearthed evidence to suggest that America's involvement with UFO research began when General Donovan took a personal interest in the foo-fighter mystery. Donovan and his staff eventually concluded that the foo-fighters were 'unusual, yet harmless, phenomena'.[5]

The RAF and Foo-fighers

Although the American aircrews' experiences with foo-fighters have been extensively documented, very little has been written about the British experience of the phenomena and nothing at all about how the Air Ministry or government viewed the matter.

Some airmen told fantastic tales about foo-fighters at post-operation intelligence debriefings and recorded them in their flight logs. Others were more circumspect, certain about what they had seen but unwilling to make official reports, fearing they might be branded as psychologically unbalanced or grounded for suffering hallucinations.

In the years following the historic Kenneth Arnold UFO sighting of 24 June 1947, when the term 'flying saucer' was coined (*see* page 47), former RAF personnel began to recall their wartime aerial encounters and wonder if they too had seen UFOs. Few of these encounters were recorded in the books written by ex-aircrews, but amazing stories were told to friends and relatives and eventually reached the ears of UFOlogists. Slowly but surely, first-hand accounts of UK foo-fighters began to appear in print.

UFOlogists were confident that if serving members of the RAF had reported these strange phenomena to intelligence officers there must be some official documentation concerning the matter. But despite years of searching, they could find no trace of foo-fighter type reports in official War Office and Air Ministry records. The Air Historical Branch of the RAF stated simply, 'We have nothing on our index relating to the phenomenon,' and official RAF histories gave no mention of the subject.[6]

It was not until researcher Jenny Randles interviewed former *Goon Show* star Michael Bentine in 1986 that anyone who had been in a position of authority within the RAF publicly acknowledged the existence of these World War II UFOs. Bentine had served in RAF Bomber Command as an intelligence officer responsible for debriefing crews after raids. On several occasions he had been told of lights which were 'pulsating and had flown round the aircraft'.[7]

Official reports to intelligence officers had obviously been made, but where were they? Had the RAF destroyed them, believing them to be of no relevance? Had they been covered up because the UFOs were German secret weapons? Or, worse, were aircrews reporting intrusions into our skies by something genuinely inexplicable, something truly alien?

That the matter was taken seriously enough by intelligence officers to warrant recording implies that the British government took an interest in these early UFOs. Any contemporaneous documentary evidence would, therefore, shed considerable light on a neglected area of World War II aviation history and indicate the way in which subsequent governments would treat UFOs when they became widespread in the years following 1947.

The First Encounters

One of the first recorded RAF foo-fighter encounters comes from B. C. Lumsden, who observed two classic UFOs while flying a Hurricane interceptor over France in December 1942.

Lumsden had taken off from England at 7 p.m., heading for the French coast. An hour later, while cruising at 7,000 feet over the mouth of the River Somme, he discovered that he had company – two steadily climbing orange-coloured lights, one slightly above the other.

Lumsden at first thought the lights might be tracer flak, but discarded the idea when he saw how slowly they were moving. He did a full turn and saw the lights astern and to port but now they were larger and brighter. At 7,000 feet they stopped climbing and stayed level with his Hurricane. The frightened pilot executed another full turn, only to discover that the objects had stayed with him. He then tried nose-diving to 4,000 feet, but the lights followed his every manoeuvre. Finally they descended to about 1,000 feet below him until he levelled out, at which point they climbed again and resumed pursuit. The two lights seemed to maintain an even distance from each other and varied only slightly in relative height from time to time. One always remained a little lower than the other. At last, as Lumsden's speed reached 260 mph, he was gradually able to outdistance the UFOs.

'I found it hard to make other members of the squadron believe me,' Lumsden said, 'but the following night one of the squadron flight commanders in the same area had a similar experience with a green light.'[8]

Lumsden's account was one of a growing number which reached the Air Ministry in 1942. By early autumn enough sightings had been reported to warrant an official statement and on 25 September a report classified as 'Secret' was issued by the Air Ministry's Operational Research section entitled 'A Note on Recent Enemy Pyrotechnic Activity over Germany'. It discussed the possible causes of the phenomena and concluded, not entirely convincingly, that they were new or misperceived types of German anti-aircraft shells. The report referred to them as 'Phenomena 1' and 'Phenomena 2' and suggested that more suitable names be given to them in a report being prepared by MI14.[9]

While some of the sightings discussed in this report may have been new types of flak such as 'scarecrow' (designed to mimic an aircraft in flames) or flak tracers, none of these prosaic explanations can account for the following sighting, which took place on the night of 28 November 1942.

Turin, November 1942

Recorded in a document stamped 'Secret', this sighting was thought to be of such significance that it was sent to the headquarters of Bomber Command. The covering letter, from the Air Vice Marshal of No. 5 Group, RAF, read:

```
'Herewith a copy of a report received from a
crew of a Lancaster after a raid on Turin. The
crew refuses to be shaken in their story in the
face of the usual banter and ridicule.'¹⁰
```

The document referred to an unusual sighting made by the entire crew of aircraft 'J', piloted by Captain Lever of 61 Squadron, based at Syerston in Lincolnshire. If a sighting such as this were made by the whole crew of an aeroplane today it would make headline news in every country in the world. As it is, this fascinating report has remained hidden for over half a century in a drab file deep in the heart of the PRO. The account, by an anonymous intelligence officer, reads:

'The object referred to above was seen by the entire crew of the above aircraft. They believe it to have been 200-300 feet in length and its width is estimated at 1/5th or 1/6th of its length. The speed was estimated at 500 m.p.h., and it had four pairs of red lights spaced at equal distances along its body. These lights did not appear in any way like exhaust flames; no trace was seen. The object kept a level course.

The crew saw the object twice during the raid, and brief details are given below:

After bombing, time 2240 hours, a/c height 11,000 feet. The aircraft at this time was some 10/15 miles south-west of Turin traveling in a north-westerly direction. The object was travelling south-east at the same height or slightly below the aircraft.

After bombing, time 2245 hours, a/c height 14,000 feet. The aircraft was approaching the Alps when the object was seen again traveling west-south-west up a valley in the Alps below the level of the peaks. The lights appeared to go out and the object disappeared from view.'[11]

Had this incident been a one-off sighting it could perhaps have been dismissed. But two distinct sightings of what appears to be the same object travelling in different directions raise more questions than answers. Even more baffling was the final paragraph, which soberly stated:

'The Captain of the aircraft also reports
that he has seen a similar object about
three months ago north of Amsterdam. In this
instance it appeared to be on the ground and
later travelling at high speed at a lower
level than the heights given above along the
coast for about two seconds; the lights then
went out for the same period of time and
came on again, and the object was still seen
to be travelling in the same direction.'[12]

It is difficult to know what to make of this sighting. Bomber Command was impressed by the sincerity of the report and the fact that the airmen were bold enough to repeat their fantastic story to their incredulous colleagues. The object resembles no known aerial craft of the time and cannot easily attributed be to misperception of astronomical or meteorological phenomena. The case remains one of the most unusual UFO mysteries of World War II on file at the PRO.

Pursuing 'Rockets'

Most foo-fighter sightings were 'passive' in that the phenomena simply appeared from nowhere and vanished just as mysteriously, having no interaction with the airborne witnesses. But there are several cases where aircraft were 'chased'.

An extract from Flight Lieutenant Mortimer's Berlin raid report from the night of 2 January 1944 gives a detailed account of one such pursuit:

'Engaged by two rockets in vicinity of
Halberstadt and later near Hanover, 90
degrees alteration of course made and
definitely established that rockets altered
course. Overtook us slowly, appearing with a
fiery head and blazing stern on a parallel
course. Initial velocity seemed to be fairly
great. Duration approximately one minute.
Disappeared without explosion.'[13]

Mortimer's use of the word 'rocket' to describe his encounter begs many questions. Although foo-fighter sightings were widespread, aircrews had yet to come up with a catch-all name for them. Because they were small and fast-moving, rockets were the enemy weapon the foo-fighters most closely resembled and so they were often called rockets. However, it is unlikely that they were actually rockets or jets of any kind. German technology was insufficiently advanced to develop any form of ground-to-air or air-to-air rocket which could 'chase' an aircraft. The German jet fighter, the ME262, only played a limited role toward the end of the war and was easily spotted by Allied aircrews. None of the foo-fighter witnesses who observed the phenomenon closely saw the outline of a rocket or aeroplane; nor did the foo-fighters ever shoot at Allied bombers or fighters – they just appeared and then 'disappeared without explosion'.

Another frightening aerial pursuit took place on the night of 27 January 1944. The officer commanding 49 Squadron was so mystified by the account that he personally asked the pilot, Pilot Officer Simpson, to amplify his initial report so it could be forwarded to the Headquarters of No. 5 Group. The report read:

> 'At 52 32N 13 03E, 2037 hours, 20,500 ft.,
> heading 082 True. A red ball leaving trail
> of yellow/red flames and black smoke at
> about 1,000 yards and at the same height
> dead astern. It was seen closing in. I dived
> to starboard and the object followed,
> appearing to fizzle out and then immediately
> to reappear. I turned hard to port and it
> followed us round in a tighter turn than we
> were in. When within 100 yards or less of
> the aircraft, it finally fizzled out.'[14]

On the surface this sounds as though it could have been a very bright long-lasting type of meteor known as a bolide. But bolide meteors are natural phenomena which do not chase aircraft. Moreover, these foo-fighter 'chases' were often of great duration.

Perhaps the most remarkable case of an aircraft being pursued by unknown aerial phenomena comes from the penultimate year of the war.

The Essen UFO

On the evening of 26 April 1944 Flight Lieutenant Arthur Horton taxied his Lancaster bomber onto the runway at RAF Mildenhall, Suffolk in preparation for a raid to Essen in Germany. It was, he thought, just another routine, if terrifying, mission. When interviewed in 1987 Horton claimed he had not heard about any unusual aerial phenomena and as usual was only concerned with the task in hand: find the target, drop the bombs and return home as quickly and safely as possible. He had no idea what was to happen in the next few hours and how 'the thing', as he called it, would almost cost him and his crew their lives.

The raid went as exactly as planned, despite the potentially fatal distractions of Luftwaffe night-fighters and the flak in the searchlight beams. Bombs dropped, the Lancaster turned for home and the crew allowed themselves to relax slightly. But shortly after leaving the target Horton's intercom crackled into life with a panicky warning from his rear-gunner. Unidentified lights had appeared from nowhere and were following the plane. Horton asked the gunner if he was certain. Yes, he replied, four orange balls of light were tailing them, two on either side of the aircraft, accelerating in short powerful spurts. According to the frightened gunner they were about the size of large footballs and had a fiery glow to them. Intercom reports made it clear that other crew members could see them now and Horton knew they must be real, not hallucinations brought on by combat fatigue. One gunner thought he could see small stubby wings and possibly an exhaust glow from the rear of the objects. Now Horton was getting worried. He had never experienced anything like this before and while the UFOs were not showing any signs of aggression, he couldn't take the risk.

Forty-three years after the event Arthur Horton could still recalled exactly what he did next:

> 'I of course immediately dropped the aircraft out of the sky. My gunners didn't know what they were. Should they fire? By this time I was standing the aircraft on its tail and beginning a series of corkscrews and turns with the things following everything I did – but making no move to attack us. By this time we had the throttles "through the gate". The gunners were still asking what they should do. Apart from flying the thing, I had to try and answer them. But were [the objects] some form of flying contraption that would explode at some specific distance from us, or on contact? Did they want us to fire at them to cause an explosion? Out of the kaleidoscope of thought the only answer was, "If they are leaving us alone, leave them alone..." [15]

Horton's term 'through the gate' refers to a technique by which Lancaster pilots could move the throttle sideways and forwards, breaking a wire, 'the gate', in the process. This would then give considerable extra power. But the strain on the engines was immense and three minutes was the maximum amount of time recommended. Horton continued evasive action for ten minutes, during which time all the crew except Horton and the bomb aimer saw the phenomena. Whatever the objects were, they stayed close to the Lancaster, duplicating its every move, until they reached the Dutch coast, when, in the words of one of the gunners, 'They seemed to burn themselves out.'

Exhausted but relieved, Horton flew the Lancaster back to England. His dramatic evasive manoeuvres had caused a serious mechanical fault which resulted in having to land at a different airfield. Horton and his crew were baffled by their mystery visitors and could only presume they had been chased by a secret weapon, perhaps a radio-controlled anti-aircraft rocket or shell. Upon reporting their experience to the intelligence officers at debriefing, however, they were met not with interest but with ridicule. Still Horton stuck to his account and wouldn't be persuaded that his crew had imagined the glowing orange balls.

We have been unable to locate a reference to this sighting in government files, but evidence that it took place does exist. In his log book for the flight Horton recorded they had been 'Chased by rockets – 4.'[16] Bernard Dye, the mid-upper gunner, also noted the incident in his log book as 'Rocket attacks lasting ten minutes...'[17]

Although Horton and his crew never heard of anything similar, the phenomena they witnessed are entirely consistent with other foo-fighter experiences. Perhaps if Horton's rear-gunner had opened fire on the UFOs we might be a lot wiser about the nature of foo-fighters. But then again, perhaps not. It was a risk Flight Lieutenant Horton was not prepared to take.

The Loch Ness Monster of Emden and Other 'Phenomena'

Occasionally a service newsletter reported an aerial oddity. The 31 December 1943 issue of *Bang On*, the newsletter of 115 Squadron, ran a short piece simply titled 'Phenomena':

'Under this heading there occur from time to time reports of
weird and wonderful apparitions seen during our (and the
American) attacks on Germany. We have asked our local Inner
Circle bloke to comment on the latest species of wizardry. Here is
his story ... believe it or not...

On the 11th December the Yanks paid one of their daylight visits to Emden. Visibility was GOOD and the weather clear. An unidentified object was seen in the target area. It was about the size of a Thunderbolt and passed 50/75 yards beneath the formation. It flew STRAIGHT AND LEVEL (no, chaps, it was not a Lanc gone mad) at a terrific speed, leaving a streak like a vapour trail which was all white and which remained visible for a long time. The object passed so quickly that the observer could not determine it more accurately.'[18]

The newsletter went on to note:

'In another attack, this time on Bremen, there were many reports of "silver and red discs above the formations". These have been seen before but up to now no-one has been able to decide their purpose. Suggestions please.'[19]

Although the introductory paragraph makes it clear that 'weird and wonderful apparitions' were not uncommon, no one in 115 Squadron was aware of their origin and the newsletter's editor wrote, 'Suggestions will be welcome, serious ones, as to what this Loch Ness Monster of Emden might have been.'[20]

'Silver discs' were also noted in the book *Black Thursday*, which dealt with the 14 October 1943 US Air Force (USAF) bombing raids on the German ball-bearing manufacturing plants at Schweinfurt. Author Martin Caidin describes how aircrews were at first frightened and then puzzled by clouds of strange discs which appeared from a clear sky with no enemy aircraft overhead. Caidin quoted directly from a War Office memo, giving a very specific reference number,[21] but this could not be located by UFO or aviation researchers and the case was widely thought to be a hoax. However, in July 2000, after years of searching, we finally located the original document, compiled by British Air Intelligence and forwarded to American intelligence:

```
'...348th Group reports a cluster of disks
observed in the path of the formation near
Schweinfurt, at the time there were no E/A
above. Discs were described as silver
coloured - one inch thick and three inches
in diameter. They were gliding slowly down
in very uniform cluster. A/C 026 was unable
```

```
to avoid them and his right wing went
directly through a cluster with absolutely
no effect on engines or plane surface. One
of the discs was heard striking tail
assembly but no explosion was observed... Also
observed 2 other A/C flying through silver
discs with no apparent damage. Observed
discs and debris 2 other times but could not
determine where it came from.'²²
```

Although, on the surface, this event seems to refer to flak or the radar-confusing 'window', none of the aircrew or intelligence officers interpreted it as such. Besides, 'window', or its German equivalent, was neither circular nor an inch thick.

By now the Air Ministry's intelligence officers were totally perplexed both by the sheer number of foo-fighter reports being received and the apparent lack of aggression displayed by the phenomena. Michael Bentine summed up the situation:

> 'When I was an intelligence officer in Bomber Command in the winter of 1943–44, I debriefed several crews about some lights that had attacked them when they were over the Baltic. They fired at the lights, which didn't shoot back. These lights didn't seem to do anything, just pulse and go round. We put it down to fatigue, but later, after I had sent the reports in, an American G2 intelligence officer told us that their day bombers saw lights in the sky – "foo-fighters" he called them.'²³

In another interview Bentine told how he debriefed a Polish bomber unit based in England. They claimed that silver-blue balls appeared near their wing on six missions in the autumn of 1943. These tailed the planes as they raided the Nazi secret weapons base at Peenemünde. The crews told Bentine it must be a new weapon. 'But what did it do to you?' Bentine enquired. 'Nothing,' they replied. 'Well, it was not a very effective weapon, was it?' he pointed out.²⁴

Rocket Phenomena

As the war progressed, RAF Air Intelligence specialists monitored the growing number of inexplicable UFO reports from all the theatres of war.

No.5 Bomber Group's branch of Air Intelligence had been carefully studying the myriad of reports from several squadrons and by early 1944 felt they had to make a statement. On 8 February a 'Secret' document entitled 'Rocket Phenomena' was issued to 15 RAF stations in the 5 Group area. The two-page document took a pragmatic view of the reported phenomena, opening its analysis with:

'Reports by aircrews suggesting the use by the enemy of some form of anti-aircraft rocket projectile have been received many times during the past year, and with increasing frequency during recent months. Observations have often been characterised by a visible trace and many of the reports have referred to changes of course enabling the rocket to follow in the path of the aircraft under attack.'[25]

The report discussed the numerous types of known German flak and rocket development, noting that pursuits as recorded by aircrews could not have been German rockets because:

' these rockets are fitted with the standard German S-30 clockwork fuse. Since this fuse must be set on the ground before take-off, it is obvious that there can also be no question of these rockets changing course and following the path of the bomber.'[26]

The report's main conclusions were simple and stark, giving no concessions to the weight of reports by experienced observers.

'(i) No aircraft of Bomber Command have as yet returned from an operation having sustained damage by rockets.

(ii) No ground rocket projectors have as yet been identified in any photographic cover.

```
(iii) There is no evidence whatever
      available, nor is it considered
      practical, that any rocket fired from
      the ground would be capable of
      following an aircraft.'[27]
```

The final conclusion attributed all reports of the 'rocket phenomena' to rockets fired from aircraft or to parachute flares. Direction changes and 'chases' were identified as instability in the rockets caused by a defect in manufacture or as the misperception of light flak tracer observed at the point where the flak shell reached its maximum trajectory and began its descent to Earth.

All of these explanations were superficially plausible when viewed from the comfort and security of a cosy Air Intelligence office, but they failed completely to account for the 'chases' lasting up to ten minutes, the sightings of multiple foo-fighters apparently holding formation and the certainties of the gunners and pilots who reported the phenomena.

The Massey Project

Although the RAF intelligence branch received hundreds of accounts of foo-fighter phenomena, there is no documentary evidence of an official government-level investigation into the matter. Neither was former intelligence officer Michael Bentine aware of any such study. Yet in 1960 author Frank Edwards made the astonishing claim that there *had* been a super-secret British study into the foo-fighter phenomena and his claims have been subsequently repeated by UFOlogists as if they were actual fact. Edwards wrote:

'As early as 1943, the British had set up a small organisation to gather information on these objects. It was under the direction of Lieutenant General Massey and it had been inspired to some extent by the reports of a spy who was in reality a double agent, working under the direction of the Mayor of Cologne. He had confirmed that the foo-fighters were not German devices but that the Germans thought they were allied ranging instruments, which of course the British knew they were not. The British Air Ministry, in 1966, told me that the Massey Project was officially terminated in 1944. Perhaps it is only coincidence that the double agent was exposed and executed in the spring of 1944.'[28]

Figure 2: **The Public Record Office, Kew, London. The central repository for all records produced by the British Government. Hundreds of files dealing with UFOs, dating from 1950, are available for study at the PRO under the '30-year rule'.**
(Authors' collection)

Edwards' announcement of the so-called 'Massey project' caused a great deal of excitement among UFO researchers and can be seen as the genesis of the belief in a cover up of sensitive UFO-based government research. However, Edwards was unable to provide any documentary proof during his lifetime and intensive research has failed to validate his claims. No one by the name of Massey served in the British forces at the rank of Lieutenant General, and Air Marshal Sir Victor Goddard, who had been the first Deputy Director of Air Intelligence at the Air Ministry in 1935 and expressed strong beliefs in the extraterrestrial origin of UFOs, has also expressed doubts that a British foo-fighter study existed. He stated:

> 'To the best of my knowledge there has never been any official study of the foo-fighters. This implies Treasury sanction; it suggests that in the middle of the war against Germany when we had our hands full and it was far from certain that we could survive, the Air Ministry was concerned that a UFO menace existed; it most certainly was not.'[29]

Of course, this does not mean a top-level study did not take place, but on the basis of evidence available it would appear that investigation of foo-fighter phenomena was limited to the higher echelons of Air Intelligence dealing with Bomber and Fighter Commands. That their investigations were never taken further is almost certainly due to the fact that the foo-fighters displayed little or no aggression and therefore, in the terms of the Ministry of Defence today, had 'no defence significance'.

Scientist R. V. Jones, who was deeply involved in British Scientific Intelligence during World War II and later in the 'ghost rocket' events of 1946 (*see* Chapter 2), took a deeply sceptical view of foo-fighters. Prior to his death Jones was in correspondence with a number of researchers and repeatedly stated there had been no 'official' study into the phenomena, writing to one researcher:

> 'In answer to your letter there was no Committee on "foo-fighters" during my time with the Air Ministry during the war or with the Ministry of Defence afterwards. If there had been any such enquiry, it would have been primarily an Air Force matter...'[30]

But just what were the foo-fighters? Despite the 'Secret' reports and analyses, Air Intelligence was unable to reach a conclusion which accounted for all the sightings. The official claim that the phenomena were misperceived flak or rocketry can only account for a fraction of the reported sightings. But Air Intelligence staff were in a difficult position. If they let slip that aircrews were seeing genuine unidentified flying objects which had the ability to outpace and possibly outgun Allied planes, morale would have plummeted and fear would have spread rapidly through the RAF airfields. Nor could they suggest that the sightings were down to hallucinations or fatigue. That would have demeaned the observational abilities of aircrews and would have meant that trained and experienced personnel would have been grounded for medical reasons.

Taking all the evidence into consideration, both from the aircrew witnesses and the Air Ministry reports housed at the PRO, it is clear that no one knew what was being seen. In that respect the situation was identical to the post-war UFO problem: incredible reports being made by credible witnesses. The result was a puzzle with no apparent solution. In the heat of World War II, with German victory a possibility, it was one which would have to be addressed at a later date.

By the time hostilities with Germany ceased in May 1945, foo-fighter reports had tailed off. World War II ended later that year with the surrender of Japan and by then the world had changed forever. In the fall-out, the political climate was cooling rapidly into conflicting ideologies armed with weapons of total destruction. The Cold War was on the horizon and with it came a new aerial mystery to plague the European skies, baffling governments and witnesses alike.

The ghost rockets had arrived.

Chapter 2

GHOST ROCKETS FROM EREHWON

'There seems to be something about
rocketry that arouses the deepest
of human emotions.'

R. V. Jones[1]

Reports during World War II of the phenomena known as 'foo-fighters', 'the thing' and 'the light' forced the British government to confront the fact that aircrews were encountering UFOs in large numbers. The Air Ministry's conclusions that all the sightings were explicable as misperceptions of natural phenomena, enemy weaponry or hallucinations were not accepted by the witnesses, many of whom went on to become fully-fledged believers in extraterrestrials. Other service personnel who were baffled by the foo-fighter mystery rose to high-ranking positions in the RAF, Air Ministry and government, and in the immediate post-war period there were many people in positions of authority with direct experience of UFOs. For these individuals, all highly experienced observers, seeing was believing and a widespread belief was emerging that if an aerial phenomenon was reported it must have a physical origin which in turn must be controlled by a living agency.

Ghost Rockets

This entrenchment of experience-based belief soon demonstrated itself when the Western world was confronted with thousands of sightings of what became known as 'ghost rockets'. The phenomena were reported mainly over Sweden but also over Norway, Finland, Germany, France and Greece during the summer of 1946. Some UFO researchers have attempted to minimise the importance of the ghost rocket wave and of the governmental conclusions about the nature and origin of the phenomenon. However, the ghost rocket saga is closely connected and highly relevant to later belief in flying saucers, UFOs and extraterrestrials. In 1951 a secret British intelligence report considered the ghost rockets to be of sufficient importance to include them in their criteria for and analyses of the UFO problem as a whole, stating:

> 'Unidentified flying objects were first reported after the war from Sweden in the summer of 1946, and for some months there was a considerable number of alleged sightings, mostly in Sweden, but a few also in Norway, Finland and Germany. The descriptions given were usually of some sort of wingless missile travelling at very high speed, cigar-shaped or circular, sometimes emitting bright lights, and occasionally sound. The reports attracted considerable attention in the press, where the objects became known as "ghost rockets" or "spook bombs". The reports died away after the summer of 1946, and very few have appeared since the end of that year.'[2]

Between the late spring and early autumn of 1946 the British and American media were saturated with accounts of sightings and speculation about the source and purpose of the ghost rockets. It is not generally known that the British government and its various military technical and intelligence departments played an important role in the saga.

The British Government's Response

Records discovered in London's PRO reveal the ghost rocket sightings brought forth a tangle of confusion and barely suppressed panic at the Foreign Office. There was an obvious schism between those who clearly believed the ghost rockets were harbingers of a new superpower conflagration and those who thought they were on a par with the Loch Ness monster. As R. V. Jones noted:

'The general interpretation ... was that these were long-range flying bombs being flown by the Russians over Sweden as an act of intimidation. This interpretation was accepted by officers in our own Air Technical Intelligence...'[3]

Exactly when the British government first became involved is unclear. Evidence at the PRO is fragmentary, but one of the first documents dates from July 1946 and demonstrates the Foreign Office had been keeping a weather eye on the situation for some time. A Mr Jerram at the British Legation in Stockholm was in discussion with the Foreign Office about the possibility of sending two 'secret agents' to Sweden to investigate the phenomena. Although initially the British officials in Sweden did not feel there was a need for this, the War Office was 'anxious to follow up' the spiralling number of sightings and wanted 'an expert to contact ... six of the eye witnesses to consolidate some apparently common characteristics of their non-technical observations'.[4]

Figure 3:
Professor R.V. Jones.
As Director of Scientific Intelligence at Air Ministry, Jones was involved in the investigation of the 'ghost rocket' phenomena in 1946. His sceptical conclusions were applied to reports of 'flying saucers' made by the RAF during his time as Director of Scientific Intelligence at MoD 1952–54.
(Courtesy of Robert Jones)

On 12 July the *Daily Telegraph* ran a piece entitled 'Ghost rockets over Sweden: V weapon rumours', which comprehensively described the phenomena:

> 'For some weeks a fair number of "ghost rockets" going from
> south-east to north-west have been reported from various parts of
> the eastern coast of Sweden. Eye witnesses say that they look like
> glowing balls and are followed by a tail of smoke more or less
> visible. So many reports cannot be put down to pure imagination
> and the General Staff has started a thorough investigation in the
> matter. As there is no definite evidence that the phenomena are
> of meteoric origin, there is a growing suspicion that they are a
> new kind of radio-controlled V weapon on which experiments are
> carried out.'[5]

Carried out by whom? The *Telegraph* didn't say, but the inference was clear. It could only be the Russians.

On 13 July Jerram cabled the Foreign Office in London with details of a major series of sightings which had taken place on 9 July. In one of these sightings, at Njurunda, a ghost rocket was seen to fall to the ground and pieces were allegedly collected for analysis by the Swedish authorities. The Njurunda event led to widespread newspaper publicity for the ghost rockets and persuaded Sweden's General Staff to issue a communiqué requesting that the public report all similar occurrences. As Jerram noted, 'This official recognition has naturally had the effect of opening the flood gates of publicity and has given rise to speculation of a somewhat "silly season" variety.'[6]

This was a problem which has plagued UFO investigations ever since. Once the media latch onto a 'wave' of UFOs, whether ghost rockets or flying saucers, the public is immediately alerted to the possibility that there *may* be something to see. Consequently people look up into the sky for what they have been told is there. Also, when UFOs are given some form of official validation or, as in this instance, requests are made for further sightings, people then believe the government is fully aware of the unidentified flying objects' existence. This in turn leads to increasing numbers of aerial phenomena being seen and reported, with little dis-crimination or quality to the accounts. As a result of the ghost rockets' publicity, the Swedish General Staff received over 300 accounts of the phenomena seen on 9 July.

By 16 July Mr Jerram in Stockholm was becoming concerned about the number of reported sightings and cabled to tell the Foreign Office that he had discussed the matter with the Swedish Chief of Combined Intelligence. The Swedes were worried that the Russians were behind the ghost rockets, but were unwilling to make a public statement, stressing 'the vital importance of utmost secrecy and delicacy of the position regarding other nations'. Clearly it would not look good if Sweden, a neutral country, were to openly accuse Russia of testing advanced rockets over its territory or to let slip that its authorities were in close communication with the British Foreign Office about the matter. A decision was made to send the secret agents to Stockholm immediately in an attempt to get to the bottom of the situation.[7]

Secret Agents Go to Sweden

The two men chosen for the task were Squadron Leader Heath of the Air Ministry and Major Malone of the War Office. These officers had been selected because of their recognised scientific expertise in missiles and rocketry. Malone was from MI10(a), a military intelligence department which dealt, among other things, with enemy artillery and rocketry. This was further confirmation that the War Office had grave suspicions that the Soviets were responsible for the Scandinavian ghost rocket sightings.

Just how sensitive the Swedish government was about other countries, especially Russia, knowing of its liaison with the British over the ghost rockets is indicated by the fact that when Malone flew to Sweden it was proposed that he did so in plain clothes, travelling 'as a mere tourist until the Air Ministry Mission arrives'.[8] His service dress was to be 'concealed' in his luggage. It was also suggested that Mrs Malone accompany him, presumably to reinforce the illusion they were just two post-war British tourists. The secret telegram which outlined details of Malone's visit ended with: 'Swedes stress need for utmost secrecy and object of Mission to be confined to selected members of British and Swedish General Staffs only.'[9]

Malone and Heath landed in Stockholm on 18 July and rushed to a meeting at the Swedish Air Ministry, where they were appraised of the latest ghost rocket information. They reported back to Jerram in Stockholm, who, though initially sceptical, now believed there was a physical component to the sightings. Following Malone and Heath's debriefing, Jerram's telegram to the Foreign Office claimed, 'Too many missiles have been observed and described to allow of explanation as meteorites.'[10]

Permutations of this statement were uttered repeatedly throughout the ghost rocket saga by government officials from Britain, the USA and Sweden. No one could believe that something as 'simple' as, say, astronomical phenomena could result in so many independent sightings. This official statement is one which flying saucer enthusiasts would echo down subsequent decades. The belief that something existed as described because a large number of people have reported seeing it is a powerful one and is the driving force behind belief in UFOs as extra-terrestrial craft.

Meanwhile the Foreign Office issued a comprehensive summary of what was known about the ghost rockets so far, based on information received up to 6 July. This document, 'Reports on Suspected V-Weapons over the Baltic', was designated 'Top Secret', its title alone indicating that Britain believed the sightings to be V-weapon tests. The suspicion of Russian origin is confirmed by the statement that analysis of the sightings so far showed 'the countries concerned were not conducting experiments themselves'.[11] The report also gives credence to the objectivity of witnesses: '…although observers were not trained they were competent to distinguish between natural and artificial phenomena.'[12] So far, so good, but the section of the report which breaks down the sightings into duration, behaviour and characteristics is inconsistent and seems to bear no relation to actual V-weapons. Terms used to describe the phenomena include 'ball of fire with tail', 'wingless, cigar-shaped flying horizontally, sparking every ten minutes', 'queer phenomenon' and 'like meteor'. These ambiguous phrases are only slightly balanced by other reports describing a 'large ball of fire resembling a V1' and a 'wingless projectile'. Accounts of duration are equally inconsistent and differ widely from ten seconds to ten minutes. Some witnesses describe the phenomena making a noise, others claim they were silent. All that could be usefully drawn from the reports was that a great many people were seeing *something*.[13]

Whatever was being seen over Sweden was also visible further north in Finland. On 22 July the British Legation in Helsinki cabled the Foreign Office in London with details of 'strange lights in the sky' at several locations in Finland. The Finnish newspapers were speculating wildly about their origin and, like other countries, had concluded they must be 'rockets of an unknown source'.

Meanwhile, Squadron Leader Heath was working closely with the Swedish authorities on several ghost rockets believed to have crashed into Swedish lakes. One was seen to crash into the sea at a point where the water was only 3 feet deep. Heath was unimpressed with the Swedish way of working and the analysis of his progress so far stated: 'It must be appreciated that Swedish methods of operation are extremely slow and probably unproductive.'[14] He also bemoaned the lack of quantitative data with which to work: 'We have not obtained an acceptable assessment of size, description or speed. We are doing everything possible to foster attention to accurate details.'[15] The Swedes had, however, indicated to Heath they would be more than willing to accept the offer of underwater search equipment.

The increasing British involvement, while welcomed by the Swedish government, was also causing concern. A telegram sent on 27 July by the British air attaché was almost panicky:

```
'I have been asked by the Swedish Air Staff
to take all possible measures to prevent the
Americans finding out about Swedish full co-
operation with us in investigating
mysterious missiles. Italian Air Attaché has
been making enquiries in Swedish Air and
General Staffs and has been given evasive
replies. Leakage of information about our
co-operation would seriously embarrass
Swedish authorities.'16
```

An American Arrives

On 24 August General James Doolittle arrived in Stockholm. At the time, he was vice president of the Shell Oil Company and was ostensibly in Sweden on business. He was travelling with the legendary World War II fighter ace Douglas Bader, also a Shell employee. However, as Anders Liljegren wrote in 1997, 'The visit to Sweden of the American General James H. Doolittle has, for fifty years, been the subject of some surmise and speculation among ufologists.'17

There have been many rumours about Doolittle's alleged involvement in early UFO history. Some anonymous sources have claimed that he headed up a secret USAF investigation into foo-fighters, others that he was somehow involved with the famous 1947 Roswell UFO crash (*see* page 52–3).

Doolittle's role in the ghost rocket saga has been hotly debated by UFO historians, with some believing that he was in Sweden on a covert intelligence mission. Certainly Sweden's Chief of Defence Staff, Colonel Kemf, indicated that he would be interested in speaking to Doolittle about the ghost rocket mystery and would make all reports available to him. However, no documentary evidence has been found to support the claim of an intelligence mission and an elderly Doolittle said he could not recall the purpose of his visit to Stockholm, adding in 1984: 'I have no firm knowledge of actual rockets or "ghost rockets" in Sweden.'18

Radar Experts Are Called In

Following Malone and Heath's secret mission to Sweden and their con-clusions that the ghost rockets were physical in nature, the Foreign Office's nervousness increased. Desperate to get to the bottom of the mystery, the Air Ministry decided to despatch a party of radar experts to Sweden. Superficially this was in response to a request by the Swedish government for training in the use of Vampire aircraft, which had recently been sold to the Swedes. However, a 'Top Secret' memorandum dated 3 August reveals that this was a cover story, Robin Hankey at the Foreign Office writing,

> 'Strictly for your own information the radar
> sets installed will be used to assist Swedes
> to obtain further information regarding
> recent projectiles seen over Sweden.'[19]

This government cover up was confirmed in another 'Top Secret' document of 22 August, where the writer states:

> 'It was necessary, at this point, to decide
> on a "cover" for the RAF party and, by good
> luck, the same open cover was decided in
> Sweden as that suggested by the Air
> Ministry, namely that the party had come out
> at the invitation of the Swedish Air Force
> to help them with radar and signals
> equipment for the Vampires.'[20]

One of the 'radar experts', Wing Commander Jennings from the Directorate of Radar, made two exploratory visits to Sweden, eventually deciding on two possible sites for the radar on the island of Gottland. The British radar party and its specialist equipment were ready to leave for Sweden on 22 August, but the mission was thwarted at the last moment when the Swedish Prime Minister blocked it on undisclosed 'political' grounds.[21]

However, details of the mission had already been leaked to the British media, which immediately exposed the Air Ministry's intentions. The

Swedes were horrified at this breach of security and issued the statement that: 'There has been no question of foreign help.'[22]

These claims and counter-claims threw the Foreign Office into a barely concealed and uncharacteristic rage. Disgusted that the Swedes should renege on the arrangement after considerable time and expense had been invested, officials began to circulate vitriolic memos. On one draft memo there is the handwritten note: 'Mr Jerram has seen this despatch and agrees that the Swedish Prime Minister has been both stupid and cowardly.'[23]

Clearly the Swedish government did not want to risk offending the Russians in any way by involving Britain in attempts to trace the source of the ghost rockets. Documents also reveal that the Swedish military was just as disappointed as the British. In his report on the embarrassing incident, Group Captain Simpson, the British air attaché in Stockholm, wrote that military co-operation between the British and Swedish services was better than ever and the Swedes would 'probably deal with a similar situation at a later date *without reference to the Political department at all*'.[24]

This situation was regarded as so politically embarrassing that the British Prime Minister, Clement Atlee, demanded to know what was going on. He was sent a long and detailed letter of explanation by Mr Henderson at the British Legation in Stockholm speculating why it was thought the offer of radar assistance had been turned down.[25]

Russian 'Spook Bombs'

Whatever political games were going on behind the scenes, little seemed to detract from the way the UK press viewed the matter. For the sabre-rattling *Daily Mail* there was no doubt who was responsible for the ghost rockets – it had to be the Soviet Union. In early September the *Mail* devoted the majority of its front page to the mystery, leading with the headline 'Spook bombs over Sweden'. The article continued:

> "The *Daily Mail* has sent its most famous war correspondent,
> Alexander Clifford, to investigate these reports. In his dispatch
> below he examines all the evidence and concludes that the
> missiles have been fired by the Russians "beyond reasonable
> doubt". They are, in his opinion, not merely super V-2s but
> something quite new – maybe developments of the mysterious
> "butterfly" or the "waterfall" which were two of the more fantastic
> German projects.'[26]

Although apparently convinced that the Soviets were behind the ghost rockets, the language used by both the *Daily Mail* and other newspapers belied their uncertainty. Unable to come up with physical or documentary

evidence that the Russians were responsible, but equally unable to coun-
tenance the possibility that thousands of witnesses and several world
governments were being fooled by misperceptions of natural phenomena,
the press seemed to categorise the mystery projectiles more as supernatural than physical phenomena. Words such as 'ghosts', 'spooks' and
'phantoms' were all used by the *Mail*, with 'rocket' or 'bomb' tagged on in
a attempt to add some reality to an increasingly surreal situation.

Clifford penned one significant and insightful sentence concerning
attitudes towards the ghost rockets: 'Deep in the heart of Sweden the
peasants are weaving a new folklore around them.'[27] Obsessed by the Cold
War and fear of all things Russian, neither Clifford nor the *Daily Mail*
could see that they were 'weaving a new folklore' just as much as the
country-dwellers of Sweden. The media's reasoning, like that of some
sections of the British and Swedish governments, was not based on careful
analysis of the sightings, but revolved round an implicit belief in witness
testimony and the as yet unfounded fear of Soviet aggression.

Even when the behaviour and characteristics of the ghost rockets failed
to match the known flight characteristics of rockets or missiles, the *Daily
Mail* continued to shoe-horn these anomalous experiences into the Cold
War scenario:

> 'That is the eeriness of it all. The Russians, with tightly sealed
> lips, are experimenting publicly with a machine that leaves no
> trace whatever and apparently defies several scientific laws.'[28]

Clifford's description of the ghost rockets' transient nature and apparent
defiance of scientific laws has been reworked time and time again in the
past 60 years and applied to every other form of UFO. Within a few short
years media commentators, government spokespersons and military
renegades would be suggesting that ghost rocket-like phenomena,
reframed as 'flying saucers', were piloted by extraterrestrials.

Clifford's estimate of the situation concluded:

> 'So the Swedes look uneasily into their skies and guess. But all the
> time the Russians know. The mystery is no mystery to them. And
> how they must laugh when they read articles like this.'[29]

The Russians were probably laughing, but at the stupidity of the West in
believing them to have the technology or desire to waste money and
missiles over a neutral country at a time when a third world war was a real
possibility.

In some quarters, however, imagined Russian laughter had already
turned to irritation at the West's insistence that the mystery projectiles

were of Soviet origin. 'No one has thought of verifying the truth of the statement,' the Russian *New Times* pointed out, going on to say that the allegations that the Russians were launching the ghost rockets were part of an organised campaign of slander against the Soviets.[30] Clearly Russian intelligence agencies were not aware of the confusion and hysteria the ghost rockets were causing among the higher echelons of the British Foreign and War Offices.

Substance or Scare?

On 9 September the RAF intelligence department AI2(g) distributed a document to over 100 Air Ministry, Admiralty, War Office and Ministry of Supply departments. The document was also circulated widely to American and European government agencies. It was apparently written by R. V. Jones and was entitled 'Investigation of Missile Activity over Scandinavia'.

After carefully analysing the possibility that the ghost rockets were of Soviet origin, Jones compared the entire ghost rocket saga to various pre-war social panics such as the rumours that the Nazis had developed rays which could stop cars, bring aeroplanes down or kill people. He concluded:

> 'The large bulk of evidence, whilst at first sight impressive, therefore loses weight in the light of our earlier experience of earlier scares, and scares at the present time are natural enough in a country near to Russia... Great importance, therefore, attaches to the results of analysis of the small fragments alleged to have fallen from missiles. If any of them turn out to be substances whose origin cannot be ascribed to innocent activities, they will form the most important piece of evidence we have...'[31]

This, then, was the nub of the matter. What was sorely needed was something more than witness testimony and wild speculation. Just one piece of a Russian rocket retrieved from Scandinavia would have been enough to settle the matter once and for all, in the same way that post-

1947 one piece of an extraterrestrial craft would have resolved the debate about the nature of flying saucers.

There had been several instances where the press had claimed physical evidence of the ghost rockets had been retrieved, but these had always turned out to be ambiguous or material unconnected with the actual sightings. Many people thought that proof was getting closer when on 6 September the *Daily Telegraph* devoted a large portion of its front page to a remarkable image. The photograph, taken from some islands just outside Stockholm, showed a bright streak of light plunging downwards.

Set in the context of ghost rocket reports and assumptions that the Russians were launching advanced V-weapons, the photograph was interpreted by some as being a missile on the point of impact. However, shorn of its connection to rumours of rockets, it also looked exactly like a bolide meteor passing through the outer edges of the Earth's atmosphere. The *Daily Telegraph* also reported that photographic analysis had determined that the projectile was in the midst of the flame track rather than in front of it. This should have set alarm bells ringing immediately, as a rocket would not have such an appearance within the Earth's atmosphere.[32]

September 1946 also saw a meeting of the secret British Joint Intelligence Committee, which spent considerable time debating the events of the summer. Minutes of the meeting included the heading 'Alleged Flights of Missiles over Scandinavia'.[33] Members were so perturbed by the number of ghost rocket reports that they suggested, contrary to earlier government policy, that all information pertaining to the mysterious phenomena should now be passed on to the Americans.

But this was to be a pointless gesture. As summer became autumn, although ghost rocket sightings continued, attitudes in His Majesty's Government were changing.

Piecing It Together

The final nail in the coffin of the belief that the ghost rockets were of Russian origin, or intelligently created machines of any origin, came with the intervention of the scientist R. V. Jones. Jones described the ghost rocket saga as a 'diversion of an Intelligence nature, which no doubt arose from the general atmosphere of apprehension that existed in 1945 regarding the motives of the Russians, and which anticipated the flying saucer'.[34] He concluded that only physical evidence would satisfy the debate and reasoned that as there had been thousands of ghost rocket sightings there ought to be, at the very least, a few crashed ones. During World War II the Germans only had a 90 per cent reliability in V-weapon trials. Had the Russians managed to attain even a 99 per cent reliability, there should have been several ghost rocket crashes on Swedish territory.

Based on this probability, Jones made it widely known that he 'would not accept the theory that the apparitions were flying bombs from Russia until someone brought a piece into [his] office'.[35]

Shortly after issuing this challenge Jones was telephoned by his colleague in the Directorate of Intelligence, Air Commodore Vimtras, who told him that the Swedes had retrieved some fragments which had allegedly fallen from a ghost rocket. Jones had the 'debris' sent to him and assessed it before forwarding it to the chemical analysis section at RAF Farnborough. The scientists there thoroughly analysed the material and sent the results to Air Commodore Vimtras. Jones records:

> '[Vimtras] phoned … in triumphant mood exclaiming, "There, what did I tell you! Farnborough has analysed the stuff you sent me, and one of the lumps consists of 98 per cent of an unknown element!"'[36]

Jones was shocked by this announcement, but Vimtras was correct. The analysis showed that the 'ghost rocket' fragments were composed of iron, nickel and copper, but these only accounted for less than 2 per cent of the sample. The analytical chemists had failed to identify the remaining 98 per cent. It appeared that the fears of many in the Air Ministry and the predictions of the *Daily Mail*'s war correspondent were being proved right – whoever was firing the ghost rockets had even developed a new chemical element which defied laboratory analysis.

With excitement mounting among the British air staff at the implications of this devastating news, Jones, still confident of his original instincts, spoke directly to the scientists at Farnborough and enquired whether they were playing a joke. 'No,' came the answer, they were genuinely baffled by the mystery substance. Astonished, Jones then enquired whether they had perhaps considered that the fragments resembled an ordinary piece of coke?

> 'There was a gasp from the other end of the telephone as the penny dropped. No one had stopped to look at the material, in an effort to get the analysis made quickly, and they had failed to test for carbon. The other lumps had similarly innocent explanations.'[37]

This seemed to burst the ghost rocket bubble completely. The admission that a mundane piece of coke had been misperceived as a fragment of a ghost rocket allowed for other, more prosaic explanations for the ghost rockets to be offered and accepted. This, combined with the diffidence shown by the Swedish Prime Minister toward British assistance in tracking the ghost rockets, now cast a long shadow across the British government's attitude towards the phenomena. Throughout the Foreign Office and Directorate of Intelligence people were reviewing the evidence and changing their minds as to what the ghost rockets really were.

A 'Top Secret' cypher telegram of 16 September dropped any pretence that the government believed there was something physical behind the ghost rockets, noting:

```
'*We find it impossible to believe that all
  observations are genuinely of missiles,
  when there is as yet no confirmed case of a
  missile crashing on land. This would imply
  an unheard of reliability of missiles or of
  self-destructive process.

*We are not convinced that there have been
  any missiles over Scandinavian territory
  (or over Greece, France, etc) at all. A
  very high proportion of all observations
  are accounted for by just two meteors
  visible, one by day and one at sunset, in
  Sweden on 9th July and 11th August
  respectively.'[38]
```

In analysing these multi-witness sightings the writer states, 'These must be genuine observations of single incidents and meteors are the simplest explanation,' before concluding:

```
'The residue of observations are random in
 time, place and country and can not
 unreasonably be attributed to fireworks,
 swans, aircraft, lightning etc and
 imagination. Such mass delusions are in our
 experience not unusual in time of public
 excitement.'[39]
```

A pencilled note from Robin Hankey adds simply, 'Rather an anti-climax!'

This no doubt sums up what many people in the Foreign and War Offices felt. There had been such a strength of feeling that some genuine, physical, probably Russian-controlled device was being intentionally demonstrated to them that the slow realisation it had all been a complicated series of misperceptions must have been anti-climactic at best, an embarrassment at worst.

By October 1946, with the sightings tailing off in the wake of revised ideas and damning evidence, the ghost rockets rapidly became just a footnote in the hidden history of the Cold War.

Observations...

Eric Malmberg, who was secretary of Sweden's 'ghost rocket committee', later expressed the ambiguous nature of the sightings:

> 'I would like to say that everyone on the committee, as well as the chairman himself, was sure that the observed phenomena didn't originate from the Soviet Union. Nothing pointed to that solution.
>
> On the other hand, if the observations are correct, many details suggest that it was some kind of a cruise missile that was fired on Sweden. But nobody had that kind of sophisticated technology in 1946.'[10]

Clearly – and not for the first or last time – the 'observations' were not correct.

It's easy, and for some convenient, to forget that many thousands of witnesses, several governments and scientists and politicians of the highest integrity were completely fooled into believing the ghost rockets were a Soviet threat. The episode consisted of misperception on a gigantic and dangerous scale and that is what makes it so relevant to the history of UFOs as a whole. If such dramatic misperception could happen in just a few months during 1946 it must be a possibility that the same subtle forces have been at work with all subsequent UFO sightings and beliefs.

In retrospect the ghost rocket episode needs to be set within the broader context of UFOs seen over the centuries and Sweden's other experiences of anomalous aerial phenomena. Veteran Swedish researchers Anders Liljegren and Clas Svahn have spent years analysing ghost rocket sightings and Swedish government and media sources. In their essay 'Sweden's Ghost Rocket Delusion of 1946' they set the drama firmly against the backdrop of historical Swedish fears of Russian invasion.

Liljegren and Svahn note that unusual and unidentified aerial phenomena over Sweden have by no means been confined to the summer of 1946. Throughout the previous decade, particularly in 1933 and 1934, the Swedish skies played host to 'ghost fliers'. At a time when there were few aeroplanes in Sweden, hundreds of reports were received of unmarked monoplanes flying over remote areas of the countryside, often in appalling weather conditions. Belief was strong that these planes were solid physical objects piloted by humans, yet no physical or documentary evidence was ever found to substantiate those claims.

Similarly, beginning in January 1946, peculiar phenomena were noted in the Swedish skies. Meteors, comets, glowing clouds and spectacular auroral displays were all recorded by astronomers. These phenomena passed with little comment outside a few newspapers and journals until May, when witnesses began to report fireballs with tails and cigar-shaped objects. The Swedish media quickly turned to phrases such as 'rocket bomb', 'projectile' and 'remote-directed bomb'. As Liljegren and Svahn noted, 'Media speculation that some sightings were of guided missiles provided a label with which to classify unfamiliar phenomena.'[41]

Liljegren and Svahn also make the point that there is a historical fear of Russian aggression which may underlie both the 'ghost flier' and 'ghost rocket' manifestations. Fears that itinerant Russian artisans were involved in spying missions during the 19th century have mutated through various folkloric motifs in Sweden and have latterly, since the 1980s, manifested in thousands of Swedish reports of alleged Soviet submarines. These too, despite intense investigation, have proved as intangible as phantoms, and Liljegren and Svahn regard them as the latest psychic manifestations of tension between a traditionally peace-loving nation and a traditionally warlike one.[42]

This way of categorising anomalous human experiences is not popular with those who believe what is described is what is seen, or those with a deep-seated belief that UFOs are extraterrestrial craft. However, the facts speak for themselves, and despite the thousands of sightings and the seriousness with which world governments treated the ghost rocket situation, it seems that sightings of meteors and other astronomical phenomena became conflated with deep-rooted fears of Russian rocketry. And, as with the flying saucer era of the 1950s and beyond, many scientists, politicians and media moguls were prepared to put their beliefs and fears before rationalism and hard evidence.

The ghost rocket saga taught the British government some useful lessons about the nature of UFOs, lessons which would later be used in dealing with the post-1947 'flying saucer' reports. But human nature and the desire for supernatural intervention in the affairs of mankind are strong. The ghost rockets had crashed leaving no trace, but 1947 was just around the corner and 'flying saucers' were coming. The world would never be the same again.

Chapter 3

THE COMING OF THE SAUCERS

'flying saucer n (1947) a disc- or saucer-shaped object reported as appearing in the sky and alleged to come from outer space.'

John Ayto, *20th Century Words*[1]

By the end of 1946 the euphoria of victory in World War II was fading and the British people were turning their attention towards rebuilding the nation's economy. Military strategists, however, were trying to consolidate Britain's defences against a wartime ally that was now perceived as a new aggressor: Soviet Russia. With the crisis growing between East and West, Winston Churchill, now in opposition, defined the beginning of the Cold War in his famous address: '...from Stettin in the Baltic to Trieste in the Adriatic, an iron curtain has descended across the continent.'

After almost six years of war Britain was impoverished and unprepared for another international crisis. With six million unemployed and an economy heading for disaster, the Labour Cabinet drew up plans to dismantle the last remnants of empire in India and to reduce the UK's military commitments across the world. On the home front, wartime conditions remained in blitzed towns and cities, with both fuel and food rationing still in force.

The Chain Home System

As the threat of a confrontation with the Soviet Union increased, Britain relied upon the Royal Navy and the war-weary RAF squadrons to defend its coastline. An integrated radar and fighter defence system was the key to these defences and this was based upon the Chain Home (CH) early warning system that had been built up around the British coastline during the war.

By 1945 there was a string of 34 static CH stations stretching from Ventnor on the Isle of Wight to the Firth of Tay in Scotland on 24-hour watch for enemy planes. They relied upon simple aerials erected on tall towers, the transmitters 'floodlighting' the English Channel with radio energy. At this point CH radar was the most advanced in the world, with a 3D sweep and height-finding capability. During the war the first plan position indicators (PPIs) had been developed, circular screens that allowed operators to 'see' the total area surveyed by radar. Echoes from aircraft appeared on the glowing screen as luminous blips as the trace rotated about the centre like the hands of a clock, an image that has become an enduring symbol of the Cold War.

The CH system had two main problems, however. First, the radar beam was unable to pick up targets at low altitudes, and second, its success at identifying the height of aircraft varied.

As technological advances continued, the CH system was supplemented by Chain Home Low (CHL) and ground-controlled interception

Figure 4: **Winston Churchill, British Prime Minister 1951–55, giving his famous wartime victory signal as he leaves Downing Street for the final time. Following a 'flap' of UFO sightings over Washington DC in the summer of 1952 Churchill asked the Air Ministry: 'What does all this stuff about flying saucers amount to? What can it mean? What is the truth?'** (Hulton-Deutsch Collection/CORBIS)

(GCI) stations which specialised in directing fighters towards enemy aircraft. High ground could produce permanent echoes on the PPI, so GCI stations were situated near the sea or in flat, low-lying areas such as East Anglia. The oldest and most important GCI station is that at RAF Neatishead in Norfolk, which began operations in 1941 and continues to play a major role in Britain's air defences today.

During World War II a central 'filtering' system was developed to pool information on aircraft movements from the GCI and the CH stations. By 1947 CH and CHL stations reported to the GCIs and their plots were 'told' to the central filter room at RAF Bentley Priory, Middlesex, where a chief controller collated the information.

All the early radar equipment operated on metric wavelengths and relied upon transmitters that were based upon pre-war valve technology. It was not until the late 1950s that this ageing system was re-engineered by Marconi experts in the projects codenamed 'Rotor' and 'Green Garlic'. The new high-powered centimetric radar this produced would eventually become the lynchpin of Britain's modern air defence network.[2]

A 'Ghost Plane' over East Anglia

The first post-war test of Britain's air defences came during the winter of 1947, which was one of the most severe on record. Temperatures fell to below freezing and there were gale force winds and six weeks of snow. The country ground to a halt and a 'crisis Cabinet' was set up as the heavy snow brought power cuts and chaos.

In the midst of this ferocious winter eastern England began to receive visits from what RAF Fighter Command described as 'an unidentified high-flying aircraft'. This 'aircraft' was never identified, however, and was therefore classified as a UFO. It should be borne in mind that use of the phrase 'flying saucer' to denote unexplained aerial phenomena was still several months away. As reports of this 'aircraft' came hard on the heels of the wave of 'ghost rockets', Britain's air defence chiefs naturally believed that they were dealing with a new Russian aircraft or guided missile.

The matter first came to the attention of the British public as a result of a 'leak' from the Air Ministry to a journalist. Once again it was the *Daily Mail* that splashed the story across its front page, under the headline 'Ghost plane over coast, RAF spot it – can't catch it':

> 'A "ghost" plane which flies in over the East Anglia coast near Norwich at midnight at a great height and disappears inland is puzzling the Royal Air Force. All attempts at interception have so far failed. Crack night-fighter pilots have been sent up in Fighter Command's latest Mosquitoes, but the mystery aircraft has got

away every time. It always crosses the coast at roughly the same spot, and it has used such effective evasive tactics that it is thought to be equipped with radar to give warning of the approach of intercepting aircraft. Time and again Fighter Command radar operators plotting the ghost plane's course over East Anglia have watched the "blip" go right across their screen and disappear as the plane penetrated deep inland. They have watched vainly for the "trace" to reappear, moving in the opposite direction, as the plane flew back out to sea. Some experts suspect that the plane is engaged in a highly organised and lavishly financed smuggling operation, using one or more secret landing places. According to authoritative information the plane – of unidentified type – has a speed of nearly 400 mph and a fast rate of climb.'³

Characteristically, the Air Ministry refused to comment other than to admit that Fighter Command had twice received what it described as 'some extraordinary plots' from its coastal radar stations. Speculation continued that the Soviets were testing a long-range missile in the North Atlantic, although Air Ministry officials stated publicly that they had ruled out this possibility.

The 'ghost plane' displayed 'enormous height range and remarkable speed variations' of between 400 and 425 mph, in excess of the top speed of Britain's fastest night-fighters, the Mosquitoes. It was listed in RAF records as 'X-362'. 'X-tracks' were allocated to unidentified radar blips that were assumed to be hostile. In this case, officers in the Fighter Command operations room had also invented a nickname for the elusive aircraft – 'C for Charlie' – and the exercise to track and intercept the target was known as 'Operation Charlie'.

Operation Charlie

During the big freeze of 1947 the CH radar system was operating during daylight only. Once or twice per month it was also switched on for a time during the evening for 'Bullseye' exercises organised by Bomber Command. These consisted of Lancasters and Lincolns flying south along the east coast from their bases. They would cross the North Sea to the Low Countries and GCI stations would guide Mosquitoes onto their tails to simulate interceptions.

On the evening of 16 January 1947 Flight Lieutenant David Richards was a senior controller of the 11 Group filter room, situated in the grounds of Bentley Priory, and a Bullseye exercise was in progress. The first inkling that something unusual had occurred came when Richards received a call from the GCI station at Trimley Heath, near Felixstowe. He recalled:

'Trimley came up on my direct phone to report a strange plot which was either stationary at a great height or moving erratically at a great speed and then stopping again. If this was a conventional aircraft it would have travelled in a straight line, but it did not do that. This was not an aircraft, it was something very odd. Somebody – either at one of the [radar] stations or at Uxbridge – had computed speed between the rather intermittent plots and had come up with a startling figure of 1,000 mph.'[4]

A speed of 1,000 mph was truly startling, for it was not until October 1947 that US test pilot Chuck Yeager first broke the sound barrier (760 mph at sea level) in a Bell X-1 rocket plane. Yet the target plotted at Bentley Priory had exceeded this speed at 38,000 feet above the North Sea near the Dutch coastline. Richards continues:

'They were looking at the tube and could judge if the echoes were the same object or a new one. This probably gave rise to the estimated speed, based on reappearances in a different place and a different height. [Trimley Heath staff] were interrogated on this both by ourselves and Uxbridge, but stuck to their guns. After some talk between Uxbridge and the scientific officers at the stations making the observation on the validity of their plots, not a meteorological balloon etc (which I had already done), it was decided to scramble a Mossie to investigate.'[5]

If the target was a plane, it was displaying unheard-of flight characteristics. Yet if it wasn't a plane, what could it be?

Details of the incident that followed have been preserved in RAF operations record books (ORBs). This was unique because in later years ORB records of 'unidentified' radar trackings are conspicuous by their absence from the official files. In other instances log books have been removed and have never formed part of the 'official history' of the RAF stations. As a result, the records of this 1947 incident are the single surviving example of the system used by the RAF to investigate UFOs during this early phase of the Cold War.

The ORB for Eastern Fighter Sector Headquarters, RAF Neatishead, on 16 January 1947 records:

'An unidentified aircraft had been plotted in
WC 9585 at 38,000 ft., and Eastern Sector
Ops were requested by Group [11 Group HQ,

Bentley Priory] to scramble a Mosquito of 23
Sqdn. to intercept. However, as there was no
aircraft available with oxygen this was
impossible, and Sector Ops were informed by
12 Group that an aircraft of 11 Group which
was already airborne on a Bullseye exercise
would try to intercept under Trimley Heath
Control.'[6]

Before the chase began, ground radar watched the target descend 21,000
feet, placing it at level altitude with the prop-driven bombers participating
in the Bullseye exercise. The fighter diverted to the intercept was a
Mosquito from RAF West Malling. According to an Air Ministry report to
the US Army Air Force (USAAF), the action began when the Mosquito was
vectored towards the blip at 22,000 feet. According to the USAAF, 'a long
chase ensued' across the North Sea towards Norfolk [7]

At Trimley Heath GCI radar operators reported:

'...five other contacts [were] obtained in quick
succession on X. 362 (OPERATION CHARLIE)
which was chased from 2120 hours until 2202
hours when interception was abandoned due to
A.I. [air interception radar] trouble. This
target was completely unidentified. Height
at the commencement of the interception was
17,000 feet and target descended to 6,000
feet by 2202 hours.'[8]

According to the USAAF account, during the chase two brief contacts were
made by the Mosquito's onboard radar, but these 'faded quickly' and 'the
UFO appeared to take efficient controlled evasive action'.[9] Neatishead's
report suggests the interception was unsuccessful because the Mosquito
developed engine trouble and a radar problem. Flight Lieutenant
Richards recalls the crew had great difficulty holding the contact, which
'faded and reappeared and sometimes stood still, before fading again'.[10]

'Evasive action' implies intelligent control and the encounter triggered
immediate fears that an enemy aircraft had been observing the exercise.

However it was apparent that no Russian aircraft could match the performance displayed by this 'flying object'

The incident caused great concern at the Air Ministry and afterwards Flight Lieutenant Richards was asked to write 'a confidential report' for Fighter Command, a report that remains 'secret' to this day and is not available at the PRO.

Richards told us:

> 'The event has always stuck in my memory as my only "encounter of the third kind" and although the term "UFO" was not in use then, we wondered if the wily Russians had produced some secret aircraft from a rapid development of German technology which we in the RAF were beginning to realise was so far ahead of our own.'[11]

Another 'High-Flying Aircraft'

In July 1947 the FBI agreed to help the USAAF's new study of 'flying discs' and the North Sea incident was one of a number forwarded to the FBI. The details were transmitted by a telex from the Air Ministry in London which stated: 'No explanation has been forthcoming, nor has it been repeated.'[12] The Ministry was actually misleading the USAAF, because a very similar incident *had* occurred just 24 hours after the dramatic North Sea chase.

As a result of the events on 16 January, Fighter Command immediately extended its night radar watch for an additional half hour after the normal shutdown. On 17 January Squadron Leader S. L. Cruwys, commanding officer at RAF Neatishead, reported that a Mosquito from 23 Squadron had been 'scrambled just before midnight to intercept an unidentified high-flying aircraft'.[13]

Earlier, at 7.45 p.m., radar stations on the Yorkshire coast had tracked an unidentified target for 30 minutes. The station log at Humberston records:

```
'U. 306 [unidentified plot] was followed
continuously for 90 miles at 10,000 feet,
moving east to west over the North Sea
before changing direction towards the south,
moving once again across the Wash towards
the Norfolk coast.'¹⁴
```

The tension can be measured by an entry that says this was 'the longest watch period ever experienced since the termination of hostilities, operational six and a half hours, being released at 01.30 hrs'.[15]

According to Neatishead, an attempt was made to intercept the object when contact was made at 18,000 feet, but 'the observer was unable to hold it as the target was jerking violently'. Further contacts were obtained as the target fell rapidly to 2,000 feet, at which point both the 'unidentified' blip and the Mosquito disappeared below radar coverage.[16]

The pilot of the Mosquito was a World War II night-fighter veteran, Flight Lieutenant William Kent. His log book confirms the incident, with a red ink entry recording an unusual night sortie of 1 hour, 45 minutes – 'a scramble interception'. Kent recalled:

> 'I, being one of the very few pilots with any wartime experience and therefore having some understanding of the request, yelled for my navigator and the duty ground crew and leapt off the ground in under four minutes. On a "scramble" we never listen to any briefings on the ops phone – speed in the air is paramount – and so I had no idea what was brewing until, climbing to height and taken over by the close controller, I was given a brisk brief on the R/T [radio telegraph]. The ORB record is correct except that on reflection with hindsight the unidentified "aircraft" was almost certainly not an aircraft... At no time at any height despite sporadic radar contacts did I sight anything visually, but on a dark night closing on a target at a speed of 10–20 knots [11–23 mph], extreme care is needed to avoid colliding and then only by steering a few degrees off centre does one's night vision show a darker silhouette – often frighteningly close!'[17]

The plot faded shortly after midnight and Flight Lieutenant Kent and his navigator continued to patrol without seeing anything unusual.

Afterwards Kent discussed the bizarre incident with Neatishead and a report was sent to the commanding officer of 12 Group. His theory was that the 'aircraft' was in fact a burst meteorological balloon, the radar returns being produced by reflections from its metal canisters as it descended towards the ground. 'The report, which I saw, had no comment except a margin sketch of a pricked balloon,' Kent recalled.

This scepticism was typical of Fighter Command's pragmatic attitude both to the 'ghost plane' mystery and the later flying saucer enigma – it refused to reach conclusions that were not supported by hard evidence.

More East Coast Ghost Planes

The intrusions continued. On the night of 23 January three officers from the Central Fighter Establishment were visiting Neatishead to control a high-speed interception exercise, when at 11.15 p.m. 'an unidentified high-altitude aircraft' suddenly appeared on the GCI radar. Mosquitoes from 264 Squadron at Linton-on-Ouse in Yorkshire were scrambled to intercept, but before they could reach the area the target faded from the radar screen.[18]

This was the third night that unidentified flying objects had been tracked by stations defending England's east coast and the third time that interception attempts had ended in failure. On each occasion the UFOs came in over the North Sea towards Norfolk before descending from great height, disappearing beneath radar cover.

It may be relevant that the aerial phenomena appeared immediately before the arrival of a deep cold weather front over southern England on 24 January. At this time knowledge of the role played by unusual weather conditions, thunderstorms and charged clouds in the creation of 'spurious' echoes and 'UFOs' on radar tubes was in its infancy. Several years later the USAF's consultant astronomer, Dr J. Allen Hynek, studied the English 'ghost plane' reports. His conclusions were: 'Weather effects on radar.'[19]

By the end of January 1947 the Air Ministry began to act on the puzzling reports of unidentified aircraft reported from the east coast. The ORB records note that a RAF signals officer was sent to Neatishead to undertake a study 'on the unidentified high-flying aircraft that have been plotted in recent months'. His report commented that 'evidence appears to be strong' that the unidentified tracks were caused by radiosonde balloons released from a Meteorological station in Norfolk.[20] But doubts remained. The Air Ministry may have decided it could dismiss the majority of mysterious radar plots as weather balloons, but it continued to classify one incident – the 'aircraft' tracked by Trimley Heath at 32,000 feet on 16 January – as 'unexplained'.

The Press Response

We can only speculate on whether unidentified radar tracks continued to plague the RAF as the 'ghost plane' era moved into the age of the 'flying saucer'. By the time the story reached the national newspapers in April the Air Ministry was actively denying the reports. A spokesman told the *Daily Telegraph* they were taking no further action. 'We have found no evidence to support the reports at all,' he said.[21]

The *Yorkshire Post* was less inclined to dismiss the mystery completely and its editorial looked at the problem from a different angle:

'Radar has plotted some strange things in its time, from children's kites and raindrops to formations of geese. But it surely never plotted a stranger thing than this. What is the aircraft? Speculation takes us into those regions where the scenes are laid for so many thrilling stories in the boys' magazine. Is it a diamond or drug smuggler? Is it conveying a secret agent from one foreign Power to another? In that event it would of course have the secret papers and probably also a beautiful woman spy on board. Is it a guided missile?'[22]

The newspaper compared the ghost plane mystery with the reports of phantom German Zeppelins that had circulated before the outbreak of World War I and observed: 'It seems to be established that it is only at times of peculiar stress that the public is in the psychological state to receive and circulate such stories.'[23]

The practical steps to solve the mystery were clear:

'Fast RAF fighters must continue trying to intercept the visitor if it should return. Our air service has the fastest fighters in the world and should not find it impossibly difficult … meanwhile we may enjoy the atmosphere of mystery and imagination which surrounds the ghost aircraft.'[24]

This perceptive article was the first time after World War II that the appearance of UFO phenomena had been linked with social or political stress and the first time a non-physical origin for unidentified aerial phenomena had been suggested by the press.

Kenneth Arnold's Flying Saucers

The 'ghost aircraft' returned in another guise later in 1947, triggering the greatest mystery of modern times: 'flying saucers'. The time was right for their arrival. The scene was the north-eastern seaboard of the United States.

Shortly before 3 p.m. on 24 June 1947 light aircraft pilot Kenneth Arnold was cruising above the Cascade mountains of Washington state, searching for the wreckage of a downed C-46 transport plane. Suddenly his attention was drawn to a 'tremendous bright flash'. Scanning the skies, he spotted a group of nine 'peculiar-looking aircraft' moving towards him at tremendous speed. The objects were semi-circular or crescent-shaped, with a lead object at a higher elevation than the rest. The formation flashed brightly as the objects reflected the sun. They appeared to be 50 feet long and 3 feet thick. Timing them as they moved between mountain peaks, Arnold was amazed to find that they were moving at around

1,700 mph, more than 1,000 mph faster than the fastest aircraft in existence at that time. Eventually they disappeared towards Mount Adams in the south.[25]

Arnold abandoned his search for the C-46 and radioed his sighting through to the airfield in Pendleton, Utah. By the time he landed, the story had reached the press and he was surrounded by newspaper reporters who asked him to describe what he had seen. Arnold was always emphatic that he never described the objects as 'saucers', but the story that entered modern folklore is that he described their movements as 'like a saucer skipping on water'.[26] The term 'flying saucers' was created by a sub-editor and within days the story was picked up by the US wire services. The phrase became a household word overnight and would eventually become synonymous with 'interplanetary spacecraft'. But in 1947, at least publicly, it had none of those connotations.

This is borne out by the first ever Gallup Poll on the subject of flying saucers, published on 14 August 1947.[27] The direct question: 'What do you think these saucers are?' obtained the percentage responses as follows:

No answer, don't know	33%
Imagination, optical illusion, mirage, etc.	29%
Hoax	10%
US secret weapon, part of atomic bomb, etc.	15%
Weather forecasting devices	3%
Russian secret weapon	1%
Other explanations	9%

The answers gave no hint of the tidal wave of belief in extraterrestrials which was to develop in the early 1950s, but they do reveal a public both fascinated and puzzled by this seemingly new phenomenon. Gallup determined that within a few months of the term 'flying saucer' being coined, nine out of ten Americans had heard of them.

Arnold himself assumed the aircraft he saw were a secret US government project, either guided missiles or new jet planes. 'I felt certain they belonged to our Government,' he wrote in his official report. Later he came to believe UFOs were 'sky creatures' who lived in the upper reaches of the atmosphere.[28]

The Flying Saucer Phenomenon

By 4 July 1947 flying saucers had appeared in newspapers from London to Sydney to Cape Town. The *Daily Express* in London, in a story entitled 'Flying saucers ablaze in sky', defined a saucer as 'a round projectile without propeller, wings or tail', quoting the description of Richard

Rankin, an experienced pilot who claimed to have seen ten flying in formation over California.[29] His sighting had occurred before the publicity surrounding Arnold's report and he said he had kept quiet until others came forward. Now so many had reported sightings of 'discs' and 'saucers' that the USAAF had ordered an investigation.

The first flying saucer report from the British Isles came from Mrs Marjorie Hyde, the wife of a clergyman from Deal in Kent. She said she had been waiting at a level-crossing near Sandwich on the afternoon of 30 June when she saw 'more of a ring than a saucer' in the heavens. As she explained to the press:

> 'I saw it for only a second or two. I called out to my husband but he didn't hear me above the noise of the gates and traffic. By the time I had attracted his attention it had disappeared. It was dark against the clouds – like a grey shadow a little darker than the cloud. I think it was revolving, but I am not sure. It was going at a fairly high speed. I am positive it was not a smoke ring from the passing engine.'[30]

Examining the reports it becomes clear that many of the 'flying saucer' sightings did not describe saucer-shaped objects at all, but were classified as such because of the media hype. On the other hand, it is of interest that although Kenneth Arnold did not describe the nine objects he saw as 'saucers', many thousands across the world subsequently reported seeing saucer-shaped flying objects as often as they reported seeing disc or rocket-shaped flying objects.

Credible Witnesses

UFO reports were often taken seriously by public and government alike because of the social status of many of the witnesses. Arnold himself was both an accomplished private pilot and successful businessman. Many other witnesses were also pilots who, it was assumed, would easily be able to make the distinction between 'flying discs' and natural phenomena such as planets, balloons and other aircraft.

One such 'credible witness' was Captain Norman Waugh, who had served with RAF Bomber Command during the war. Waugh was flying a Vickers Viking over the Bay of Biscay on 11 July 1947 when he saw 'an object travelling at lightning speed that looked like a grey tadpole'. He told a *Daily Express* correspondent at Gibraltar that:

> '...within 15–20 seconds it passed about six miles off and vanished, leaving a long vapour trail. We estimated the object

> [was flying at] 600 miles an hour at 15–16,000 feet over the sea. It
> made no interference on our radio and I ordered my radio
> operator to inform Air Traffic Control in London.'[31]

Waugh's description is a classic example of a daylight meteor or bolide
burning up in the atmosphere and leaving a trail of debris in its wake.
Bolides are very rare and it is unlikely that even a commercial pilot with
thousands of hours of flying time would have encountered one. If this is
what Waugh did experience, it is easy to see how, in light of the media
hysteria at the time, he chose to report it as a 'flying saucer'. When a
phenomenon occurs which is outside usual human experience the brain
seeks to find a 'pigeonhole' in which to put it. Interviewed later, Waugh
said, 'The crew and I came to the conclusion that it could only be a flying
saucer.'[32] Months earlier Waugh may well have framed his experience as a
'ghost plane', or, had the sighting been during 1944 or 1946, a 'foo-
fighter' or 'ghost rocket'.

Thousands of flying saucer reports now began to pour into official
channels both in the USA and Britain, and sightings by 'credible witnesses'
added weight to the notion that the flying saucers must be physically real.
And if they were real, just what were they and who was piloting them?

Early Hypotheses

In the post-war period the USA retained its dominant position as the
world leader in military technology, so it was natural for witnesses like
Kenneth Arnold to speculate that the saucers were American secret
weapons. This technological superiority was challenged in 1949 when the
Soviets tested their first atomic bomb. As Western fears of Soviet intentions
increased, it was logical for some military minds to suspect that some of
the 'flying saucers' could be of Russian origin.

When it became apparent that terrestrial aircraft could not account for
the saucer phenomenon, the extraterrestrial hypothesis was the next
logical step. This was already being discussed by both the US military and
public by the end of the 1940s.

In Britain there was little or no official interest in flying saucers until
1949, when both the Air Ministry and the MoD's Scientific Intelligence
branch first began to collect reports and news cuttings on the subject. As
we have seen, UFOs were frequently encountered before this, but categorised as the unknowable 'ghost planes', and after the British
government's experiences with the foo-fighters and the ghost rockets, it
was unwilling to become embroiled in another mystery with no physical
solution.

'Estimate of the Situation'

In the USA the situation was markedly different. Shortly after Kenneth Arnold's sighting Lieutenant General Nathan F. Twining was asked to look into the matter. His response to Brigadier General George Schulgen of the USAAF was unequivocal: 'The phenomenon reported is something real and not imaginary or fictitious.'[33] It was recommended that a detailed study of flying saucers be undertaken and on 30 December 1947 Project Sign came into existence.

Sign, known to the public as 'Project Saucer', began work immediately. The group's first major investigation was the legendary Mantell Incident of 7 January 1948, in which a young Air National Guard pilot, Thomas Mantell, crashed his F-51 jet while pursuing a 'gigantic UFO' over Kentucky. The investigation decided that Mantell had chased the planet Venus, prominent in the same part of the sky as the 'UFO', until he lost consciousness due to lack of oxygen.[34] This explanation was said to be definitive when the USAF exchanged UFO data with British intelligence in 1950.[35] But two years later the case was reopened by a new UFO project, Blue Book, and the 'UFO' was correctly identified as a Skyhook balloon released by the US Navy from a base in Minnesota.[36] The Mantell incident demonstrated how radical misperception could lead even trained pilots into believing a mundane object was a UFO.

A second major sighting was made by two commercial pilots from a DC-3 passenger plane over Alabama on 24 July 1948. Clarence Chiles and John Whitted reported that a torpedo-shaped wingless object emitting flames like 'one of those fantastic Flash Gordon rocket ships' shot past the plane before disappearing into clouds. This sighting further persuaded some of Sign's personnel at the Air Technical Intelligence Center (ATIC) that UFOs were of extraterrestrial origin[37] As a result, an intelligence briefing document was prepared, known as the 'Estimate of the Situation'.

'Estimate' has become legendary within the UFO community, mainly because of its sensational conclusions, which seemed to prove that the US government was taking the extraterrestrial possibility seriously. It is also legendary because, despite the prominence it has been given in the UFO community, no copies have survived. Nor are there any records, other than anecdotal ones, of its existence.

However, rumours concerning 'Estimate' have an interesting pedigree and its conclusions, if not its actual existence, appear to have some basis in reality. Captain Edward J. Ruppelt, who would lead the USAF's Project Blue Book from 1952, stated that he saw a copy of it and it was 'a black-cover document, stamped TOP SECRET'.[38]

In a draft of his 1956 memoirs Ruppelt again claimed that 'Estimate' 'concluded that UFOs were interplanetary' and summarised the contents, which appeared to be a collection of disparate reports of aerial phenomena that displayed no consistency either in shape or behaviour. According to Ruppelt, the list of 'unexplained' incidents included several that occurred before June 1947 such as the English 'ghost planes' tracked by radar in the January of that year.[39] Nebulous though these reports were, they were being used as supporting evidence for an interplanetary origin for the flying saucers.

Another highly placed military source informed UFOlogist Kevin Randle that 'Estimate' contained references to the alleged crash of a flying saucer at Roswell. The same source told Randle that Air Force Chief of Staff General Hoyt S. Vandenberg ordered that any reference to the Roswell incident be removed from the 'Estimate of the Situation'.[40]

The Roswell Incident

For believers and sceptics alike, Roswell has everything that characterises the UFO subject: alien cadavers, flying saucers, government conspiracies and witnesses being 'silenced'. The basic premise – that an extraterrestrial craft crashed in the New Mexican desert and was retrieved by the US military – has survived for over 50 years. The story originated from a hasty press release issued by Roswell Army Field at the height of the flying saucer craze on 8 July 1947. The statement said a disc-shaped object had landed (not crashed) on a ranch near the town and was later removed and 'lent to higher headquarters'. The news was picked up by the Associated Press and the next day the story was splashed across the front pages of newspapers across the world.[41] The excitement was dampened within hours when the Eighth Army Headquarters announced that the 'flying disc' had been identified as a lowly weather balloon. It has only been since the 1970s, when the Roswell incident was revived, that UFOlogists have been gathering 'evidence' for the crash of an 'alien craft'.[42]

That *something* happened at Roswell is not in doubt. Even the US government accepts that an incident did occur, but claims the 'flying disc' was actually part of a covert project, code-named Mogul, that used specially-adapted high-altitude balloons to track Soviet nuclear tests. As in the case of the Skyhook balloons, the Mogul project was so secret that staff at Roswell army air base, who were responsible for the initial press release, did not have sufficient 'need to know'.

The release of the 'weather balloon' story was a typical Cold War tactic to cover a public relations blunder. However, an investigation by the General Accounting Office following senatorial pressure in 1994–95 found no evidence that:

```
'... [the Roswell incident] was a UFO event nor
was there any indication of a cover-up by
the Government.... No records indicated or
even hinted at the recovery of "alien"
bodies or extraterrestrial materials.'⁴³
```

Many relevant records from the era have been destroyed, so it is unlikely that conclusive evidence will ever be found to satisfy those who believe an extraterrestrial (ET) craft was recovered. However, the failure to provide definitive proof of the balloon theory, combined with the initial statement that a 'flying disc' had been captured, set in motion a train of belief which has spread like a virus through contemporary American folklore. Whatever the US government says about the event is now undermined by their earlier claims and for many nothing short of an admission that an alien craft did crash will suffice. One salient fact about the Roswell incident remains constant: as yet not one piece of physical evidence or one genuine government document has emerged to back up the claims that an 'alien' craft crashed and was retrieved by the US military.

'Don't Believe It'

Following the unpalatable conclusions reached by the 'Estimate of the Situation', those within Project Sign who believed interplanetary visitors were the most likely explanation for UFOs were marginalised. Although Sign officials had recommended that UFO specialists should be located at every air base, this proposal was rejected by air force officials.

On 16 December 1948 Project Sign became Project Grudge. Captain Ruppelt summed up Grudge's philosophy in describing how UFO reports were being evaluated 'on the premise that UFOs couldn't exist. No matter what you see or hear, don't believe it.'⁴⁴

Meanwhile the British Air Ministry was belatedly taking an interest in flying saucers. Scientific and Technical Intelligence branch files dating from 1949 contain news cuttings and magazine articles on flying saucers that were categorised as 'unorthodox aircraft'.⁴⁵

Initially some intelligence sources suspected that the saucers could be Russian prototypes developed from Nazi designs for a 'saucer-shaped' aircraft captured at the end of World War II, but this theory was quickly dismissed. The Air Ministry would shortly arrive at its own conclusions about flying saucers. The story of how those conclusions were reached and the views of those who took part in the process would form the template for Britain's handling of the UFO subject for the next 50 years.

Meanwhile, into the melting pot of tension and paranoia came an international wave of interest in 'flying saucers'. The subject stole newspaper headlines almost every day on both sides of the Atlantic. It is not surprising that from 1950 onwards the Western powers began to regard UFOs, as they became known, with extreme seriousness, and subject them to a high level of secrecy.

Britain's First Saucer Scare

Flying saucers arrived in the British Isles in October and November 1950, when two popular weekend newspapers, the *Sunday Dispatch* and the *Sunday Express*, launched the first pro-'saucer' media campaign (see Figure 5).

Both papers serialised the first 'saucer' books, published in 1950, that would have a huge impact on public belief. They were *The Flying Saucers are Real* by retired Marine Corps Major Donald Keyhoe,[46] Frank Scully's *Behind the Flying Saucers*[47] and Gerald Heard's *The Riddle of the Flying Saucers* (published in the USA as *Is Another World Watching?*)[48] Scully's book was a sensational account of a flying saucer containing 'little men' that had crashed in the New Mexico desert in 1948 and been secretly recovered by the US government. The source was later traced to two confidence tricksters who admitted the story was a hoax. Despite this revelation, Scully's book continued to contribute to the growing rumour that the US authorities had captured alien technology and were engaged in a conspiracy of silence.

Keyhoe was a veteran of World War II and his stories were taken seriously because of his contacts in the US military. He was the first person to publicly push the claim that the US government held evidence that the saucers were extraterrestrial but was concealing it from the people for reasons of its own. For Keyhoe, the saucers were a means of ensuring America's superiority in the arms race because 'if [our] scientists and engineers can learn the source of the space ship's power and adopt it to our use, it may well be the means of ending the threat of war'.[49] He believed that the policy of secrecy was necessary to conceal the US military's determination to obtain the secret of the saucers' propulsion system before the Communists. This secret was to Keyhoe more important than the hydrogen bomb because 'it may one day be the key to the fate of the world'.[50]

Figure 5 (*opposite*): ***Sunday Dispatch***, 1 October 1950: 'Flying Saucers': This was the newspaper headline that launched the first 'flying saucer' craze in Britain. Newspaper editor Charles Eade was pursuaded to publish a series of articles on sightings in the US by his friend Lord Mountbatten, who had become convinced the saucers were extraterrestrial spacecraft. (By permission of the British Library.)

Sunday Dispatch

1 Year.   OCTOBER 1, 1950.   Price 2d.
7,769.   Radio Page 6.

The Story That May Be Bigger Even Than Atom Bomb Wars

FLYING SAUCERS

Full Inquiry Into The No. 1 Sensation Of The Age

BY THE EDITOR OF THE SUNDAY DISPATCH

I HAVE decided to publish in the SUNDAY DISPATCH a series of the most sensational articles ever printed in any newspaper. The word "sensational" is much overworked, but I use it deliberately today because there is no other expression that can properly describe either the subject or the articles.

For the question is the most "sensational" in the world today—WHAT ARE THESE FLYING SAUCERS?

Millions of people laugh at newspaper reports of Flying Saucers. They do not believe they exist; they do not believe anyone has seen one; they dismiss the whole subject as nonsense not worth a minute's serious thought.

But not everyone takes that view, and I have found that many intelligent and distinguished people in all parts of the world are intensely interested in Flying Saucers and treat such reports very seriously indeed.

Some months ago I published in this newspaper an article entitled "The Day They Saw The Flying Saucer at Orangeburg." It consisted of extracts from a local paper in a small American town over which a Flying Saucer had appeared a few days earlier.

Personal Letter

A few days after I had printed that article I received a personal letter from one of the most famous men alive today. I will not give you his name, but I must ask you to accept my word that you, your family, and all your friends would certainly know of him. He is a man who commands universal respect and admiration.

"These extraordinary things have now been seen in almost every part of the world—Scandinavia, North America, South America, Central Europe, etc. The reports are always vague and the newspapers generally try to ridicule them. As a result it is difficult for any seriously interested person to find out any much about them. I should therefore like to congratulate you on having had both the intelligence (and, incidentally, the courage) to print the first serious helpful article which I have read on the Flying Saucer."

A few weeks ago I had a long talk about Flying Saucers with the writer of that letter, and it was as the result of that discussion that I decided to place before the readers of the Sunday Dispatch all that is known about the Flying Saucers and all the theories about them no matter how sensational and fantastic.

Some people will scoff at the very idea, but I promise this—no intelligent person who reads these articles with an open mind will laugh at the end.

The United States Government has taken the Flying Saucers seriously. Have you ever heard about Project Saucer? That is the name of the special investigation set up by the U.S. Air Force to inquire into 375 separate Flying Saucer reports.

Do you know that although they were able to explain away the majority of the incidents there were 34 for which it was impossible to find any explanation?

Suddenly Silence

No one has ever cleared up the mystery of Captain Thomas Mantell, a U.S. pilot with 3,000 flying hours to his credit. He and two other pilots were given orders to chase a Flying Saucer near Fort Knox, Kentucky. The others were outdistanced by the strange object, but Mantell went on. He described the chase by radio to the one below when he was closing in on the Flying Saucer. Then, suddenly silence. His plane disintegrated in mid-air, and his body was found near Fort Knox. Mantell died chasing something that neither he nor any other pilot could identify—AND THERE WAS NO JOKE OR HOAX ABOUT MANTELL'S DEATH.

Two American aviation experts were not satisfied that the U.S. Air Force's "Project Saucer" was giving the public all the facts that had been collected as independently and unknown to one another they started personal investiga-

U.S. Veteran

One is Donald Keyhoe, a former Chief of Information for the aeronautics branch of the U.S. Department of Commerce. After many months of research he wrote a book called "The Flying Saucers Are Real."

The other is Frank Scully, a veteran of journalism. His investigation and report, as complete as Keyhoe's, his book is entitled "Behind The Flying Saucer."

I have bought the rights to publish their reports in this country, and the essential parts of both books will form part of the Sunday Dispatch series beginning next week.

Although Keyhoe and Scully worked separately they reach the same general conclusion—and a sensational conclusion it is.

But of one thing I am quite certain—I am not sure that I myself... I myself. I just do not know. But of one thing I am quite certain—no one need be ashamed of holding a serious and intelligent interest in Flying Saucers, and it would be a mistake to dismiss the stories about them with a laugh. The first man to see some strange object which, he said...

(Continued in Column 4)

The Girl In The Park
By Thomas Stillwell

The 25-year-old labourer who was acquitted in the police court after a "private prosecution" charging him with the murder of Joan Woodhouse, aged 27, in Arundel Park in August 1948.

WHAT of the girl I so very loved saving? If he meeting our awaited ervicing my continuing with each other...

Here is exactly what happened.

I was walking along that day from the direction to the park on a path and right across the bit weight, time.

As I walked I came across Pack Diamonds back at white-face caretaker at the hallway, and with those leaving and the house kept each

As I walked on with him I saw the little girl had come up, and her pretty smile as she smiled and I ran over with the idea of showing her. I saw once with the little girl and I could see right across the water...

Near Walnut Tree

It was after a had passed an outer remark on the girl I saw that as I had told saver taking the field in the third. I made to the prep a saver and the biggest part of his path...

Exclusive

Stillwell Tells His Own Story

State May Pay First Child

By Sunday Dispatch Political Correspondent

THE Government are considering paying a family allowance for the first child.

By this means they hope to avoid a clash at the Socialist annual conference at Margate this week on wages and the high cost of living.

But Ministers would announce their plans only if the storm on the wage - freeze threatened to defeat the National Executive.

TWO-AND-A-QUARTER HOUR BATTLE FOR LIFE

Vet Saves Terrier Si... In Lake Mud

By Sunday Dispatch Reporter

POLICE, firemen, and R.S.P.C.A. officials fought for two and a qua... day to save a dog slowly sinking in seven feet of mud in Kelsey P... mere, which had been drained for dredging.

When R.S.P.C.A. veterinary officer Thomas Gibbs-Murray reached the dog over a bridge of fire ladders and brushwood only above the surface.

The dog, Simon, a curly-haired fox-terrier belonging to Mrs. ...ford-road, Beckenham, was being taken for a walk by eight-year-old old Muriel Caird, of Lake-road.

Inspector Gibbs-Murray drags Simon to safety.

Ex-Baths Attendant Weds Daughter Of Countess On Riviera

From Our PARIS Reporter

A YOUNG Australian who was once a swimming baths attendant was married at Nice yesterday to a member of one of the oldest families in British aristocracy.

The ex-baths attendant, who swam for Australia in the Olympic Games, was Mr. Frank O'Brien, of Sydney, New South Wales. His bride was the Hon. Patricia Cavendish, daughter of the widowed Countess of Kenmare and sister of the seventh Lord Waterpark.

The bride, given away in marriage...

THE BEST
BIG
PICTURE IN TELE...

DECCA
TELEVISION MODEL

Keyhoe's ideas were highly influential and this 'government cover up' would soon become a major belief within flying saucer mythology. Keyhoe also expressed his views in an article in *True* magazine, published in January 1950, which was read by hundreds of thousands of people across the globe and scrutinised by the British Air Ministry and the Scientific Intelligence branch of the MoD.[51]

Tens of thousands of British people read these sensational UFO stories and the circulation of the *Sunday Dispatch* reflected the level of fascination the subject had aroused. Before the paper began its flying saucer campaign its circulation was 50,000, but in 1957, after seven years of sensational saucer headlines, it had risen to 2,500,000.[52] As rival *News Chronicle* columnist A. J. Cummings put it, the flying saucer phenomenon had become a worldwide talking point:

> '...partly because of the sinister implication that it signifies the appearance of hostile visitants from another planet, partly because it may be the trying out of a new secret weapon – American or Russian – and partly, perhaps, because after the splitting of the atom most of us are ready to believe that anything can happen.'[53]

The public was fascinated and the Air Ministry was monitoring the situation, but there was no department specifically responsible for investigating reports of flying saucers. That was soon to change.

The Asmara Sighting

On the morning of 6 April 1950 there was great excitement in the streets of Asmara in Eritrea, East Africa, when hundreds of people, including the British chief administrator, saw two disc-shaped objects spinning through the skies.

The sightings began when the captain of an Aden Airways aircraft reported seeing 'an object in the sky in the nature of a silvery disc suspended from [a] parachute' as he approached Asmara airport. Soon the airport's meteorological staff were watching two flying saucers through a theodolite, 'one moving so quickly and erratically that it soon went out of the field of view, one moving steadily', but it proved impossible to estimate their height.[54] The chief meteorological officer, F. A. Sharp, saw two similar objects with the naked eye and concluded one was the planet Venus, with the rapid movement of the other being the result of an optical illusion.

Before this solution was offered, the British administrator's report had reached Sir Nelson Johnson of the Meteorological Office at the Air

Ministry, London. He suggested the silvery disc seen from the aircraft was probably a balloon used by the army for testing radar. Johnson's letter was rejected by the chief administrator, who explained there were no army testing stations in the territory. He concluded: 'It is not felt, in view of the uncertainty of the Air Ministry's views, that a satisfactory explanation of the phenomena is yet forthcoming.'[55]

'Useful for Analysis'?

The Asmara sighting effectively marks the beginning of the Air Ministry's involvement in the flying saucer mystery. It would also become the first of many subsequent controversies sparked by glib public statements which offered seemingly ludicrous explanations for saucer sightings. Writers such as Keyhoe drew parallels between this UK policy and the public stance adopted by the USAF as evidence that both governments were involved in suppressing saucer information. In fact, claims of a high-level cover up were based upon rumours that were often without foundation and what evidence has survived indicates that official unconcern was the order of the day.

An Air Ministry file dating from 1950 – the earliest on record at the PRO – illustrates this point. Although the sighting was of a 'light in the sky', the observer was an experienced airman and the file provides an insight into the way early UFO reports were investigated. The file heading, 'Unidentified Aircraft', was altered by hand in later years to read: 'Unidentified Objects', indicating how perceptions of aerial phenomena at official level were evolving.

The file contained a report by RAF Group Captain R. Cartmel of 'an unusual occurrence' that he witnessed on a Sunday evening, 10 December 1950, from the Wildernesse country club near Sevenoaks in Kent. Cartmel had flown 1,400 hours in 81 different aircraft and was a classic example of a 'credible witness'. He and two friends had watched a bright light in the sky moving east to west at a steady height of 3,000 feet below the cloud base. It travelled at a speed of around 150 mph and was visible for five minutes before it passed out of sight behind the club buildings. 'The matter which really drew my attention to it was the complete absence of sound,' Cartmel emphasised in his report to the Air Ministry. 'I would be interested to know if this information is of any value and whether or not there is an explanation to the phenomena of straight and level flight without sound.'[56]

Cartmel's report was passed round various Air Ministry departments, the first being DD Ops (AD), where it was discovered that the radar system was 'non-operational' in the Southern Sector on the night in question. A comment appended to the file provides an insight into the mindset of Air

Ministry officials at the time:

> 'I suppose reports of this sort, if kept and added to other reports of similar phenomena, might one day be useful for analysis. I can't think of anything else we could do with this one.'[57]

Although it was suggested that more information might be obtained by interviewing Cartmel, no one seems to have made the effort to do so.

Despite the Air Ministry's lack of interest in UFOs, by the spring of 1950 there were some senior figures in the MoD and intelligence departments who were beginning to treat the subject in a serious manner. The most important influence was the extensive coverage newspapers were devoting to the sightings. With flying saucers in the headlines every other day, some of the world's most influential politicians, scientists and military minds were beginning to make enquiries of their own.

Chapter 4

FLYING SAUCERS: BY ROYAL APPOINTMENT

'...these extraordinary things have now
been seen in almost every part of the
world: Scandinavia, North America, South
America, Central Europe, etc... It seems
clear that the overwhelming weight of
opinion from every part of the world will
show that some new thing definitely
exists which is capable of flying at very
slow speed or even perhaps of hovering
and accelerating at an unheard of speed
several times the speed of sound.'[1]

Sunday Dispatch, London, 1 October 1950

These are the views of one of the most powerful military leaders of the 20th century, revealed in a letter to an influential media tycoon. The writer was Lord Louis Mountbatten. Like many other military leaders and thinkers of the time, he was fascinated by flying saucers.

In recent years it has been claimed that Mountbatten had access to 'Top Secret' photos of flying saucers held in the files of the Royal Navy, or that he was directly involved in the investigation of a UFO which crashed in Britain during World War II. In reality, his interest in UFOs simply overlapped with his fascination for rockets and space travel in general. Ziegler's biography notes that Mountbatten was an atheist who rejected the supernatural and believed flying saucers were open to rational study

Figure 6: **Admiral of the Fleet Lord Louis Mountbatten, Earl of Burma (1900–1979) and Chief of Defence Staff 1958–65. Mountbatten believed that 'flying saucers' were extraterrestrial spacecraft and encouraged his friend, the journalist Charles Eade, to publish a series of pro-UFO articles in the *Sunday Dispatch* newspaper during 1950–51. Later in his life he became more sceptical and dismissed stories of 'little men' and claims that the Government had captured a crashed UFO as 'nonsense'.**
(Hulton-Deutsch Collection/CORBIS)

and explanation.[2] However, Mountbatten became an influential figure among the British aristocracy and military who took a keen interest in the subject. Other household names within this élite circle included the Battle of Britain mastermind Air Chief Marshal Sir Hugh Dowding, the British army general Sir Frederick 'Boy' Browning, wartime pilot Sir Arthur Barratt and Mountbatten's nephew Prince Philip, Duke of Edinburgh. By 1952 a significant number of this discreet 'gentleman's club' had become convinced the Earth was under observation by aliens.

Collecting the Evidence

In 1950 Mountbatten began collecting reports of flying saucer sightings, using his contacts in the armed services. Unsurprisingly, his official papers, preserved in the Broadlands archive, do not contain photographic evidence of alien spacecraft, but simply accounts of lights and objects in the sky that were no different from those published in the newspapers. Mountbatten's writings on the subject of UFOs have been preserved in letters to his friend Charles Eade, then editor of the *Sunday Dispatch*, who was fascinated by the flying saucer stories that were appearing almost daily in US newspapers.

British government and senior military figures such as Mountbatten initially took the saucers very seriously, as they were concerned about the threat which UFOs – or belief in UFOs – might pose to the fragile peace between the West and the Soviet Union. In Britain, as in America, military leaders and their scientific advisors were divided in their attitude towards the UFO phenomenon. Some feared the saucers could be advanced Soviet aircraft, but the consensus among scientists was that they could be explained by misidentification, mass hysteria and natural phenomena. Mountbatten, however, belonged to a small group of high-ranking military personnel who believed that flying saucers were from another world. His theories about the origin of UFOs were clearly stated in letters to Charles Eade:

> '... the available evidence will show that they are not of human agency, that is to say that they do not come from our Earth. If that is so then presumably they must come from some heavenly body, probably a planet ... Maybe it is the Shackletons or Scotts of Venus or Mars who are making their first exploration of our Earth.'[3]

More telling was the revelation of Mountbatten's own personal feelings concerning the nature of the intelligence which animated the saucers themselves:

> 'My own view is that we should think of the possibility of these Flying Saucers being not a form of aeroplane from another planet but being the actual inhabitants of that planet!'[4]

Sensing the media headlines which sensational statements such as these would produce, Mountbatten asked Eade to keep his private opinions out of the newspapers:

> '...I know this sounds ridiculous and I am relying on you as a very old and loyal friend not to make any capital out of the fact that I have put forward such a far-fetched explanation. Such an explanation, however, would apparently fill all known cases in which the Flying Saucer has so far been seen...'[5]

Mountbatten's writings reveal that he felt that persuading the public to take the subject seriously was more important than providing the tangible proof which scientists such as R. V. Jones demanded. Early in 1950 he urged Charles Eade to 'employ someone … to collect all the evidence that at present exists' and to put the reports together in a 'proper scientific way'[6] and pressured him to publish a series of weekly articles on flying saucers in the *Sunday Dispatch*. Mountbatten said he would 'be interested to hear what the reaction of the public is to them'.[7]

He did not have to wait long. On 1 October 1950, the series began as the front-page splash in the *Dispatch*, the highlight of which was a long editorial written by the editor describing flying saucers as 'the story that may be bigger than atom bomb wars'.[8] Eade described how the subject had been dismissed as nonsense, but, 'Many intelligent and distinguished people in all parts of the world are intensely interested in Flying Saucers and treat such reports very seriously indeed.' He quoted from a letter he had received 'from one of the most famous men alive today' whom he could not name but who 'commands universal respect and admiration'. It was a discussion with this mystery man, Eade said, which led to his decision 'to place before the readers of the *Sunday Dispatch* all that is known about the Flying Saucers and all the theories about them, no matter how sensational and fantastic'. We now know that the 'mystery man' was Lord Mountbatten.

Following publication of these stories, accounts of flying saucers and UFOs poured into newspaper offices across the British Isles. In hindsight it is clear that the aggressive newspaper campaign had created a new template for a timely 'idea' which had finally come of age. People were actively looking for strange things in the sky. And of course they saw them.

The impact of this level of press attention upon popular opinion in Britain has never been adequately quantified, but it is no exaggeration to suggest that October 1950 saw the 'launch' of the flying saucer in Britain.

A Flying Saucer at Broadlands

Mountbatten's papers illustrate the evolution in thought which has become an established tradition among the more rational scientific minds who have been drawn to the study of UFO reports. Initially Mountbatten was overwhelmed and impressed by what appeared to be an irrefutable mountain of evidence from 'credible witnesses', including pilots and police officers. That certainty was replaced by doubt when the reliability of both the 'evidence' and the testimony upon which it was based was called into question. Most importantly, Mountbatten became alarmed by the growing numbers of cultists, charlatans and publicity-seekers who were gravitating towards the subject.

Alarm bells began to ring for Mountbatten when he found himself caught up in a flying saucer contact on his doorstep. On 23 February 1955 a bricklayer called Briggs claimed to have encountered a saucer hovering in the grounds of Broadlands, Mountbatten's Hampshire residence, making him late for work. Mountbatten's fascination with UFOs was well known and Briggs was persuaded to furnish his employer with a full account.

Briggs was 'still dazed' when Mountbatten first saw him and 'worried no one would believe him'.[9] He claimed that he hadn't believed in flying saucers before that morning. In a signed statement he claimed the UFO was shaped like a child's humming top and was 20 to 30 feet in diameter and aluminium in colour, like a saucepan but with portholes in the side. Briggs had dismounted from his bicycle as the saucer hovered and was amazed to see a tube descend from its centre. A platform appeared in the tube, containing a man. He was wearing a dark suit or overalls and a close-fitting helmet. As he watched, Briggs was suddenly overcome by an 'unseen force' which caused him to stumble. The tube retracted into the flying saucer, which suddenly shot straight up into the sky and disappeared.

Mountbatten records how he interviewed Briggs before visiting the scene of the sighting with an electrician. Although they found marks in the snow consistent with Briggs' account of his movements, there was no physical evidence of the flying saucer.

Briggs was either favoured by the aliens or, more likely, encouraged by the attention he received from his employer, as later he reported a second close encounter, this time with the occupant of the flying saucer, with whom he communicated via telepathy. On this occasion he was invited on board the spacecraft and taken to see the Egyptian pyramids, a round trip which lasted just ten minutes. Before he was returned to Hampshire, the aliens told the bricklayer: 'If Lord Mountbatten met us he could change the world.'[10]

Mountbatten's role and belief in the Broadlands landing were frequently misrepresented by UFO writers during the next few years and he often found himself in the difficult position of having to give out information only to refuse to endorse its credibility when the news seemed certain to reach the press. One writer, Margaret Church, was invited to lunch with Mountbatten's secretary and was pressurised to omit certain details from an article she intended to publish which claimed both Mountbatten and his wife endorsed Briggs' flying saucer contact.[11]

By 1961 Mountbatten had begun to realise that nothing he could say would stop the UFOlogists from using his name to endorse Briggs' claims and the beliefs which they helped to support. However, in a letter to a persistent UFO enthusiast he stated: 'I did not express any belief whatever in the story, which remains completely unproven.'[12]

Mountbatten and the 'Flying Ship'

Lord Mountbatten and his nephew Prince Philip, Duke of Edinburgh, were among the first people to receive copies of the magazine *Flying Saucer Review (FSR)*. *FSR* was founded in 1955, at the height of the flying saucer craze, by RAF pilot Derek Dempster. In that year the magazine's publicist, Brinsley le Poer Trench, wrote that he had been contacted by Lord Mountbatten and the Duke of Edinburgh, who both wanted to receive the magazine. Gordon Creighton, the current editor, writes: 'They were both at once put on to our free list, and the Duke has consequently been receiving his regular copy of *FSR* at Buckingham Palace ever since.'[13]

Dempster's workload soon led him to relinquish the editorship of *FSR*, which was taken up by Brinsley le Poer Trench (who, as Lord Clancarty, was to chair a House of Lords debate on UFOs in 1979). The magazine's prestigious board now included a former Foreign Office official, Gordon Creighton, who had high-level contacts of his own. During the next 50 years, Creighton would become the source of a series of rumours connecting the British royal family with a high-level conspiracy to conceal the truth about UFOs. He claimed various royals were 'believers' from an early stage in the UFO controversy, basing his claims upon Prince Philip's early association with *FSR*. Implicit within this was the assumption that the royal family took UFOs seriously as a direct result of being privy to 'secret' information which was being withheld from the public.

Creighton has also been responsible for disseminating rumours concerning the British government's involvement in the alleged cover up of UFO secrets. One story came from a distant relative of Creighton's (unnamed) who had served in the Royal Navy and had heard it from another (also unnamed) naval officer who had worked at the Admiralty after World War II. He happened to visit the office of a very senior officer (unsurprisingly not named) and saw, on his desk, files dealing with UFOs, including 'photographs of strange disc-shaped objects on the surface of the sea'.[14]

If this evidence had ever existed, Lord Mountbatten would certainly have had access to it, given his position in the Admiralty and later the MoD. Similarly, if there had been a government cover up of UFOs and aliens during the late 1940s and 1950s, Mountbatten would have been aware of it. But the evidence we found in his personal archive suggests that not only was he unaware of any 'Top Secret' UFO evidence but that initially he was as easily misled by the reported sightings as the average man in the street.

The UFO rumour mill, however, lost no time implicating Mountbatten in a British version of Frank Scully's 'crashed flying saucer' hoax. This began as a story cabled to America from the International News Service's

London office in 1955 by Dorothy Kilgallen, a syndicated columnist with the New York *Journal-American*. The story claimed scientists and airmen were examining the wreckage of a 'mysterious flying ship' which had crashed in Britain and were convinced 'these strange aerial objects are not optical illusions or Soviet inventions but are flying saucers which originate on another planet'.[15] The tale was later embroidered with claims that the saucer was crewed by 'small men, probably under four feet tall'.[16]

Kilgallen was told the British government was holding back on issuing an official report on the matter 'because it does not want to frighten the public'. She claimed her source for this story was 'a British official of Cabinet rank' who wished to remain anonymous. Immediately rumours spread that this source was Lord Mountbatten. Creighton, writing in 1996, revealed that this was the assumption made by the *FSR* editorial team.[17]

Kilgallen collected many of her stories and celebrity gossip at cocktail parties where she mixed with royalty, aristocracy and military top brass. FBI and CIA documents obtained by Nick Redfern reveal that she was being closely watched because of her apparent influence with a number of foreign officials, and at one stage in the 1950s was cultivated as a potential intelligence source.[18] Given such connections, it is quite plausible that Kilgallen could indeed have spoken to Mountbatten, but it is unlikely that he would have let slip a piece of ultra-secret information to a gossip columnist at a cocktail party.

Creighton's letter to Kilgallen asking for further details went unanswered, leading him to conclude she had been 'effectively silenced', and the fact that she never made any further comment upon the story was enough to establish its authenticity in the opinion of the UFO believers. Kilgallen's sudden – and some claim mysterious – death in 1965 only added to the suspicions of those who were convinced there really was a conspiracy to hide the truth about UFOs.

The Kilgallen story can also be interpreted as a 'contemporary legend' defined by the folklore scholar Professor Jan Brunvand as 'the Secret Truth' – that of a cosmic secret 'accidentally' revealed by a powerful politician or military leader to a journalist at a cocktail party.[19] In a similar case, UFO believer and author Georgina Bruni claims she was able to discuss alien technology with former Prime Minister Margaret Thatcher at a charity cocktail party in 1997. Bruni claims Baroness Thatcher treated the subject with the utmost seriousness, repeating the comment 'UFOs? You must get your facts right, and you can't tell the people' twice before abruptly changing the subject. This ambiguous phrase was interpreted as evidence of the former PM's knowledge of UFO secrets and eventually became the title of Bruni's book on the Rendlesham incident (*see* Chapter 12), *You Can't Tell the People*.[20]

If the British 'crashed saucer' story was not simply invented by

Kilgallen during the 'silly season', then it could have been a joke or even a piece of deliberate disinformation planted by the intelligence services. Whatever its source, rumours connecting Mountbatten with the crashed saucer and the little men multiplied during the 1950s and in recent years the yarn has been resurrected in a series of books and articles, often with the unsupported claim that the crash occurred during the later stages of the war. In March 1957 New York UFOlogist Ted Bloecher wrote to Mountbatten asking whether the story were based upon fact. In response, Mountbatten's private secretary at the Admiralty stated bluntly:

> 'The Admiral of the Fleet asks me to say that he has no information about Her Majesty's Government having possession of a flying saucer… Indeed, he would go further and asks me to say that he has not heard any rumours to this effect in this country.'[21]

UFOs at Buckingham Palace

> 'British agriculture and defence officials want to know more about the mysterious crop circles which have appeared across the countryside … so does Queen Elizabeth, who is said to have sharply questioned Prime Minister Margaret Thatcher about the circles recently. While those talks are kept secret, a Buckingham Palace spokesman says the Queen took a hurriedly published book about the circles to her summer palace in Scotland this month.'[22]

This story appeared in the *Wall Street Journal* in 1989 at the height of the craze for spotting rings of flattened cereal crops in fields across England. Although it emerged later that the majority of the circles were created by hoaxers, during the 1980s *FSR* was at the forefront of a campaign to link them with UFOs and extraterrestrials. The first book dealing with the phenomenon, *Circular Evidence*, was written by *FSR* contributors Colin Andrews and Pat Delgado. It was published in 1989 and the authors presented copies to Buckingham Palace and 10 Downing Street.[23]

No one has been able to establish whether the royal interest in the crop circle mystery was genuine or simply the product of a tabloid newspaper editor's imagination. However, as late as the mid-1990s, film director John McNeish stated that he had received an order from Buckingham Palace for a copy of his book *Crop Circle Apocalypse*. This is just one example of the Palace's interest in 'fringe' subjects. Another dates from the late 1960s, when it was claimed that Prince Philip had been sent a copy of the newly-released Colorado University study of UFOs.[24]

There is no doubt that Prince Philip's interest in UFOs and flying saucers was at one time second only to that of his uncle, Lord Mountbatten. One of the prince's equerries, the late Sir Peter Horsley, wrote:

> 'Prince Philip was open to the immense possibilities of new technology leading to space exploration, while at the same time not discounting that, just as we were on the fringe of breaking out into space, so other older civilisations in the universe might already have done so.'[25]

In the summer of 1955 *Sunday Express* columnist Ephraim Hardcastle revealed that the Duke of Edinburgh had requested that all flying saucer reports received by the Air Ministry should be copied to him. Hardcastle wrote: 'I had not realised that the Duke of Edinburgh's interests in mechanical contraptions extended as far as flying saucers.'[26] In a 1985 letter to UFO writer Timothy Good via an equerry, the Duke claimed Hardcastle's story was 'a case of gossip columnist inaccuracy'.[27] He did, however, confirm a report which appeared in US family magazine *McCalls*, in 1962, entitled 'How Queen Elizabeth II entertains her friends', which carried a paragraph detailing Prince Philip's interests. This read:

> 'He talks animatedly of new inventions, argues farming techniques with Lord Dorchester, yarns about sport … discusses sputniks, atom bombs, space travel. The subject of flying saucers came up at one dinner party. "I'm sure they exist," Philip insisted. "All the evidence points to it. So many people say they have seen them. You should read the book *Flying Saucers Have Landed*." '[28]

So, while the *Sunday Express*'s report may have been factually incorrect, it was certainly correct in substance.

Sir Peter Horsley's autobiography also revealed how reports of flying saucers were enthusiastically discussed among the staff at Buckingham Palace throughout his time as equerry, first to Princess Elizabeth and, after the death of King George VI in 1952, to the Queen and finally to the Duke of Edinburgh. Horsley recounts how in that year Prince Philip 'agreed that I could investigate the more credible reports [of flying saucers] provided I kept it all in perspective and did not involve his office in any kind of publicity or sponsorship'.[29]

As a result of his position in the RAF, Horsley was given '*carte blanche* to read any reports and interview pilots'.[30] He was also able to draw upon the experience and contacts of colleagues in Fighter Command, the USAF and the civilian airlines by virtue of his 'unofficial' capacity as royal UFO investigator. Keeping an open and objective outlook throughout, Horsley arrived at the same conclusions as official investigations by the USAF and, covertly, by the RAF, namely that most UFO reports had logical explanations but that a small residue, a 'hard core' of around 5 per cent, could not be satisfactorily accounted for.

The case which impressed Sir Peter the most involved two pilots from 25 Squadron who observed a flying saucer while on patrol in a Vampire jet from RAF West Malling, Kent, one afternoon in November, 1953. Horsley investigated the sighting as thoroughly as he was able, using a subterfuge to the visit the base and quiz both airmen. He submitted a report to the Duke of Edinburgh, saying that he was 'satisfied that the Vampire crew was perfectly reliable' and the two airmen had seen 'a genuine UFO'.[31]

Horsley has since played down Prince Philip's direct encouragement of his UFO enquiries, claiming he was acting on his own initiative. The RAF airmen, however, both independently recalled being informed – by their station commander – of Prince Phillip's personal interest in flying saucers. Flying Officer Geoffrey Smythe said:

> '[Prince Phillip] sent his equerry to interview us at West Malling.
> Funny thing about that was that the equerry, a squadron leader,
> seemed to be just going through the motions and was not really
> interested...'[32]

During Sir Peter's time as equerry a number of other UFO witnesses were invited to the Palace, including the captain of a BOAC airliner, James Howard, who, along with other crew members and passengers, had reported a formation of UFOs while flying over the north Atlantic.[33] The most unusual visitor was 11-year-old Stephen Darbishire from Coniston in the Lake District, who had taken two photographs of a 'saucer-shaped' object as it hovered above the slopes of Coniston Old Man in February 1954.[34] In both these instances, it was the equerry who sent out invitations to Buckingham Palace after he saw reports of the sightings in the national press. There can be no doubt, however, that he was encouraged to do so by the Duke of Edinburgh and that his reports detailing these sightings are still preserved in the royal archives.

Horsley explains his reason for inviting UFO witnesses to the Palace was partly to 'put them on the spot' and test their honesty in the presence of royalty – as effective as any truth serum in the context of the day and age. In respect of Captain Howard, he intended the civilian pilot should be overawed by his invitation to the equerry's office, for 'if he was solely seeking publicity, this experience might unnerve him'.[35]

Like Mountbatten, Sir Peter was less impressed by what he described as 'the growing body of people promoting sightings for mercenary reasons or self-advertisement'.[36] Among these less than objective influences he included Desmond Leslie, who had become a friend of Lieutenant General Sir Frederick 'Boy' Browning. Browning was a distinguished soldier who had led the British airborne forces during the ill-fated Operation Market Garden in 1943. After the war he was made Controller of the Royal Household and like many other British aristocrats became fascinated by the flying saucer mystery. Eventually he was introduced by Desmond Leslie to the American contactee George Adamski, with whom Leslie had written the 1952 bestseller *Flying Saucers Have Landed*. It is possible that it was through Browning that Prince Philip was introduced to Adamski's claims of contact with the benevolent inhabitants of Venus and Saturn. Sir Peter said he eventually met both Leslie and Adamski and was not impressed by either. He felt that Desmond Leslie was 'probably sincere but gullible, sucked into the saucer cult by people who hoped to profit from it such as Adamski' and he warned 'Boy' Browning against having anything to do with the pair of them.[37]

'I Believe in Flying Saucers'

'Boy' Browning and another World War II veteran, airman Sir Arthur Barratt, along with Lord Dowding and others, formed a group of senior military figures who found refuge in a range of 'fringe' beliefs in retirement. Among their number could also be counted Squadron Leader Peter Caddy, who was instrumental in founding Findhorn, the international spiritual centre in Scotland. Bored by the austerity of post-war Britain, these former military men sought excitement and spiritual fulfilment by escaping into the world of flying saucers and space people. Their beliefs may have been unusual, but their influence and the respect they commanded, both among their peers and the public at large, cannot be underestimated.

Dowding became interested in theosophy, spiritualism and flying saucers, and made several pro-UFO statements to the press. His finest hour came not in the skies of 1941 but in the *Sunday Dispatch* of 11 July 1954, with his unequivocal article 'I Believe in Flying Saucers' (*see* Figure 7, page 70). Using the number of UFO sightings and the status of many of their witnesses as his yardstick for belief, Dowding wrote:

> 'I say then that I am convinced that these objects do exist and that they are not manufactured by any nation on earth. I can see no alternative to accepting the theory that they come from some extra-terrestrial source.'[38]

Sunday Dispatch

LONDON: NORTHCLIFFE HOUSE   FOUNDED 1801   MANCHESTER: NORTHCLIFFE HOUSE

CENTRAL 6000   BLACKFRIARS 6000

TANFIELD HOUSE   EDINBURGH   CENTRAL 2535

JULY 11, 1954.

I Believe In Flying Saucers

By
Air Chief Marshal
LORD DOWDING,
Air Officer Commanding-in-Chief Fighter Command In The Battle of Britain

Case Of Dr Cort

IN the House of Commons the Home Secretary, Sir David Maxwell Fyfe, has finally refused to reconsider his decision concerning Dr. Joseph Cort.

Dr. Cort is an American citizen. He was once a member of the Communist Party. He came to Cambridge to continue his researches as a physiologist.

The important point is this—he came on a temporary footing and not as a resident alien.

He was, however, allowed by the Home Office to extend his stay to the end of June, so that he could take up a post at Birmingham University.

Clamour

Now the United States authorities want him to return home. They allege that he has evaded military service.

Immediately there is a clamour among the extreme Left - Wingers here to preserve him from the judgment of his fellow nationals.

Why? Is it because Dr. Cort has any legal claim to sanctuary here? No. It is clearly because he has at least once held Communist convictions, and also that to keep him here would be a further feeding of grit into the machinery of Anglo-U.S. relations.

Sir David Maxwell Fyfe has refused to be swayed by sectional clamour.

Had he been a less resolute character, he could more easily have turned a blind eye to facts and bowed to the instinct, so easily roused, of sheltering "an innocent victim."

This is not the first time the Conservative Home

I HAVE never seen a "Flying Saucer," and yet I believe that they exist. I have never seen Australia, and yet I believe that Australia also exists. My belief in both cases is based upon cumulative evidence in such quantity that, for me at any rate, it brings complete conviction.

More than 10,000 sightings have been reported, the majority of which cannot be accounted for by any "scientific" explanation, e.g., that they are hallucinations, the effects of light refraction, meteors, wheels falling from aeroplanes, and the like.

Best Evidence

THE best available evidence, perhaps, is contained in Major Donald Keyhoe's recent book, "Flying Saucers From Outer Space."

I say this because most of the incidents which he records have been checked by the Intelligence Branch of the United States Air Force. They endorse the accuracy of the evidence, but they put forward no explanation. The critics who deny the existence of these objects must produce some alternative theory which will account for the observed facts.

In a brief article I cannot deal at length with the suggestion that they are new types of aircraft under development by Russia or the U.S. They have been tracked on radar screens in America—on one occasion by three screens simultaneously—and the observed speeds have been as great as 9,000 miles an hour.

No earthly materials that we know of could be forced

make human life as we know it, impossible.

I say then that I am convinced that these objects do exist and that they are not manufactured by any nation on earth. I can therefore see no alternative to accepting the theory that they come from some extra-terrestrial source.

And why should this be considered to be such a ridiculous idea? In ten

This is the outstanding picture in the Flying Saucer debate.

years' time we shall probably have shot a rocket to the moon. In a hundred years we may have made the return trip with a manned projectile. In 500 years we may have reached the nearer planets. Are we so arrogant as to maintain that the inhabitants of no planet are as much as 500 years ahead of us in scientific development?

A Warning

IF I say that I believe that the majority of the visitors are actuated by friendly and helpful motives. I cannot produce the same volume of evidence in support of my opinion as I have done for the physical reality of the Saucers; but the fragmentary and uncer-

occupants in visiting the Earth's atmosphere?

I think that we must resist the tendency to assume that they all come from the same planet, or that they are all actuated by similar motives. It might be that visitors from one planet wished to help us in our evolution from the basis of a higher level to which they had attained.

Another planet might send an expedition to ascertain what have been these terrible explosions which they have observed, and to prevent us from discommoding other people besides ourselves by the new toys with which we are so lightheartedly playing.

Other visitors might have come bent solely on scientific discovery and might regard us with the dispassionate aloofness with which we might regard insects found beneath an upturned stone.

---

object," his machine disintegrated in mid-air and his body was found among the wreckage.

This brings me to the most important thing which I have to say. It is to give a warning against attempts to open fire either with guns or aeroplanes on these objects. Looked at from the purely selfish aspect, such gratuitous folly might well turn neutral curiosity into active hostility, and it may be assumed that those who visit us from outer space can well look after themselves and will have the means of making us sorry that we compelled them to defend themselves.

But it is not on this note that I wish to finish. It seems possible that for the first time in recorded history intelligible communication on the physical level may become possible between the earth and other planets of the solar system.

Such a prospect is epoch-making in the literal sense of the word, and we should be guilty of criminal folly if we were to do anything to hinder a contact which may well bring untold blessings to a distraught humanity.

£300 Car Is

By J. D. S. ALAN

CAN Harry Ferguson, the tractor genius, make an all-round utility car for £300? There are many ways to produce cheaper cars. A well

---

Figure 7: **Sunday Dispatch**, 11 July 1954: 'I believe in Flying Saucers' Air Chief Marshall Lord Dowding achieved a place in history by leading the Royal Air Force to victory against the Luftwaffe in the Battle of Britain. After retirement in 1942 he became deeply involved in spiritualism, theosophy and flying saucers. In the 1950s Dowding and a number of other retired RAF and army officers fell under the spell of American contactee George Adamski who claimed to have taken trips in spaceships piloted by benevolent Venusians. Their message of peace and love was a antidote to the fear of nuclear destruction that characterised the Cold War.

(By permission of the British Library)

He went on to expound his belief that the saucer occupants were peace-loving, echoing the 'saucers as salvation' message believed by hundreds of thousands of people and railing against the idea that the RAF should attempt to shoot them down: 'We should be guilty of criminal folly if we were to do anything to hinder a contact which may well bring untold blessings to a distraught humanity.'[39]

Much in the same way that spiritualism flourished in the wake of World War I, when people flocked to séances, desperate to contact their slain loved ones, so it seemed that saucers were fulfilling a similar role after World War II. Intervention by aliens appeared to be an appealing antidote to the threat of an imminent atomic war with the Soviet Union. In both cases supposedly hard-headed rationalists became involved. Arthur Conan Doyle, creator of the rigorously logical Sherlock Holmes stories, was a fervent believer in spirit mediums, while Lord Dowding had been the architect of Britain's air defence in the Battle of Britain. Similarly, when proof for either life after death or the physical reality of flying saucers was not forthcoming, belief continued unabated.

A Strange Encounter

As royal equerry and in his later role as Assistant Chief of Air Staff (Operations), Sir Peter had the opportunity to scrutinise official UFO reports which have remained a secret until the present day. He also had the confidence of some of the country's most senior military officials. Like his contemporary Mountbatten, never once did Sir Peter receive even so much as a whiff of evidence that the MoD had a tangible piece of evidence of UFO reality – such as a crashed flying saucer – which was being concealed from the public.[40]

But even Sir Peter's sense of objectivity was sorely tested when he found himself face to face with someone he believed may have been a visitor from another world! This extraordinary meeting was arranged by Sir Arthur Barratt, who worked at Buckingham Palace as Gentleman Usher to the Sword of State. It was Barratt who introduced Sir Peter to a twilight world inhabited by a mysterious General Martin, who believed UFOs were visitors from an alien civilisation which wanted to warn us of the dangers posed by atomic war.

Soon Martin had arranged for Sir Peter to meet an enigmatic Mrs Markham at a flat in Chelsea. Arriving from Buckingham Palace one night in 1955, he was ushered into a second-floor drawing-room on Smith Street occupied by a man referred to only as 'Mr Janus'. Janus asked Sir Peter to tell him everything he knew about UFOs. In return, Sir Peter asked, equally directly, what was his interest in the subject. The answer was simple: 'I would like to meet the Duke of Edinburgh.'

Understandably thrown off guard by this request, Sir Peter went on to explain that a private audience was not easy to arrange. He and Mr Janus proceeded to discuss a variety of esoteric subjects, including the mission of the flying saucers and the perils which faced mankind as a result of technological progress. Sir Peter recalls that although Mr Janus never claimed to be from another planet, he gave the impression that he was visiting Earth as 'an observer'. Throughout the meeting, the royal equerry was given the distinct impression that his thoughts were being read – and scrutinised – via telepathy.

Peter Horsley was acutely aware of his responsibility to report any evidence of plots against the royal family to the security services. However, he was sufficiently swayed by Mr Janus' otherworldly presence not to take this seemingly obvious step. Instead he decided to hand his report to 'Boy' Browning. Browning was at this point heavily influenced by the 'space brother' stories of Adamski and, naturally enough, wished to arrange his own personal audience with Mr Janus.

At this point an already surreal story took a further step into the twilight zone. For when Sir Peter tried to contact Mrs Markham, he found she had vanished and his other contact, General Martin, 'suddenly became distant and evasive'. Puzzled, Sir Peter retraced his steps to the Smith Street address where he had met Mr Janus – and found it empty. Neighbours told him its occupant had 'left in a hurry'.[41]

Was the royal UFO investigator the victim of a joke, a cruel hoax or even an elaborate set-up by MI5 to test his vulnerability? When we posed this question to Sir Peter he insisted that none of these explanations fit the facts as he remembered them, but the Janus story sits uneasily alongside his careful and objective investigations of the UFO mystery on behalf of Prince Philip.

Sir Peter said that his meeting with Mr Janus helped to focus his mind on two great puzzles: the nature of God and the existence of alien visitors. 'I never saw Mr Janus again. But ... I don't care what people think – it happened.'[42]

Perhaps this evolution in belief can account for the change of heart noticed by the RAF aircrew from West Malling whom Sir Peter had quizzed back in 1953. Speaking in the year 2000, one of the airmen said:

> 'He seemed hardly interested at the time, but he must have gained some interest, because quite recently he featured in a TV programme about UFOs and he appeared to have a near-religious belief in them.'[43]

Celebrity Gossip or Sincere Interest?

Prince Philip was again drawn into the public eye to comment about flying saucers in 1959. In April of that year George Adamski, now world famous as a result of his books about his contacts with aliens, visited Holland, where he had discussed his experiences with Queen Juliana and Prince Bernhard. At a press conference in The Hague on 20 May Adamski made the bold claim that the British royal family was also keen to meet him and: 'Prince Philip so far has been the most interested.'

Whatever the truth behind Adamski's statement, Buckingham Palace had other ideas. A statement was issued to the effect that there were no plans for any member of the royal family to meet Adamski.[44]

On one level, the many accounts of royal and aristocratic involvement with the early development of the flying saucer myth in Britain may be read as just celebrity gossip. But the influence of the British Establishment upon the formation of public opinion during the 1950s was immense and should not be underestimated. Ordinary people who were reporting UFOs and setting up UFO study groups took heed of what key figures in the Establishment believed. Their endorsement put the stamp of authority on UFO sightings and belief in visitors from space and helped validate the development and expansion of those beliefs.

In contrast, the level of involvement of members of the Establishment in the growing UFO subculture shows the depth of penetration that flying saucers and everything synonymous with them had achieved at the highest levels of society. The symbiotic relationship between the two was instrumental in the study of UFOs during the next 50 years.

Chapter 5

BRITAIN'S FLYING SAUCER STUDY

'We have had at least thirty
instances of this sort of object
being seen … they have all been
successful in leaving their point
of departure and returning somewhere out of the sight of man.'

Air Chief Marshal Sir Philip Joubert, 1950[1]

By the summer of 1950, with war in Korea and Soviet atomic bomb tests adding to international tensions, the Western powers were growing increasingly worried by the flying saucer mystery. Sightings were making newspaper headlines every day on both sides of the Atlantic and placing the subject firmly on the military agenda.

In the USA Major Donald Keyhoe's writings were contributing to the rumours that the authorities were hiding the fact that the saucers were interplanetary spacecraft, while across the world, nervous fingers were hovering above buttons that could trigger a devastating nuclear exchange. Those entrusted with weapons of mass destruction had only seconds to decide if an unidentified radar blip was a Soviet bomber, a guided missile or simply a 'phantom'. Flying saucers, whether they existed or not, quite clearly had the potential to trigger a third world war.

The Woodman Report

When the first flying saucer rumours reached Britain in the late 1940s they had received a sceptical reception from officers of the RAF. One of those who found the stories difficult to believe was Wing Commander R. G. 'Tim' Woodman. In 1950 Woodman was deputy superintendent of test flying at RAF Boscombe Down in Wiltshire. During World War II he had been a night-fighter ace and member of the secret 100 Group that flew night-time intruder missions above Germany. Later in the campaign he tested advanced airborne radar equipment in combat situations, achieving a record nine 'kills'. After the war as a test pilot he flew the most advanced jets and made personal friends of aviation legends such as Chuck Yeager.[2]

Writing in 1967, Woodman said that in thousands of flying hours he had never seen a flying saucer and had not known they existed until he read about them in the *Sunday Dispatch*. His no-nonsense approach to aviation made him sceptical, but his personal curiosity was aroused by the claims appearing in newspapers:

> 'I'd been test flying ever since the war, met up with the world's leading test pilots and aeronautical scientists and had acquired myself an exceptional background of knowledge of aerial phenomena, and yet here I was being told by a Sunday newspaper that there were curious objects up there in the air which somehow had not come my way.'[3]

Figure 9:
**Squadron Leader
RG 'Tim' Woodman.**
World War II night-
fighter ace. As Deputy
Superintendent of Test
Flying at RAF Boscombe
Down Woodman was asked
by the MoD to under-
take a study of the
'flying saucer' phe-
nomenon in 1951–52.
(Courtesy of Clive
Williams)

During his posting to Boscombe Down Woodman received an unusual 'request from the Government'. He told us:

> 'On a visit to Air Ministry at that time I was asked if I would
> submit a report on the subject [of flying saucers]. It was an
> unofficial investigation, [but] aircrew from the RAF and Navy were
> asked to submit reports to me. Three American test pilots at
> Boscombe Down were astounded and amused that the British
> should take an interest in such a matter, which they treated as
> rubbish.'[1]

Two of the test pilots, Major Chilstrom and Captain Clemence, told Woodman they 'thought that flying saucers had died out two years ago' and were 'very much surprised' to see the story revived in the British press.
Woodman wrote:

> 'There was a hot state of flying saucer fever on at that time in
> Britain because of the articles in the newspapers and nearly
> everyone I talked to had seen them – or what they thought were
> them – but not me. Then the hoaxers got cracking – a Boscombe
> Down pilot, up in a Vampire, left his VHF transmission on a test
> frequency, reporting that he was formatting on a flying saucer –
> green men in it, purple glow from portholes – and that evening
> I had to entertain two chief test pilots from the Midlands who
> had been airborne at the same time and who rushed down to
> Boscombe Down, furtively trying to find out all about it.'[5]

Woodman's sense of humour led him to carry out a spot of hoaxing of his own. In 1952, when he received a Soviet delegation of air attachés, he inserted the silhouette of a flying saucer on his wallchart of aircraft currently under test at Boscombe Down. 'Longitudinal stability, I think I said it was undergoing,' Woodman quipped. 'And honestly, the attaché chaps spent the rest of the day peering over hessian-draped hide-outs of secret aircraft trying to find it!'[6]

The Woodman study was just one of a number of 'unofficial' investigations initiated by various branches of the services as a result of enquiries made by the Scientific Intelligence branch of the MoD during the period 1950–52. Fifty years later, the papers they produced are still not available at the PRO and the level of secrecy that surrounds these early studies has contributed to the popular belief that an official cover up existed. But a cover up of what?

Woodman concluded: 'Nothing was established as being other than well-known phenomena, man-made objects and human errors of observation.'

Woodman's 'secret report' may not have been made public, but its contents seem to have been used in the preparation of another classified study that was underway at the MoD in the early 1950s.

The Flying Saucer Working Party

One outcome of the 'ghost rocket' scare of 1946 was that unknown aerial phenomena could no longer be dismissed, as they just might be cutting-edge Soviet technology. Finding a solution to the flying saucer mystery became a priority for the CIA and their British counterpart, the MoD's Directorate of Scientific Intelligence (DSI). The DSI advised the Joint Intelligence Committee (JTIC), which ultimately answered to the Prime Minister. Throughout the 1950s the MoD tried to calm public fears by debunking flying saucer sightings as meteorites or weather balloons, but in private they had launched an intelligence study drawing on the best scientific and military minds available.

One of those involved was the wartime head of Air Ministry Scientific Intelligence, R. V. Jones. As a result of his investigations into the 'ghost rockets', he had become sceptical of unexplained aerial phenomena. However, his mentor, Sir Henry Tizard, did not entirely share his views. Tizard was a key figure in the development of radar and had great influence in Whitehall. When, in the summer of 1950, he asked the DSI, Dr Bertie K. Blount, to launch a study of 'flying saucers', the MoD had no choice but to act.[7]

Blount's specialist team investigated the first 'official' report of a flying saucer in Britain. This sighting had been made by the pilot of a Meteor jet on an exercise from RAF Tangmere near Chichester and had leaked to the press. The *Daily Herald* headline for 7 June read 'First flying saucer reported here' and described how the 'shining, revolving disc-like' object had flashed past the jet at 40,000 feet. Cross-examination by squadron intelligence failed to shake the pilot's account and a report was sent to Fighter Command, where it was 'considered by senior officers and weather experts'.[8]

The *Daily Mail* claimed the saucer was tracked by a radar station in Sussex. Confronted by this claim, an Air Ministry spokesman would only say, 'It cannot be confirmed,' adding, 'The report received from the pilot is no evidence to confirm that what was observed was anything more than natural or meteorological phenomena.' The *Mail* told its readers this was evidence that 'a curtain of secrecy' had been drawn over the subject of flying saucers.[9]

The first mention of the Flying Saucer Working Party appears in a 'Top Secret' minute of a meeting held on 15 August 1950 in the Metropole Building, Northumberland Avenue, London. Chaired by Hugo Young,

TOP SECRET

- 4 -

SECRET

9. WORKING PARTY ON FLYING SAUCERS

THE CHAIRMAN said that Sir Henry Tizard felt that
reports of flying saucers ought not to be dismissed
without some investigation and he had, therefore, agreed
that a small D.S.I./J.T.I.C. Working Party should be set
up under the chairmanship of Mr. Turney to investigate
future reports.

After discussion it was agreed that the membership of
the Working Party should comprise representatives of D.S.I.1,
A.D.N.I.(Tech.), M.I.10 and A.D.I.(Tech.). It was also
agreed that it would probably be necessary at some time to
X consult the Meteorological Department and O.R.S. Fighter
Command but that these two bodies should not at present be
asked to nominate representatives.

THE JOINT MEETING:-

(1) Approved the setting up of a Working Party
on Flying Saucers.

(2) Invited the branches mentioned at X above to
inform Mr. Turney of their nominations to the
Working Party.

TOP SECRET

**Figure 10: Excerpt from minutes of DSI/JTIC, MoD, 1950–51,
referring to the Flying Saucer Working Party** (Public Record Office DEFE 41/74)

Deputy Director of Intelligence, it was attended by representatives of the
major scientific and technical departments of the MoD, including the
Secret Intelligence Service (SIS) (*see* Figure 10). The technical intelligence
branch of the Air Ministry was represented by Wing Commander Myles
Formby, who would become a central figure in the Flying Saucer Working
Party. Item 9 on the agenda that day was 'the Working Party on Flying
Saucers':

'THE CHAIRMAN (Mr Young) said that Sir Henry
Tizard felt that reports of flying saucers

ought not to be dismissed without some
investigation and he had, therefore,
agreed that a small DSI/JTIC Working
Party should be set up under the
chairmanship of Mr Turney to investigate
future reports.'[10]

It was agreed that membership of the Working Party would include representatives from the DSI and the technical intelligence branches of the Admiralty, War Office and Air Ministry. Consultants from the Meteorological Office and the Operational Research section of Fighter Command would also be involved, but would not be asked to nominate representatives.[11]

The aims and objectives of the Working Party were, according to Wing Commander Formby:

'1. To review the available evidence in
reports of "Flying Saucers."

2. To examine the evidence on which future
reports of British origin of phenomena
attributed to "Flying Saucers" are
based.

3. To report to DSI/JTIC.'[12]

Formby contacted Project Grudge in the USA and informed Fighter Command that all reports of aerial phenomena were to be reported to the new Working Party.[13]

The members of the Working Party included the chairman, G. I. Turney of DSI, and G. E. G. Graham, whose expertise was in the field of radar. Wing Commander Formby represented by the Air Intelligence department DDI (Tech), with Commander E. R. Wilson of Naval Intelligence and Major B. M. O'Brien of MI10 completing the panel of experts.[14] Both DDI (Tech) and MI10 were branches dedicated to the analysis of technical intelligence collected from the Soviet air force and army. MI10 was involved in obtaining photographs and pictures of Russian tanks and military equipment through espionage.[15]

Internal MoD memos make it clear that members of the intelligence team felt they were wasting their time studying flying saucers. In an October 1950 letter updating Tizard on progress, Hugo Young reports:

> 'In general, the members of the Flying Saucer Working Party are not very enthusiastic, but we are keeping the pressure on them as much as we can... This is not a very exhilarating progress report, but we have at least kept the moss off our boots!'[16]

The Working Party spent eight months sifting through hundreds of reports, including those submitted to the Air Ministry by members of the public and service personnel. Trips were made to foreign countries to interview witnesses and intelligence was gathered by Wing Commander Formby through his contacts at the USAF 'saucer' investigation team at Wright-Patterson air force base in Ohio. Surveys were made of early sightings, including the 'ghost rocket' wave of 1946, and the CIA allowed access to its own 'Secret' UFO data, compiled by the USAF's studies, Projects Sign and Grudge.

Report No. 7: Unidentified Flying Objects

In June 1951 the committee produced its final report at a joint meeting of DSI/JTIC. In attendance was a senior scientist from the CIA's Office of Scientific Intelligence, Dr H. Marshall Chadwell.[17] The Flying Saucer Working Party's conclusions were set out in a six-page document, DSI/JTIC Report No. 7, with the security grade 'Secret/Discreet', one level below the highest security grade of 'Top Secret'. Its title, 'Unidentified Flying Objects', reflected the American influence (the acronym UFO having been coined by the USAF), as did its methodology, conclusions and recommendations.

The report produced by the Working Party was the last of seven completed by the joint DSI/JTIC working parties. The previous six were all concerned with Soviet technical developments, including electronics, the manufacture of nerve gases and remote-controlled missiles. The inclusion of UFOs in this grouping reflects Cold War concerns that flying saucers could be some form of foreign technology, presumably Soviet in origin.[18]

Copies of the report were circulated within the MoD and to intelligence agencies in the USA and Canada. These quickly vanished and the

Figure 11:
Wing Commander Myles Formby.
Formby was a wartime Technical Intelligence Officer with the RAF. In 1950 he joined the Flying Saucer Working Party created by the MoD and visited the Pentagon to discuss UFOs with his opposite number in the USAF. (Courtesy of Juliet Formby)

MoD has until recently denied knowledge of any remaining copies of the report. In 2000, we were assured by the records officer that:

> 'Attempts have been made to locate a copy but unfortunately efforts to date have proved unsuccessful... Our lack of success in locating Report No. 7 in the Defence Records archive [and] the Defence Intelligence Staff's file store and its apparent absence on the PRO catalogue lead me to conclude that, regrettably, the document has not survived the passage of time.'[19]

Despite this conclusion, we persisted in our request that the MoD search for the report and to our great surprise copy number 17 of Report No. 7 was discovered in May 2001, during 'a routine re-review' of a closed Scientific Intelligence file (see Figure 12). It was filed with five other documents relating to the Flying Saucer Working Party.[20]

For a subject that was surrounded by so much secrecy, Report No. 7: Unidentified Flying Objects, is surprising in its brevity. The text is broken into four sections containing 15 numbered paragraphs and sub-paragraphs which discuss historical sightings, USAF studies and reports from the United Kingdom during 1950. The historical 'introduction' begins with the 'ghost rocket' wave, then moves directly to American flying saucer reports from the summer of 1947:

'The first report of a "flying saucer" came
from the United States in June 1947; the
name arose because the observer (Mr K.
Arnold, of Boise, Idaho) described what he
had seen as a "saucer-like disc." The report
received much publicity, and was quickly
followed by a great many more. Since then
reports of sightings have been made at
intervals in large numbers, mostly from the
United States, but some from other parts of
the world, including Great Britain, where
there was a notable outbreak during the
summer and autumn of 1950. The objects
reported have become popularly known by the
generic title "flying saucers," but the
descriptions given have included not only
flying disc-like objects of the original
"saucer" type, but also wingless torpedo or
cigar-shaped bodies, spherical or balloon-
shaped objects, and luminous phenomena of
various types... The reported observations
have been almost exclusively visual; reports
of any associated sound have been rare.
In no case has any tangible, material, or
objective evidence, been submitted. It is
therefore extremely difficult, if not
impossible, to arrive at anything like
scientific proof of the nature of the
phenomena.'[21]

Figure 12 (*opposite*): **Excerpt from DSI/JTIC Report No. 7:
Unidentified Flying Objects, June 1951** (Crown copyright: MoD)

DISCREET

SECRET

UNIDENTIFIED FLYING OBJECTS

Report by the " Flying Saucer " Working Party

Introduction: Historical

1. Unidentified flying objects were first reported after the war from Sweden in the summer of 1946, and for some months there was a considerable number of alleged sightings, mostly in Sweden, but a few also in Norway, Finland and Germany. The descriptions given were usually of some sort of wingless missile travelling at very high speed, cigar-shaped or circular, sometimes emitting bright lights, and occasionally sound. The reports attracted considerable attention in the press, where the objects became known as " ghost rockets " or " spook bombs." The reports died away after the summer of 1946, and very few have appeared since the end of that year.

2. The first report of a " flying saucer " came from the United States in June 1947; the name arose because the observer (Mr. K. Arnold, of Boise, Idaho) described what he had seen as a " saucer-like disc." The report received much publicity, and was quickly followed by a great many more. Since then reports of sightings have been made at intervals in large numbers, mostly from the United States, but some from other parts of the world, including Great Britain, where there was a notable outbreak during the summer and autumn of 1950. The objects reported have become popularly known by the generic title " flying saucers," but the descriptions given have included not only flying disc-like objects of the original " saucer " type, but also wingless torpedo or cigar-shaped bodies, spherical or balloon-shaped objects, and luminous phenomena of various types.

3. The reported observations have been almost exclusively visual; reports of any associated sound have been rare. In no case has any tangible, material, or objective evidence, been submitted. It is therefore extremely difficult, if not impossible, to arrive at anything like scientific proof of the nature of the phenomena.

Review of previous evidence

4. A systematic and extensive investigation of all the reported incidents in the United States was carried out between 1948 and 1950 by the U.S.A.F., in conjunction with the Rand Corporation, Dr. Hynek, a well-known astronomer from Ohio State University, and other specialist consultants.
      we have been enabled to study two reports (Project " Sign " and Project " Grudge ") covering the investigation of incidents up to the beginning of 1949.

Deletion   RETAINED UNDER
             SECTION 3(4)

5. On the Scandinavian sightings in 1946, Project " Grudge " reports as follows: —

> " The Swedish Defence Staff conducted a comprehensive study of the early incidents. Several thousand reports were thoroughly investigated and plotted, with resultant conclusions that all evidence obtained of sightings was explicable in terms of astronomical phenomena."

6. Dealing with reports from the United States, Project " Grudge " quotes the opinion of the Rand Corporation after an examination of 172 incidents: " to date, we have found nothing which would seriously controvert simple rational explanations of the various phenomena in terms of balloons, conventional aircraft, planets, meteors, bits of paper, optical illusions, practical jokers, psychopathological reports, and the like."
      Dr. Hynek investigated 228 incidents and concluded that approximately 33 per cent. were astronomical with varying degrees of probability; 37 per cent. were not astronomical but suggestive of other explanations, such as birds, rockets, balloons, ordinary aircraft, &c.; the remaining 30 per cent. either lacked sufficient evidence or the evidence offered suggested no explanation, though some of these might conceivably be astronomical.

SECRET

The 'review of previous evidence' relied almost exclusively upon information supplied to the MoD by the USAF and the CIA, whose input is reflected by the fact that two paragraphs were deleted from the document released under Section 3(4) of the Public Records Act. This allows material to be retained 'within Department' for more than the 30 years laid down by the Act.

Project Grudge's Conclusions

It was as a direct result of CIA's influence that the British team was provided with copies of the reports produced by the two USAF studies, Projects Sign and Grudge, that covered the investigation of UFO incidents reported up to the beginning of 1949. In addition, 'a systematic and extensive investigation' of all reported incidents in the United States had been carried out between 1948 and 1950 by the USAF, working with a scientific think-tank, the Rand Corporation, the astronomer Dr J. Allen Hynek and other specialist consultants. All these studies, according to the report, had reached a similar result.[22]

Project Grudge's negative conclusions, based upon an examination by Rand of 172 incidents, are well-known and are widely regarded with suspicion by UFO historians. The project found nothing which couldn't be explained rationally in terms of misperceived prosaic phenomena including balloons, aircraft, meteors and hoaxes. Dr Hynek arrived at a similar conclusion in his survey of 228 incidents. The Grudge team's summary of both studies found there were 34 reports where there was no obvious explanation, but 'when psychological and physiological factors are taken into consideration, the opinion expressed [is] that all these incidents can also be rationally explained'.[23]

The report emphasised the role of the mass media in the transmission of UFO rumours and the British team shared the American view that 'peaks' in UFO sightings closely followed periods of media publicity. A frequency distribution curve drawn up by the Grudge team to illustrate reports received between May 1947 and December 1948 found a marked tendency for 'peaks' to occur in the weeks immediately following a report that received wide publicity. This was of interest to members of the British team, as they felt it indicated 'the extent to which sightings may be psychological in origin'.

Incidents 'Explained'

The more spectacular incidents reported by the British press during 1950, had, according to the report, 'been fully explained'. These included the claim that the US government had captured a flying saucer that had crashed in the deserts of New Mexico. This referred not to the Roswell incident but to a crashed flying saucer hoax presented as a true story in Frank Scully's 1950 bestseller *Behind the Flying Saucers*. British intelligence was informed by a member of the Project Grudge that 'the sensational report of the discovery of a crashed "flying saucer" full of the remains of very small beings, was ultimately admitted by its author to have been a complete fabrication'.[24] The lack of any reference to the Roswell incident is open to interpretation, but implies that had the Americans been in possession of a crashed UFO then even their closest allies did not have sufficient 'need to know'.

Of the incidents reported from Britain, the report concluded that many had emerged as a direct result of the press publicity during 1950. Half a century later, Wing Commander Formby told us how his team had received reports from as far afield as New Zealand and he personally suspected that 'a lot never saw the light of day'.[25] Statements were taken from some of those who had reported sightings, but the team remained sceptical of witness testimony. The final report submitted to the DSI and CIA admits that the team had not attempted any form of systematic investigation of all the evidence presented, but could not see any reason why simple explanations could not be found for the majority of sightings.

The committee concluded that only three sightings, all 'reported officially by experienced officers from RAF stations', were worthy of detailed investigation. The first of these was the 1 June 1950 report from Tangmere, which had been leaked to the press:

'... the pilot of a Meteor reported on landing at Tangmere that at 1430, while flying at 20,000 feet on an easterly course over the Portsmouth area, he had sighted an object travelling at very high speed on a reciprocal course, 1,000–2,000 feet above him and roughly 1,200 yards to starboard. He described the object as circular, and of bright metallic appearance. He could not give any real estimate of its speed, but thought it might be about 800 knots. He had observed it for about 15 seconds, during which period he had looked away to port and back, having no difficulty in picking up the object again.'[26]

When questioned by the *Daily Mail*, the Air Ministry 'could not confirm' that the sighting had occurred at the same time that an unidentified blip had appeared on radar screens. Report No. 7 reveals that Tangmere made enquiries at the sector GCI station at RAF Wartling, near Eastbourne. They discovered that the duty controller and three radar operators had seen 'an unusual response' on their screens 'which appeared to be due to a target moving at 1,300–1,650 knots, first approaching and then receding from the station'.[27] The controller said the target 'looked to be very thick, leaving more afterglow than a usual response', while an operator, watching a separate display, said that it was 'slim, short and weaker than an aircraft' with a series of shadows appearing in the spaces between successive points on the screen.

As a result of this apparent correlation between the visual and radar sightings, the pilot and all four radar ground crew were interviewed by a member of the RAF Fighter Command's Research branch. After careful questioning, it was established that there was a 10-minute discrepancy between the times of the two reports. As a result, the Working Party concluded that there was 'no connection between the unusual PPI response and the pilot's visual observation'.[28] Although the team found it 'impossible to be entirely definite about the pilot's report', they felt that if he had not been the victim of an optical illusion:

'... the most probable explanation, which is borne out by his description of the object as "circular", implying a spherical body, is that he saw a meteorological balloon and greatly over-estimated its speed... We can find no reason whatever for adopting any less simple hypothesis.'[29]

The radar tracking required a more elaborate explanation and this was produced by collaboration between the team's radar expert, G. E. G. Graham, and the Royal Navy. Graham concluded that the 'target' seen by radar was produced by interference from another radar transmitter on a ship off the Isle of Wight. This was, said Graham, 'a phenomenon which has been frequently observed'. It would be frequently used to explain other baffling reports in the future.

Flying Saucers over Farnborough

The two remaining 'reliable' sightings both came from the Royal Aircraft Establishment at Farnborough. This was a centre for experimental aircraft testing and also the site of one of the aeronautical industry's most important annual events – the September air show.

Both sightings at Farnborough were made by experienced test pilot Flight Lieutenant Stan Hubbard. On the second occasion Hubbard's observations were supported by other senior test pilots who were present on the airfield watch-tower. All were questioned by Fighter Command's Research branch and Hubbard was later interviewed for two hours by Scientific Intelligence officers. The witnesses were impressed by the seriousness with which their reports appeared to be treated – but none were aware of the conclusions reached until they saw copies of Report No. 7 50 years later.

The events began on the morning of 14 August 1950, 'a lovely Hampshire summer day, warm, dry and clear', as Hubbard recalled.[30] As he left the base office and walked along the airfield towards his quarters his attention was attracted by a 'strange distant humming sound' from the direction of Basingstoke. The test pilot, who was wearing sunglasses, stopped to look skywards:

> 'The noise grew more distinct and more intense and I clearly remember pausing and turning in mid-stride to see what it could possibly be. To say that I was astonished is a profound understatement. Coming directly towards the airfield was an object entirely unlike anything I had ever seen before. Edge on, it appeared to be something like a discus we used to hurl on sports day at school, and as it came closer I could see that it was indeed very similar in shape.
>
> Initially it seemed that its angular altitude and attitude, above the horizon, were enough to indicate that it was well airborne ... but its lack of identifying features made it difficult to classify or easily estimate either its size or distance away. It was coming straight towards me and was holding a straight course. But it was rocking laterally, gently from side to side, about 20 degrees or so each way ... while steadily maintaining its heading. The sound emanating from this strange object increased markedly as it got closer, to a heavy, dominant humming with an associated subdued crackling-hissing sound, which reminded me strongly of the ambient noise inside a large active electrical power generating station.

As the object came closer, its overall shape, more closely now resembling a sports discus, could be clearly detailed and its general outer surface could be seen to have a satiny shimmering mother-of-pearl sort of finish. As it rocked laterally back and forth I was reminded of the opposing segments of reflected light that rotate back and forth that one sees when a shiny aluminium pan lid is tilted back and forth to reflect ambient light... This object came very close, quickly passing directly overhead, and the first impressions of colour and surface finish were strongly reinforced. The exterior was almost entirely featureless except that the periphery was edged by a band of a darker colour with indistinct markings of some sort, which kept changing in appearance, but from which emanated strange bluish flickering of points of light, very much like the little blue plumes of flame from a gas ring on a cooking stove, but turned upside down. I also got the impression that either the main body or the peripheral rim was rotating. It also seemed quite clear that the sibilant crackling-hissing sound came from this circle of flickering light; there appeared to be a definite connection and most remarkably there was a concurrent smell of ozone, that normally is associated with heavy electrical discharges, and again like the odour inside a power station.

As the object was coming closer and then went overhead I tried to estimate its size, altitude and speed, but with the absence of any readily identifiable feature it was difficult to gauge these factors with any confidence. Taking the angle of the object above the horizon when I first observed it as a datum from which to get some idea of its height and distance away, and then connecting this with the impression as it passed overhead, I guessed that its height above ground when first seen was probably between 700 and 1,000' and since it certainly seemed to maintain altitude throughout the period of my observation, I guessed that it would have to be about 100' in diameter. Taking consideration of the time I had it under observation [estimated to be 30 seconds], and the distance it would have travelled until it went out of sight, it must have been travelling very fast, perhaps as high as 500 to 900 knots, but there was no sense whatsoever of air disturbance due to its passing.'[31]

Hubbard said his estimates were 'intuitive guesses'. According to the MoD report, he had estimated the height of the saucer to be 5,000 feet and the speed to be 800–1,000 mph on a 100 degree heading 'executing a series of

S-turns, oscillating so that light reflection came from different sections as it moved'.

As the saucer disappeared into the distance Hubbard recalled hearing 'screaming and shouting' from the flight dispatches office nearby. A dispatcher came running towards him in a hysterical state, shouting, 'Stan, did you see that awful thing?' She was comforted by another airman but was 'extremely upset, almost irrational'.

Soon afterwards, when Hubbard was interrogated by Scientific Intelligence officers from London, he asked whether they had spoken to the dispatcher, but they refused to answer and merely posed another question. Hubbard recalled:

> 'One question which I think reflects the tenor of the interview was: "What do you suppose the object was, and where would it have come from?" I replied simply that in my opinion it was not something that had been designed and built on this Earth. Clearly, from the effect it had on the team, it was the wrong answer.'[32]

The first interview lasted two hours and ended with an order from the leader of the team 'not to discuss the matter with anyone, including my boss, and that I would be hearing from them'.

Despite the admonition, news of the story evidently leaked out and Hubbard took some ribbing from other officers and aircrew. One practical joke was particularly memorable:

> 'A very neatly packed tea chest was delivered to my home. When unpacked, it revealed a somewhat smaller box, within which was a yet smaller container – and so on, each succeeding box being smaller, until at last a very small box, which contained a demitasse and a little note which read: "Put this in your saucer and have a cup of tea." '[33]

The Scientific Intelligence team, however, was confounded by testimony of such clarity and privately reached a controversial conclusion. They had no reason to doubt that the experienced test pilot had honestly described what he had seen,

> '... but we find it impossible to believe that a most unconventional aircraft, of exceptional speed, could have travelled at no great altitude, in the middle of a fine

summer morning, over a populous and air-
minded district like Farnborough, without
attracting the attention of more than one
observer.'[34]

They concluded that Hubbard 'was the victim of an optical illusion, or that he observed some quite normal type of aircraft and deceived himself about its shape and speed'.[35]

This explanation was to be soon thrown into doubt by Hubbard's second sighting. On the afternoon of 5 September he was standing with five other airmen on the watch-tower at Farnborough awaiting the arrival of Hawker's chief test pilot, 'Wimpy' Wade, who was to be the star of the forthcoming air display.[36] Suddenly, and at the same moment, they all saw a strange object appear in the direction of Guildford and Farnham. The official report described it as 'a flat disc, light pearl grey in colour [and] about the size of a shirt button'.[37] They observed it follow a rectangular flight path, consisting in succession of a 'falling leaf' another horizontal stretch, and so on; finally it 'dived to the horizon at great speed'.

Hubbard described the scenes that followed the appearance of the saucer:

'Pandemonium! Orders being shouted – "Get a camera," "Get binoculars," etc. The performance of the object was quite different from that formerly seen. From a ... fluttering, as though bordering on instability, in a hovering mode, the object would swoop off in a slight dive at incredibly high speed and in quite stable flight, then stop abruptly and go into another fluttering hover mode. This performance was repeated many times, frequently with some change of height and it appeared that all this was taking place some eight to ten miles south of us over the Farnham area. We watched these performances for over ten minutes, during which time the gathering had swelled to at least a dozen people, not one of whom had a camera ... but the display had a most notable effect on my companions and, in fact, truly made my day.'[38]

Recalling the event in 2001, Wing Commander Frank Jolliffe told us:

'We all saw this twinkling silvery object at the same instant and, as it tumbled earthwards, we were shocked to suppose it could be a cowling or some part of an aircraft that had failed in flight. Indeed, we were about to run to Air Traffic Control and have them raise a general alarm, when the object changed direction very sharply and shot skywards at very high speed. The height of the sighting was hard to assess, as was the distance ... but the fact that it was there cannot be in doubt.'[39]

This new sighting was reported to Farnborough's chief test pilot, who notified the MoD in London. Soon the team from Scientific Intelligence was travelling to Farnborough again.

Jolliffe recalls how the six witnesses were all quizzed separately by 'a suit' who introduced himself as a serving RAF technical officer employed in the Scientific Intelligence branch of MoD (RAF). This was Wing Commander Myles Formby, of the Flying Saucer Working Party. 'He told us that his role was to gather information and fully examine all "UFO" sightings and he added that the Department had never had a more reliable and authentic sighting than ours,' Jolliffe said.

'He had no doubts or reservations about our evidence and said that the follow-up action would be to cover the whole sector east of Farnborough bounded by the angle of the first and last sightings to discover if there were other witnesses to this phenomena. He was optimistic that there would be. Unfortunately, he reported to our chief test pilot weeks later that this was not the case.'[10]

When the Scientific Intelligence team arrived to interview Hubbard, the leader exclaimed: 'Oh my goodness, not you again!' The interview followed the same pattern as before, but was shorter, as the team said they had to catch a plane to Brazil to interrogate flying saucer watchers there! Hubbard added:

'The first interview lasted very nearly two hours, and I got the impression then that they did not understand what I was telling them, or comprehend the implications. We were never permitted to see any of the reports of the interviews we had from those strange people from Scientific Intelligence, and certainly did not realise there was an officer in mufti with them. We were not given their names and we were strictly warned not to ask questions of them, nor make enquiries elsewhere in the Ministry. We were also warned to not discuss the subject later, even amongst ourselves in private.'[11]

The Scientific Intelligence team's conclusions about the second sighting followed a familiar path. They had no doubt that all the experienced officers involved 'did in fact see a flying object of some sort'[42] but they cast doubt upon the circumstances by making a connection between the first and second sightings. Hubbard, they said, had claimed the objects he saw on the two occasions were identical and 'the other observers agreed that the second object fitted the description they had been given of the first'.[43] The team felt this was of little value, as the second object was seen at a great distance:

'Further, we again find it impossible to
believe that an unconventional aircraft,
manoeuvring for some time over a populous
area, could have failed to attract the
attention of other observers. We conclude
that the officers in fact saw some quite
normal aircraft, manoeuvring at extreme
visual range, and were led by the previous
report to believe it to be something
abnormal.'[44]

Thus the 5 September sighting was 'an interesting example of one report influencing another'.[45]

The team was satisfied this conclusion was sound because of an similar misperception by one of their own members, Wing Commander Formby:

"While on the rifle range at Tipner,
Portsmouth, an object having the appearance
of a "Flying Saucer" was observed in the
distance. Visibility was good, there being a
cloudless sky and bright sunshine. The
object was located and held by telescope and
gave appearance of being a circular shining
disc moving on a regular flight path. It was
only after observation had been kept for
several minutes, and the altitude of the

```
object changed so that it did not reflect
the sunlight to the observer's eye, that it
was identified as being a perfectly normal
aircraft.'⁴⁶
```

Formby's experience brought home to the Scientific Intelligence team 'the ease with which mistaken identifications can be made, even by experienced observers'.[47]

These conclusions were soundly rejected by Hubbard and Jolliffe when we provided them with copies of the Working Party's report in 2001. Hubbard told us:

> 'I find it quite strange that so much information that we thought critically relevant at the time was not only not included but misrepresented and taken completely out of context, resulting in flawed conclusions. I am not normally given to being suspicious, but I think that perhaps this was deliberate official policy.'[18]

Jolliffe was even more direct:

> 'The conclusions reached in the MoD report are ludicrous. What we saw and explained clearly was an object not of aircraft shape, travelling at speed not achievable by anything flying at the time and altering direction not in curved, sweeping manoeuvres but by acute angular changes. It was not "some quite normal aircraft" – it was not an aircraft, as we know it, at all. Wing Cdr Hubbard's previous sighting had no influence on any of our opinions.'[19]

In his view, the MoD report 'leads one to think that the Working Party was following a high-level cover-up directive'.

Occam's Razor

It is from events such as these that the belief in a government cover up originated. If the Men from the Ministry could suppress testimony from some of the RAF's most experienced test pilots, who were specially trained to observe and report critically and accurately upon occurrences taking place in the air, what did that say about their real agenda?

Of the options considered by the Scientific Intelligence team, the

possibility that UFOs were solid mechanical craft piloted by extraterrestrial visitors was rejected outright. Their report concluded:

> 'When the only material available is a mass
> of purely subjective evidence, it is
> impossible to give anything like scientific
> proof that the phenomena observed are, or
> are not, caused by something entirely novel,
> such as aircraft of extraterrestrial origin,
> developed by beings unknown to us on lines
> more advanced than anything we have thought
> of. We are ... satisfied that the bulk of the
> observations reported do not need such an
> explanation, and can be accounted for much
> more simply...'[50]

Building upon the conclusions of the investigations conducted by the
USAF during 1947–49 and Woodman's Boscombe Down study of 1950,
the British team turned to what it called 'a very old scientific principle
usually attributed to William of Occam'. The principle, known as Occam's
Razor, states that the most probable hypothesis is the simplest necessary to
explain the observations. The team concluded that the razor should be
applied to all reports of UFOs and that all sightings were therefore due
to one or other of the following causes:

> Astronomical or meteorological phenomena
> of known types.
>
> Mistaken identification of conventional
> aircraft, balloons, birds, or other normal
> or natural objects.
>
> Optical illusions and psychological
> delusions.
>
> Deliberate hoaxes.

These conclusions were revised by later MoD studies which resulted in the more moderate assessment that between 5 and 10 per cent of sightings could not be identified, simply because of a lack of information. In 1950 a more open-minded attitude was not within the Working Party's remit, however, and the team's scathing conclusions were amplified further in the recommendations made to the DSI and chiefs of staff. These maintained that 'no progress will be made by attempting further investigation of unco-ordinated and subjective evidence' and that the only effective method to settle the question of UFO reality for good would be to 'organise throughout the country, or the world, continuous observation of the skies by a co-ordinated network of visual observers, equipped with photographic apparatus and supplemented by a network of radar stations and sound locators'.[51] Such a project would be an expensive and 'singularly profitless enterprise' and instead:

```
'We recommend very strongly that no
further investigation of reported mystery
aerial phenomena be undertaken, unless
and until some material evidence becomes
available.' [52]
```

Keeping It Quiet

Unable to explain the UFO phenomenon or to admit they could not explain it, the authorities were placed in a predicament. It seemed the only remaining option was to downplay the importance of the subject and to ensure that the most puzzling reports were stifled. The Air Ministry gave out only the most perfunctory of statements when questioned by the press and the existence of any form of 'official' study was denied both publicly and to MPs for 50 years. That has remained the MoD's position.

The conclusions and recommendations of the Flying Saucer Working Party in 1951 set the tone for all future British policy on UFOs and also influenced the American approach. The presence of a senior CIA scientist, Dr H. Marshall Chadwell, when Report No. 7 was presented to the MoD underlined the close links between the British and American intelligence networks during this part of the Cold War. Chadwell's role in formulating the British conclusions would later influence the CIA's own study in 1952–3.

G. Turney of the DSI, who chaired the meeting at which Report No. 7 was presented to the DSI and CIA, said that it 'should be regarded as a final report ... and in view of the conclusions reached ... [the Working Party] should now be dissolved'.[53]

Significantly, in view of the CIA presence at the meeting, Turney went on to add, 'Following the lead given by the Americans on this subject, the Report should ... have as little publicity as possible and outside circulation should be confined to one copy to Sir Henry Tizard.'[54] On 26 June 1951 a copy of Report No. 7 was forwarded by Dr Bertie Blount to Tizard. 'This is the report on "Flying Saucers" for which you asked,' he wrote. 'I hope that it will serve its purpose.'[55]

In hindsight this final cryptic comment leaves the real motives behind the study open to speculation.

Chapter 6

THE UFO INVASION

'...Holy Mackerel! Get the
Lieutenant! That thing's doing
4,000! That can't be aircraft!
Must be a buzz bomb! I have a
bogey at two zero zero thousand
feet, four zero zero zero miles
an hour...'

Opening lines of *The Day the Earth Stood Still*, first
performed in New York City, 18 September 1951[1]

If the British intelligence services and their friends in the CIA were hoping the flying saucer craze had been exorcised by their secret study, they were soon to be disappointed. The Flying Saucer Working Party's debunking words came back to haunt them during the summer of 1952 when UFOs appeared in force above the US Capital, Washington, DC.

Over a period of ten days, unidentified blips appeared on the radar at Washington's National Airport and Andrews air force base. F-94 fighter aircraft were scrambled but were unable to make contact with the radar phantoms. More than 500 sightings were reported to the USAF in July and flying saucers filled newspaper headlines across the world. The scare led the *New York Times* to ask why 'a jet fighter of Air Defence Command, capable of a speed of 600 miles an hour, failed to catch one of the "objects" '. Unless such questions were answered, the London *Times* commented, 'Belief in visitors from outer space will be strengthened in those who cannot distinguish between speculation and scientific reasoning.'[2]

In a bid to calm public fears, the USAF took the decision to hold a press conference at the Pentagon on 29 July, where high-ranking officials, including Major-General John Samford, director of Air Force Intelligence, spent more than an hour answering questions. The conference was in fact the longest and best-attended press conference since the ending of World War II. Samford said the radar sightings were most likely the result of temperature inversions, but he was unable to account for the visual sightings by pilots. Although no definitive answer was available, he stressed there was no evidence of a threat to the United States.[3]

Behind the scenes there was far less confidence that UFOs did not pose a threat. Like Britain, the USA relied upon radar of World War II vintage to defend its vast airspace. Secretly, the US Joint Chiefs of Staff had been working on a permanent national radar network which was meant to be in place by 1 July 1952, which had been identified as 'the critical date when the Soviets would pose a dangerous threat'.[4] The UFO 'invasion' of Washington, DC, at this critical time alarmed President Harry Truman, who demanded answers from the USAF, and the CIA, which had been monitoring the air force's half-hearted investigations, now set up its own secret study group.

The following year an investigation by the Civil Aeronautics Administration found the Washington radar blips had been produced by temperature inversions created by the hot summer weather and concluded: 'They do not represent new phenomena, nor are they peculiar to the Washington area.'

In Britain, meteorologist R. F. Jones reached a similar conclusion in a secret paper circulated to Air Ministry. The air staff were reassured that the scare 'occurred during a period when the atmosphere was exceedingly superrefractive and "spotty" anomalous propagation was definitely in order'.[5]

'What on Earth Is Going On?'

Flying saucers were the last thing on Michael Swiney's mind when he climbed into the cockpit of an RAF Meteor VII on the afternoon of 21 October 1952. Swiney was a staff instructor based at the RAF's Central Flying School at Little Rissington, Gloucestershire, where his job was to provide tuition to RAF and Navy pilots. Seated behind him was his student for the day, David Crofts, a Royal Navy lieutenant. What began as a run-of-the mill exercise was soon to turn into one of the most dramatic experiences in Swiney's flying career.

In 2001 Swiney recalled how, as the jet punched through a layer of strato-cumulus cloud at 10–12,000 feet:

'I got the fright of my life because there appeared to be, smack in front of the aeroplane, three circular objects. Two of them were on a level keel and one of them was canted at a slight angle. I thought, "God Almighty, this is three chaps coming down on parachutes," and I literally took the stick, or pole as we used to call it, out of [the student's] hand so we didn't tear through these parachutes. He issued some sort of expletive, I don't know what it was, and said, "What on Earth is going on?" and I said, "David, have a look at this!" and he just said, "What's that?" [6]

What followed mixed shock with calm adherence to procedure in the face of the unknown. According to an account of this incredible incident by the late Air Marshal Sir Peter Horsley, the Fleet Air Arm pilot found it so difficult to take in the sight that he initially believed he was suffering from oxygen failure.[7] Meanwhile Swiney, who had taken control, turned the aircraft through a 45-degree turn, still climbing. He explained:

> 'They were circular and appeared to be stationary. But as we continued to climb they did in fact change position and to make sure of that we very carefully checked and these things moved across to the right-hand side somewhere. The higher we got, [the more] they lost this circular effect [which appeared] when looking at them from underneath. As they came down to your level they lost the circular effect and took on a "flat plate" appearance.'[8]

As the Meteor levelled out at 35,000 feet the three strange objects remained clearly visible. They were saucer or plate-shaped, slightly off-white in colour and emitted a fuzzy or iridescent light from their edges. There were no visible signs of propulsion; no portholes, turrets or other tell-tale signs that might have identified them as known aircraft viewed at an unusual angle. Swiney continued:

> 'I called up air traffic control at Rissington and said I had three unidentified objects fairly close and gave them my course. I had then been flying for about nine years and I had seen many funny reflections, refractions through windscreens and lots of other things, but this was nothing of the sort. By then we were feeling decidedly uneasy because we were not sure what we were looking at. We had been looking around to try and say it was some sort of reflection coming through the window, but every time we looked back they were still there.'[9]

According to Horsley's account, air traffic control (ATC) instructed the Meteor to approach the UFOs and Swiney turned the aircraft towards them, opening up to full power:

'At Mach.8 they gained quite rapidly but when the circular object filled half their windscreen, it suddenly turned on its side "like a plate" (their words) and climbed away out of sight at great speed.'[10]

Meanwhile, on the ground, Rissington had alerted RAF Fighter Command and air traffic control at Gloucester. Simultaneously, defence radar tracked 'an unidentified aircraft' crossing the southwest of England. Two Meteor fighters on 24-hour quick reaction alert (QRA) duty were scrambled from RAF Tangmere in Sussex to intercept.

The Meteors were controlled by the radars at Rudloe Manor in Wiltshire. Controllers there tracked Swiney's Meteor as it closed on the unidentified blip, which suddenly disappeared off the tube at speed estimated as 1,000 mph. The two Meteors followed as the target sped towards the Atlantic, but failed to make contact.

To Swiney and his student the disappearance of the flying objects was equally swift. 'It was quite extraordinary,' he recalled. 'The next time I looked away and looked back, they'd gone. Just disappeared.'[11]

Abandoning the exercise, Swiney returned to Little Rissington, where he was told he looked as if he had seen a ghost. Senior officers immediately separated the two witnesses, who were led to briefing rooms where they were asked to write a detailed report on their experience. Their reports, along with tracking charts from two ground radar stations, were passed from Fighter Command to the MoD intelligence branch DDI (Tech). Within 12 months of receiving Swiney's report, the Assistant Chief of Air Staff (Intelligence) delegated to this branch full responsibility for the study of UFO reports made by radar stations and aircrews.[12]

Swiney, who was to rise in rank to air commodore, heard nothing further until the mid-1970s, when, during a posting to the MoD, he decided to make some discreet enquiries of his own. At that time, the MoD's standard answer to all public and parliamentary questions was that because UFO sightings had such mundane explanations all files were routinely destroyed at five-yearly intervals. This practice, they said, had been halted in 1967 and as a result the earliest UFO records held by the MoD dated from 1962. Evidently someone was being economical with the truth, because the 1952 statements by Swiney and his student pilot were still on file with DDI (Tech)!

'I asked to see the report and I was shown the file,' Swiney explained. 'It was all there, and I know that it existed in the mid-1970s, but I don't know what has happened to it since.'[13]

Figure 13 (*opposite*): **Entries from the Operational Record Book, RAF Little Rissington** (Public Record Office: 29/2310) **and personal flying log belonging to Flight Lieutenant Michael Swiney recording sighting of three 'flying saucers' during a training exercise over southwest England, 21 October 1952** (Copyright: M.J.E. Swiney)

PLACE	DATE	TIME	SUMMARY OF EVENTS
Central Flying School (Advanced) Little Rissington	October, 1952		
	17.10.52.		Squadron Leader D. C. H. SIMMONS led a team consisting of Flight Lieutenant W. J. STACEY and Flight Lieutenant W. H. CADALY on a visit to No. 608 Squadron, (R. Aux. A.F.) THORNABY. Tests were carried out on Meteor and Harvard aircraft.
	20.10.52.		Squadron Leader H. E. WHITE, D.F.C., A.F.C., led a team from No. 1 Squadron, Examining Wing on a visit to No. 6 F.T.S. TERNHILL. The team consisted of Lieutenant E. C. SPREADBURY, R.N., Flight Lieutenant G. ALLEN, M.C., and Flight Lieutenant J. M. NICHOLSON. Tests were conducted on Harvard aircraft. Squadron Leader D. C. H. SIMMONS led a team from No. 3 Squadron Examining Wing on a visit to No. 226 O.C.U. STRADISHALL. The team consisted of Flight Lieutenant J. C. STEELE and Flight Lieutenant K. L. TEBBITT. Tests were conducted on Meteor aircraft.
	21.10.52.		Flight Lieutenant M. J. E. SWINEY, instructor, and Lieutenant D. CROFTS, R.N., student, sighted three mysterious "saucer shaped objects" travelling at high speed at about 35,000' whilst on a high level navigation exercise, in a Meteor VII. Later, A.T.C.C. Gloucester reported radar plots to confirm this, but Air Ministry discounted any possibility of "extra terrestrial objects".
	22.10.52.		The first of the D.4 Link Trainers to re-equip the Link School was installed.
	27.10.52.		Squadron leader H. E. WHITE, D.F.C., A.F.C., led a team consisting of Flight Lieutenant L. J. COOP, Flight Lieutenant W. R. HERBERT, Lieutenant E. C. SPREADBURY, R.N., and Flight Lieutenant G. ALLEN, M.C. to No. 1 Grading Unit, DIGBY. Tests were conducted on Tiger Moth aircraft.

Year 1952 Month	Date	AIRCRAFT Type	No.	Pilot, or 1st Pilot	2nd Pilot, Pupil or Passenger	DUTY (Including Results and Remarks)	SINGLE-ENGINE AIRCRAFT DAY Dual (1)	Pilot (2)	NIGHT Dual (3)	Pilot (4)	MULTI DAY Dual (5)	1st Pilot (6)	(7)
						Totals Brought Forward	152.00	685.30	17.05	101.05	46.50	500.40	9.
OCT.	21	METEOR VII	M	SELF	F/S HALL	Ex. 6.						.40	
OCT.	21	METEOR VII	M	SELF	LT. CROFTS	Ex. 18. (SAUCERS!)		3 "flying saucers" sighted by				1.10	
OCT.	22	METEOR VII	M	SELF	F.O. KEMP.	Ex. 14.		Flight Lieutenant M.J.E. Swiney &				.45	
OCT.	23	METEOR VII	H	SELF	F.O. KEMP.	Ex. 14.						.40	
OCT.	23	METEOR VII	M	SELF	F.L. NEW	Ex. 14.						.40	
OCT.	23	METEOR VII	H	SELF	LT. CROFTS	Ex. 8.						.40	
OCT.	23	METEOR VII	M	SELF	F/S HALL	Ex. 18.						1.15	
OCT.	28	METEOR VII	M	SELF	F/S HALL	Ex. 9.						.45	
OCT.	28	METEOR VII	M	SELF	F.O. KEMP.	Ex. 18.						1.15	
OCT.	29	METEOR VII	M	SELF	F.O. KEMP.	Ex. 16.						.45	
OCT.	30	METEOR VII	M	SELF	BARRACLOUGH	Revision						.40	
OCT.	30	METEOR VII	M	SELF	F.O. KEMP.	Low-level X-Ctry.						.40	
OCT.	31	METEOR VII	M	SELF	F/S HALL.	Ex. 16.						.40	
OCT.	31	METEOR VII	C	SELF	LT. CROFTS	Ex. 14.						.40	
		SUMMARY FOR	October 1952		1. METEOR VII							24.45	
		UNIT	C.F.S.	AC TYPE	2.								
		DATE	31.10.52.		3.								
		SIGNATURE	M.J. Swiney		4.								
NOV.	1	METEOR VII	M	SELF	SOLO	Air Test.						.20	
NOV.	3	METEOR VII	A	SELF	F/S HALL	Ex. 14.						.40	
NOV.	3	METEOR VII	A	SELF	LT. CROFTS	Ex. 16.						.40	
NOV.	4	METEOR VII	A	SELF	LT. CROFTS	Ex. 20.						.45	
NOV.	6	METEOR VII	A	SELF	F.O. KEMP	S.E. Landings.						.40	
NOV.	10	METEOR VII	M	SELF	F.O. KEMP.	Ex. 22.						.50	
		GRAND TOTAL [Cols. (1) to (10)]				Totals Carried Forward	2.00	685.30	17.05	101.05	46.50	515.50	

P.S. CROSBY LT. R.N.
O.C. "M" FLT.
J.C. WILTON SQN. LDR.
O.C. 5 SQUADRON.

Swiney had also kept a copy of his flying log book for 1952, which supported his story (*see* Figure 13, page 101). Under Exercise 18 an entry read: '(SAUCERS!) 3 "Flying Saucers" sighted at height. Confirmed by G.C.I.' When in 2001 Swiney attempted to obtain a copy of his original report to Air Ministry he was told by the MoD that it had 'most likely' been destroyed. However, research at the PRO revealed an entry in the ORB of the Central Flying School, dated 21 October 1952, which read:

> 'Flight Lieutenant M. J. E. SWINEY,
> instructor, and Lieutenant D. CROFTS, R.N.,
> student, sighted three mysterious "saucer
> shaped objects" travelling at high speed at
> about 35,000' whilst on a high level
> navigation exercise, in a Meteor VII. Later,
> A.T.C.C. Gloucester reported radar plots to
> confirm this, but Air Ministry discounted
> any possibility of "extra terrestrial
> objects".'[14]

The evidence suggests that in addition to the testimony of the two pilots, two separate radars had tracked an UFO and this resulted in the scramble of interceptor aircraft. How could the Air Ministry claim, so quickly after the events, that they had 'discounted any possibility' of extraterrestrial objects? Where are the records of the official investigation into this incident that were evidently seen both by Sir Peter Horsley and by Air Commodore Swiney as recently as the 1970s? If there was nothing to hide, then why was this incident kept secret for half a century?

At some point in the future these questions may be answered, but in 1952 the OSA ensured that details of this startling incident never reached the public. This level of secrecy allowed DDI (Tech) to continue their investigations, but at that point no formal orders had yet been circulated to RAF stations and personnel outlining the procedure for the reporting of sightings.

Winston Churchill's Questions

Meantime, the Washington sightings and the US government's sudden intense interest in a subject it had previously debunked worried the British Prime Minister, Winston Churchill. On the day before that reporters were gathering at the Pentagon press conference, Churchill fired off a memo

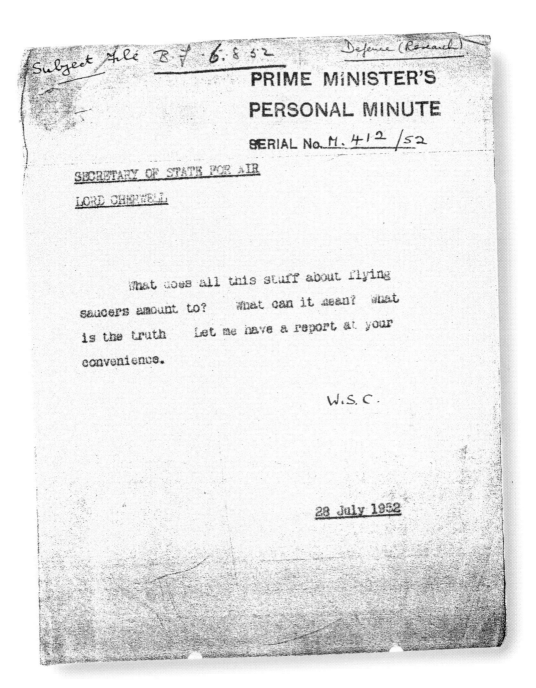

Figure 14: **PM's personal minute: Winston Churchill to Secretary of State for Air, 28 July 1952** (Public Record Office: PREM 11/855)

to his Secretary of State for Air:

> 'What does all this stuff about flying saucers amount to? What can it mean? What is the truth? Let me have a report at your convenience.'[15]

The answer reassured Churchill there was nothing to be concerned about. Flying saucers had been the subject of a 'full Intelligence study' conducted by the MoD in 1951, which had concluded that all reports could be accounted for by mistaken identity, delusions and hoaxes. The British study had drawn heavily upon the negative findings of the US Project Grudge in 1949 when reaching these conclusions and, the Air Minister wrote, 'Nothing has happened since 1951 to make the Air Staff change their opinion, and, to judge from recent Press statements, the same is true in America.'[16] Churchill's senior scientific advisor, Lord Cherwell, said he had seen the Secretary of State's minute and 'agreed entirely with his conclusions'.[17]

If the Air Ministry's response to Churchill was accurate, the subject was deemed to be of so little importance that knowledge of the USAF's policy on UFOs was being judged from press statements rather than direct intelligence contacts. Those who promote the idea of a cover up by the British government have claimed that Churchill was misinformed about the true findings of the US and British studies. In reality, Churchill was provided with what his advisors believed was the best answer available at the time. He was not, of course, made aware of contradictory evidence, such as the testimony of the RAF's own test pilots, which had been carefully hidden within the MoD's secret report.

Our interpretation of the Prime Minister's interest is supported by the testimony of Sir Anthony Montague-Browne, CBE, Churchill's private secretary from 1952 until his death in 1965. In 2000 he told us:

> 'Sir Winston's interest in the subject of UFOs was ephemeral. He wanted to know the facts in case he was questioned in Parliament. That was all. The information we received from the United States agreed with what the Secretary of State at the Air Ministry and others said – that there was nothing in it, just misperception.'[18]

Figure 15 (*opposite*): **Memo from Secretary of State for Air to Winston Churchill, 9 August 1952** (Public Record Office: PREM11/855)

Defence (Research)

AIR MINISTRY,
WHITEHALL,
S.W.1.

PRIME MINISTER

The various reports about unidentified flying
objects, described by the Press as "flying saucers",
were the subject of a full Intelligence study in 1951.
The conclusions reached (based upon William of Occam's
Razor) were that all the incidents reported could be
explained by one or other of the following causes:-

(a) Known astronomical or meteorological phenomena

(b) Mistaken identification of conventional aircraft,
       balloons, birds, etc.

(c) Optical illusions and psychological delusions

(d) Deliberate hoaxes.

2.   The Americans, who carried out a similar investigation in 1948/9, reached a similar conclusion.

3.   Nothing has happened since 1951 to make the Air
Staff change their opinion, and, to judge from recent
Press statements, the same is true in America.

4.   I am sending a copy of this to Lord Cherwell.

S.L.B.

9th August, 1952.

Put by

MC

10. VIII

Sir Anthony said Churchill's circle of friends and advisors was as divided over flying saucers as was the general public. Both Lord Cherwell and Dr R. V. Jones, Churchill's most trusted scientific advisors, said that flying saucers were nonsense. The Prime Minister's son-in-law and future Defence Minister Duncan Sandys:

> '... believed or said he believed some of the evidence... As for the stories about little men, these were just ridiculous. There was no conspiracy to hide anything because what was there to hide?
> There was some initial concern about the possibility they could be Russian aircraft, but these would have been detected by radar.
> The whole story was hyped up by the newspapers. Never during my time as Winston's private secretary did he take it seriously and the whole subject was deemed to be of little importance.'[19]

Two months after Churchill was reassured that flying saucers were a figment of the imagination, they appeared right in the middle of a major NATO exercise.

Exercise Mainbrace

Mainbrace, a major exercise to measure how effectively NATO forces could respond to a simulated attack upon Western Europe, took place in September 1952. More than 80,000 personnel in 150 ships and submarines, plus hundreds of aircraft from the forces of eight countries took part. Even before the manoeuvres began it was clear the forces of the Iron Curtain would be keeping a close eye upon the exercise. But were the eyes of another world also watching? Captain Edward J. Ruppelt of the USAF's new UFO project noted in his memoirs: 'Someone in the Pentagon had half-seriously mentioned that Naval intelligence should keep an eye open for UFOs,' but no one had taken the remark seriously.[20]

In 1967 retired Royal Navy Commander B. V. Wilson told the University of Colorado UFO project that there were five 'important sightings' of UFOs during Operation Mainbrace, 'all made by naval officers and men, and well authenticated by the Navies concerned'.[21] None of the files relating to these sightings has ever surfaced and the Royal Navy has consistently denied ever receiving or investigating UFO reports. Nevertheless there is compelling evidence that visual sightings and radar trackings of UFOs did occur throughout the 13-day exercise.

Meanwhile an unusual plot was added to the huge chart on the wall of the operations room at RAF Pitreavie in Scotland – a cut-out in the shape of a flying saucer alongside the word 'Topcliffe'. At HQ No. 18 Group Coastal Command the duty controller opened up a new signal file entitled 'Saucer Sightings and Movements'. This signal, transmitted from Pitreavie to NATO command and copied to the Air Ministry and Scientific and Technical Intelligence branch of the MoD, was seen by Ralph Noyes, who was Private Secretary to the Vice Chief of Air Staff, Air Chief Marshal Sir Ralph Cochrane. Noyes eventually rose to a senior position in the MoD and on retirement became one of the first to defy the Official Secrets Act and publicly discuss official attitudes to the UFO phenomenon. In 1988 he recalled his embarrassed unease, shared by operations staff, on reading the signal from Pitreavie, that 'our own people had begun to fall for that saucer nonsense'.[22]

So unfamiliar was the Air Ministry in dealing with saucer sightings by its own staff that there was still no formal reporting procedure in place. Evidence of this is found in a note scribbled on the signal by the Wing Commander at RAF (Ops): 'Ask PA [personal assistant] to open folder: "Unidentified a/c or Objects Reported to Air Ministry".'[23]

The headlines of the *Sunday Dispatch* of 21 September 1952 were to change all that. They read: '"Saucer" chased RAF jet plane'. The article continued:

> 'Serious investigation was being made last night by the RAF into the mystery of a silvery-white object that chased a Meteor jet-plane over Yorkshire during "Exercise Mainbrace".'[24]

Two RAF officers and three Shackleton aircrew from 269 Squadron had sighted the saucer at RAF Topcliffe in North Yorkshire. They had landed shortly before 10 a.m. and were watching a Meteor approaching nearby Dishforth airfield when Flight Lieutenant Paris 'suddenly noticed a white object in the sky at a height of between ten and twenty thousand feet some five miles astern of the Meteor'.[25] Paris drew the attention of another officer, Flight Lieutenant John Kilburn, to the UFO. Kilburn's official report has survived in a PRO file and was elaborated upon in an interview published by the *Sunday Dispatch*:

> 'It was 10.53 a.m. and the sky was clear ... when I noticed the white object in the sky. This object was silver and circular in shape and appeared to be travelling at a lower speed than the Meteor but was on the same course. I said, "What the hell's that?" and the chaps looked to where I was pointing. Somebody shouted that it might be the engine cowling of the Meteor falling out of the sky. Then we thought it might be a parachute. But as we watched the disc maintained a slow forward speed for a few seconds before starting to descend.'[26]

Kilburn's description of the 'pendular motion' of the object is remarkably similar to that of the test pilots who watched the saucer in the sky near Farnborough in 1950. This was a sighting of which Paris and Kilburn knew nothing, because details remained an MoD secret. Nevertheless, Kilburn described the same peculiar motion, 'swinging in a pendular motion … similar to a falling sycamore leaf'.[27]

As the Meteor turned to begin its landing run, the saucer first appeared to follow it but soon stopped and hung in the air, 'rotating as if on its own axis'. Then it accelerated at an incredible speed to the west, turned southeast and vanished. Kilburn reported to his HQ:

> 'The acceleration was in excess of that of a shooting star. I have never seen such a phenomenon before. The movements of the object were not identifiable with anything I have seen in the air and the rate of acceleration was unbelievable.'[28]

This report was flashed across the world, along with the airmen's conclusion that what they had seen could not possibly have been a smoke ring, weather balloon or a vapour trail left in the wake of the Meteor. Kilburn told the press:

> 'The speed at which it moved away discounts this altogether. Our combined opinion is that it was about the size of a Vampire jet – and it was something we had never seen before in a long experience of air observation.'[29]

In the face of such statements from an experienced airman, the Air Ministry was at a loss to respond, though a spokesman claimed: 'We do not believe in flying saucers.'[30] Be that as it may, base intelligence officers had already begun to interrogate the six witnesses.

A New Approach

After the Flying Saucer Working Party was disbanded in June 1951 the lack of documentary evidence implies the Air Ministry had followed its recommendations and ended any further study. That policy was rescinded in 1952, when a worldwide wave of UFO sightings triggered a high-level exchange of intelligence between Britain and the USA. This was to continue as a new approach was formulated in the wake of the Mainbrace sightings. The fear that the Soviet Union could use the new Western fascination with flying saucers as a diversion to launch a sneak attack was very real. So little was known about Soviet progress in aircraft and rocket technology that it also remained possible that the saucers themselves were of Russian origin.

It was during this period that Squadron Leader Peter Horsley, the royal equerry, discussed UFOs with the Commander in Chief at Fighter Command, Sir Thomas Pike, as part of his study of the subject. 'Their main interest was the possibility that the Russians had developed a high-speed aircraft to spy on the UK,' he admitted in 2000.[31] Horsley also made his own informal enquiries with the USAF via the British air attaché in Washington, Group Captain H. A. C. Bird-Wilson. 'I was very surprised because the Americans wouldn't tell me anything,' Horsley said. 'Bird-Wilson made some enquiries and came back and more or less hinted that the Americans were covering up something.'[32]

Whatever that 'something' was, Horsley did not have sufficient 'need to know'. According to Ralph Noyes, following the Washington sightings of 1952 Sir Ralph Cochrane asked the Air Ministry's chief scientist, Robert Cockburn, to make enquiries with his opposite number in America. He was informed that a USAF special study group were involved in a highly secret study of the mystery, based upon the premise that the saucers were Soviet aircraft.[33]

In June the British press had reported that the USAF had reactivated its moribund UFO project under a new title, Blue Book. General Hoyt Vandenberg told them many sightings had been explained, but others had not, 'and we cannot afford to be complacent'.[34] Vandenburg had played a key role in the debunking of saucer stories during the era of Projects Sign and Grudge, and this apparent U-turn puzzled the British air staff. Ralph Noyes recalled how Cochrane discussed the situation with the government's chief scientist, Lord Cherwell, and both continued the public stance that 'American public hysteria' was the true cause of saucer sightings. Both must have been shocked in September that same year when the hysteria appeared to be spreading to Britain.

Equally sceptical was Dr R. V. Jones, who remained as a consultant on intelligence matters to the MoD. In September 1952, at the invitation of Winston Churchill, he returned to full-time work as Director of Scientific Intelligence. Jones brought his vast experience of aerial phenomena, formulated during the 'ghost rocket' era, to bear upon the new flying saucer 'problem'. In a statement to an aviation historian in 1978 he said that he 'knew of no attempt whatsoever to deceive the public' over the subject of flying saucers:

'If there were any reticence at all on the part of officials, it could only have been a protective measure to save themselves from being inundated with reports of doubtful quality, such as followed the Swedish General Staff's invitation to the public in 1946 to report sightings to them.'[35]

A December 1952 memorandum prepared by the CIA scientist Dr H. Marshall Chadwell reported on Jones' efforts to debunk UFOs in the face of growing public belief. Classified 'Secret' until 2001, 'British Activity in the Field of Unidentified Flying Objects' reveals the concern generated at the highest levels of government by newspaper reports of the Topcliffe incident:

'[UFO] activity had been quiet and normal [until] the Yorkshire incident took place ...there was a demonstration to which high officials of the RAF in London had been invited. During the show, a "perfect flying saucer" was seen by these officials as well as RAF pilots. So many people saw it that many articles appeared in the public press. This is disturbing to Jones because he realizes that the ... correction of public opinion is a part of his responsibilities.'[36]

The CIA memo contained another revelation (*see* Figure 16). Officially the British government had ended all UFO investigation with the disbandment of the Flying Saucer Working Party in June 1951, at a meeting that Chadwell had attended. Yet according to the CIA, that same month the British set up a 'standing committee on flying saucers'. Chadwell revealed this committee now answered to Jones and that:

'The RAF are action people. The group has concluded that the observations are not enemy aircraft and that none have been over Britain.'[37]

Figure 16 (*opposite*): **CIA memo 'British Activity in the Field of Unidentified Flying Objects' prepared by Dr H. Marshall Chadwell, Assistant Director of Scientific Intelligence, 18 December 1952** (Copyright: Central Intelligence Agency)

SECRET
Security Information

18 December 1952

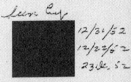

MEMORANDUM FOR RECORD

SUBJECT: British Activity in the field of "Unidentified Flying Objects"

1. On 15 December, the recently arrived messenger from ▓▓▓▓ reported the following. He had talked with ▓▓▓▓▓▓▓▓▓▓▓▓

2. The British have had a standing committee created about sixteen months ago on flying saucers. Presumably this is now under Dr. Jones through inheritance. The RAF are action people. The group has concluded that the observations are not enemy aircraft and that none have been over ▓▓▓▓▓▓

3. The activity has been quiet and normal up to about ten to twelve days ago, at which time the Yorkshire incident took place. In some RAF field, there was some sort of demonstration to which high officials of the RAF in London had been invited. During the show, a "perfect flying saucer" was seen by these officials as well as RAF pilots. So many people saw it that <u>many articles appeared in the public press</u>. This is disturbing to Jones because he realizes that the creation of the correction of public opinion is a part of his responsibilities.

4. ▓▓▓▓ reminded us of the Swedish incident (presumably he refers to the one in 1946), and reminds us of a paper on the origin of meteorites published in the French Academy of Sciences between 1760 and 1780 by Chladni.

5. The traveler told ▓▓▓ of our interest at this time, mentioned the film which had been taken by the Naval non-commissioned officer (▓▓▓▓▓▓ incident). It is possible that ▓▓▓ will write asking for a copy of the film or further on the same subject.

▓▓▓▓▓▓▓▓▓▓

H. MARSHALL CHADWELL
Assistant Director
Scientific Intelligence

Distribution:

▓▓▓▓▓▓▓▓▓▓

SECRET
Security Information

35

DDI (Tech) and UFO Investigations 1952–54

Despite what Jones may have told the CIA, the MoD, like General Vandenberg, was determined not to be complacent. In the autumn of 1952 Wing Commander Myles Formby, a veteran of the Flying Saucer Working Party, was asked to direct the new, more permanent investigation team.

In 1956, in an interview with journalist John Pitt, the MoD denied that there was a separate branch which dealt exclusively with UFO reports. This *was* correct, as DDI (Tech) was responsible for a wide range of Cold War intelligence gathering, with UFOs forming just one part of its overall responsibilities. Led by an RAF group captain, the intelligence branch had five sections dedicated to the study 'of the technical aspects of air and missile weapon systems of the Sino–Soviet bloc and all other foreign countries'.[38]

Formby's office was in the Metropole Building, where the Flying Saucer Working Party had made its deliberations in 1951. In 2001 he told us:

> 'It was the job of the committee to investigate all reports of possible unidentified phenomena and to decide what should be done about them. We never got a concrete report and I remained sceptical throughout.'[39]

Contacts with the Americans continued and in 1952 Formby travelled to the Pentagon for three weeks to work closely alongside his opposite number at USAF Intelligence, Colonel William O. Farrior, who worked in the same section as Major Dewey Fournet. This contact dated back to 1948, when Farrior had supplied Formby with information on the US investigations during his posting as a technical intelligence specialist in London.[40]

These informal exchanges were referred to by the USAF's Ed Ruppelt, who described a visit to the USAF's Air Technical Intelligence Center in 1952 by two RAF officers, one of whom was Wing Commander Formby. Ruppelt said they were in America 'on a classified mission' and brought with them 'six single-paced typed pages of questions' concerning UFOs. According to Ruppelt, the two men told him the sightings during Exercise Mainbrace 'caused the RAF to officially recognise the UFO'.[41]

Rumours of these visits leaked out and a London Sunday newspaper revealed that a reciprocal 'secret mission of American saucer experts' had recently visited Britain to discuss the growing mystery with Air Ministry experts. The mission had been led by Lieutenant Colonel Edwin Sterling and Dr Stefan Possony of the USAF's Directorate of Intelligence special studies group. Dr Possony had a high security clearance and has been described as 'the greatest strategic philosopher of the 20th century'.[42] In

May 1952 the pair had secretly visited Wiesbaden in Germany and the MoD's Joint Intelligence Bureau (JIB) in London in the hope of finding out 'something about the flying saucer problem'. It was clear that the most puzzling British UFO reports were being shared at a very high level with American intelligence.

Journalists were also on the trail of the new British 'saucer' project and a *Sunday Dispatch* story was the first to name the RAF branch responsible for the investigation of UFOs:

> 'For years the British public has been led to believe that the RAF has regarded "flying saucers" as a joke. The *Sunday Dispatch* can reveal ... that, on the contrary, ever since the first "saucer" was reported in 1947 the RAF has been operating a hush-hush investigation bureau in London. A staff of technical experts – mostly commissioned officers under the direction of a Wing Commander – are analysing every report of a flying saucer over British territory. Though the exact location of the flying saucer investigation bureau – known at the Air Ministry as the D.D.I. (Technical) Branch – is secret, I can reveal it occupies rooms in a building formerly a hotel, not five minutes' walk from the Air Ministry in Whitehall. The building is closely guarded. No one is allowed in without a pass.'[43]

It was to DDI (Tech) that ultimately the reports from RAF Topcliffe and the Central Flying School were sent. Eleven weeks later, when the *Dispatch* followed up the Topcliffe report, however, they found the department was unable to explain it. The Ministry was no longer falling back upon 'meteorological phenomena' as a catch-all explanation. 'The special branch which has been dealing with this is keeping an open mind on the subject,' a spokesman told the newspaper.[44]

The results of the technical investigation of UFO reports by DDI (Tech) during 1952–54 have never been released and the MoD claims all records were destroyed at 'first review'.[45] Questioned in 1964 by a member of the public who requested a copy of the Topcliffe report, an officer at department S6 said no such document existed.[46] However, three years after this reply was given, a member of the Defence Intelligence staff examined these 'non-existent' reports. In an internal memorandum of 1967 preserved at the PRO, Dr John Dickison said he had managed to recover 'all but two of the Intelligence files on UFOs for the period 1951–2'. The files he examined indicated that the Topcliffe-Meteor incident 'was typical of reports about such aircraft at the time' but no conclusions were ever reached and the object was 'never identified'.[47]

A number of other semi-official and private studies of 'saucer' reports by senior RAF and defence officials were ongoing during the period 1950–55 and were to influence the development of British government policy.

Whitehall also received enquiries from a number of foreign governments who had investigated 'flying saucer' sightings in their airspace and wanted their questions answered. In 1953–54 Lord Richard Casey, Minister for External Affairs and later Governor General of Australia, exchanged letters on the subject of flying saucers with Britain's DSI. He was told by the British government that they 'were not taken seriously here and no special research was carried out to try to find a simple explanation for these phenomena as the Americans are reported to be doing'.[48]

The Australians were told that Sir Frederick Brundrett, who replaced Dr Jones as Director of Scientific Intelligence in 1954, had conducted his own private study of the subject 'covering a large number of reported sightings extending over the past 30 years or so' and had decided that flying saucers did not exist.[49] Brundrett worked as a high-ranking intelligence officer for both the Royal Navy and MI5. The enquiries he made had led him to conclude that the majority of sightings were meterological and psychological in origin and he felt there was insufficient evidence to 'to justify the setting aside of money and resources for serious study ... but [he] has by no means closed his mind completely'.[50]

US Concerns

In 1997 CIA historian Gerald Haines published a study of the agency's involvement with UFOs. He found the CIA had closely monitored the USAF's investigations of UFOs since 1948.

From an early stage the West's intelligence agencies agreed that any 'outside knowledge' of their interest in UFOs would make the 'problem' worse. Haines admitted: 'This concealment of CIA interest contributed greatly to later charges of a CIA conspiracy and cover up.'[51] This policy of official silence was observed in Britain both by Bertie Blount and R. V. Jones, who followed the American lead and decided to shelve plans for a public statement on the MoD study.

In the aftermath of the sightings over Washington the Truman administration was alarmed and for a short time UFOs were considered as a potential threat to US security. In 1952 a special intelligence advisory committee was set up within the CIA's Office of Scientific Intelligence (OSI) and met USAF officials from ATIC at Wright-Patterson air force base. Project Blue Book staff told them 90 per cent of sightings could be explained, but the remainder were 'incredible reports from credible observers'. Few members of staff believed the unexplained UFOs could be Russian aircraft or 'men from Mars' and the more incredible theories had

apparently been rejected during the Project Sign era in favour of misin-
terpretations of known phenomena.

The overriding concern of the CIA was the potential use of UFOs by
the Soviets as a psychological weapon. Intelligence indicated that no
mention had been made of flying saucers in the Soviet press, which
suggested the phenomena could be 'controlled ... predicted and ... used
from a psychological warfare point of view either offensively or defen-
sively'.[52] The fear was that a cleverly-engineered UFO wave could be
targeted to overload the US air warning system to such an extent that it
would not be able to distinguish real aircraft from what the CIA called
'phantoms'.

Dr Chadwell, the Assistant Director of OSI, felt the potential for panic
and mass hysteria was reflected in the press stories, which indicated to him
that: 'A fair proportion of our population is mentally conditioned to the
acceptance of the incredible.'[53] Chadwell pressed CIA director Walter
Smith to set up a scientific research project to study the UFO problem,
but offers of help from the Massachusetts Institute of Technology (MIT)
were rejected. Eventually Smith agreed that he should 'enlist the services
of selected scientists to review and appraise the available evidence in the
light of pertinent scientific theories' and to draw up a National Security
Council Intelligence Directive.[54]

The Robertson Panel

The panel of high-flying scientists that met in January 1953 was chaired by
a physicist, Dr H. P. Robertson, who was a science advisor for the CIA. The
panel contained three other physicists, including Nobel Prize winner Dr
Luis Alvarez, Dr Samuel Goldsmit and Dr Lloyd Berkner of Brookhaven
National Laboratories. The fifth member of the panel was an astronomer,
Dr Thornton Page. Ed Ruppelt of Project Blue Book and the USAF's
astronomer, Dr J. Allen Hynek, played a minor role in the proceedings.

Meeting at the height of McCarthyism, the Robertson Panel reflected
the CIA's concerns about the Soviet threat, both to the nation's defence
and in terms of 'the enemy within'. Despite the presence of physical
scientists, the conclusions reached had little connection with the data that
were presented to the panel. As UFO historian Dennis Stacy noted, the
recommendations had more to do with national security issues 'which fell
more [in] the domain of the "soft" disciplines like psychology and
sociology'.[55]

In its final report the panel members concluded that the 'hard'
evidence they saw, including two famous movies of UFOs, showed 'no
indication that these phenomena constitute a direct physical threat to
national security'. However, they felt:

'The continued emphasis on the reporting of
these phenomena, in these perilous times,
results in a threat to the orderly
functioning of the protective organs of the
body politic.'

This was the paranoid language of the Cold War. The danger posed by belief in UFOs, if not the UFOs themselves, was summarised as:

'... the clogging of channels of communication
by irrelevant reports, the danger of being
led by continued false alarms to ignore real
indications of hostile action, and the
cultivation of a morbid national psychology
in which skilful hostile propaganda could
induce hysterical behaviour and harmful
distrust of duly constituted authority.'[56]

The recommendations were carefully worded by the CIA and followed the tradition established by the British study of 1951. First, federal agencies were asked to 'take immediate steps to strip the UFOs of the special status they have been given and the aura of mystery they have unfortunately acquired'. Secondly, the CIA recommended a public campaign to debunk UFOs and educate the public to recognise and identify 'true indications of hostile intent or action'.

Sceptics have used the Robertson Panel's conclusions to support their dismissal of UFOs, while believers in alien visitors regard the whole exercise as a whitewash designed to hide the truth from the masses.

It is true that Robertson's connections with Dr R. V. Jones stretched back to World War II, when he had been chief American liaison officer with British Scientific Intelligence and the pair had become friends. When in July 1953 Jones spent a month in America, he flew to California specifically to meet Robertson. We do not know if UFOs were on the agenda because the file on the visit continues to be withheld by the MoD.[57] However, in 1967 Jones wrote that the verdict of the Robertson Panel 'did much to restore a critical view of flying saucer stories and to offset the effort of publicity seeking charlatans'.[58] It could never entirely quell those who claimed the government was involved in a cover up, but in responding to claims that Robertson participated in a whitewash, Jones was clear:

> 'I knew H. P. Robertson well… He was as anxious as anyone I know to establish the truth, and he would never have made an attempt to suppress it if it proved unpalatable; the same is true of the other members of his Panel who are known to me.'[59]

British Scepticism

British intelligence officers who were involved in the studies of 1952–53 were more sceptical of the UFO evidence than their American colleagues. A director of DDI (Tech), Wing Commander Peter Cribb, recalls informal discussions about UFOs with USAF intelligence staff at the Pentagon during January 1953:

> 'I got the impression that they were no more convinced of the substance than I was. In my opinion our Report No. 7 is right on target and I recall no incidents which provided conclusive evidence of the existence of mysterious saucer-like flying machines, or men from Mars or Venus.'[60]

His predecessor at DDI (Tech), Group Captain Harold Collins, was similarly unconvinced. Collins told us in 2001 that he recalled studying a dozen reports of aerial phenomena during the period 1950–52:

> 'They ranged from one from a woman who reported on a man from outer space knocking on her door to two reports we were never able to explain as misidentifications… I was left with the impression that "flying saucers" did not exist.'[61]

The First 'Officially Confirmed' Sighting

News of the Robertson Panel's existence did not leak out to the public until Ed Ruppelt published his memoirs in 1956 and these were carefully phrased to avoid any mention of the CIA's key role in formulating their conclusions. By that time a number of the recommendations had been acted upon by the US Joint Chiefs of Staff. Project Blue Book continued to operate but followed a vigorous debunking campaign designed to reduce the number of reports classified as 'unknown'.

By July 1952 measures had been taken to tighten up the reporting system and ensure that UFO sightings made not only by military personnel but also by civilian pilots did not reach the public. This was achieved by an order that implemented a reporting system known as the Joint Army-Navy-Air Force Publication (JANAP) 146. This required that all UFO sightings should be reported to USAF Intelligence in a format known as the Communication Instructions for Reporting Vital Intelligence Sightings (CIRVIS). Any unauthorised leaks were theoretically punishable and offenders faced a fine or prison sentence of up to ten years.[62]

Although JANAP 146 was not implemented in Britain, a very similar order was drafted by the RAF shortly after the Robertson Panel met in the USA. This move followed the sighting of a flying saucer by two RAF airmen while on an exercise above Kent. The pilot, Flying Officer Terry Johnson, and his navigator, Flying Officer Geoffrey Smythe, knew little about saucers when they took off from RAF West Malling in a Vampire night-fighter on the morning of 3 November 1953. They were flying north at 20,000 feet towards the Thames estuary when Johnson saw a bright object 10,000 feet higher and dead ahead. The UFO was stationary for a short time and Johnson could see it was two-thirds the size of a full moon and shaped liked a doughnut with 'a bright light around the periphery'. He nudged Smythe, whose head was buried in the console of his radar screen, and the navigator looked up at the UFO.

'After about 30 seconds it moved to our right, to the southeast, at very high speed,' Johnson told us. 'It was not a "flying saucer", but it was a luminous object of some kind.'[63] Smythe said he had been using his onboard radar to scan below the horizontal at the time and had seen nothing unusual.[64]

On landing the men decided to make a report, but were unprepared for what would happen next. Their report was passed by the station commander to the squadron's commanding officer, Denis Furse, who had become a 'believer' in flying saucers following an encounter with a foo-fighter in World War II.

'When Johnson told him of our adventure he was completely hooked and reported up the chain of command,' Flying Officer Smythe told us. 'Under almost any other circumstances our story would have died there and then.'[65]

In fact the news reached a pilot with 604 Squadron, Derek Dempster, who doubled as aviation correspondent for the *Daily Express*. Dempster was also a UFO believer and in 1955 became the first editor of *FSR*. Smythe and Johnson believe that if it were not for Furse and Dempster the story would have gone no further. But, as Smythe explained:

> 'Word had got out and a small paragraph appeared on the front page of the *Daily Express*. They used the term "flying saucer". The BBC picked up the message and Johnson and I were interviewed on the evening news.'[66]

In the meantime, Dempster had discovered that at 2.30 p.m. on the same day a UFO had been tracked by a Territorial Army (TA) radar unit at Lea Green in London. Suddenly, this had become the first 'officially confirmed' sighting of a flying saucer. Sergeant Harry Waller's report to the War Office described 'a very large echo' at a height of 60,000 feet that gradually lost height over 40 minutes after the radar locked onto the target. Waller had used a telescope and seen 'a circular or spherical object' high in the sky. He said the object could not have been a balloon as 'to get a kind of signal we got, it must have been metallic'.[67]

The next day another *Express* reporter, Chapman Pincher, discovered that half an hour before the Lea Green sighting a large balloon fitted with a powerful metal reflector had been released by the Meteorological Office from Crawley in Sussex. Its course had been carefully tracked as it had passed high over London before falling into the English Channel. There was little doubt this was what the TA unit had seen.[68]

On 24 November the controversy reached the House of Commons, where the Secretary of State for Air, Nigel Birch, answered the first parliamentary question on flying saucers. Birch said both the airmen's sighting and the radar trackings were caused by 'two experimental meteorological balloons that were fitted with a special device to produce as large an echo on a radar screen as an aircraft'. The balloons had 'been allowed to escape at unusual times [and] there was nothing peculiar about either of the occurrences'. Laughter broke out when an MP asked if the Minister agreed that 'This story of flying saucers is all ballooney.'[69]

While balloons seemed a likely explanation for the TA report, the RAF crew remained unconvinced they had seen the same object several hours before they were actually released. Johnson and Smythe were interviewed at Fighter Command by a senior air staff officer:

> '[He] specifically denied a met balloon explanation and told us that investigations were in progress, that aircraft movements at that time had been analysed. In particular attention had been applied to balloon launches because of the similarity of [our] description to a balloon. But he said that nothing had come of it.'[70]

The First Formal Report Procedure

In December 1953, as a direct result of the West Malling incident, a formal procedure for reports of 'aerial phenomena' was issued for the first time to all radar and fighter stations. These instructions were combined with an earlier order that was sent to HQ Metropolitan and Southern sectors for distribution to radar units. Following the detection of UFOs all information was to be treated as 'Restricted' and this category was eventually upgraded to 'Confidential' under the OSA. All incidents, whether observed by radar operators, aircrews or civilians, were in future to be reported in writing to commanding officers and forwarded direct to DDI (Tech) at the Air Ministry.[71]

Significantly, when viewed in the context of the Robertson Panel recommendations, the orders state:

```
'The public attach more credence to reports
by Royal Air Force personnel than to those
by members of the public. It is essential
that the information should be examined at
the Air Ministry and that its release should
be controlled officially. All reports are,
therefore, to be classified "Restricted" and
personnel are warned that they are not to
communicate to anyone other than official
persons any information about phenomena they
have observed, unless officially authorised
to do so.'[72]
```

The Secret Intelligence Summary

In April 1955 the *Sunday Dispatch* revealed that the Air Ministry had been presented with a full report of its five-year investigation of the flying saucer mystery. Although the inquiry had concluded flying saucers did not exist, the newspaper claimed a senior air marshal had ordered the report was never to be made public. News editor Christian Peterson told readers:

'Fear of scepticism is one of the reasons that induced the air marshals to have report filed away… They feel that the findings cannot be explained without revealing top secret facts and that without a full explanation there would be nationwide controversy over the truth of the report.'[73]

What the 'full report' contained remains unclear, but the new Air Ministry study was based upon a modified version of the conclusions reached by the Flying Saucer Working Party in 1951 and by DDI (Tech) during the period 1952–54. The basis of the story can be traced directly to an exchange of letters between Churchill's secretary, Anthony Montague-Browne, and the future Defence Secretary, Duncan Sandys, MP. The pair had discussed fly-ing saucers at Chequers and in March 1955 Montague-Browne sent the Minister a copy of an article 'which may be of interest to you'.[74]

The article was published in a RAF publication known as the 'Secret Intelligence Summary'. This was a watered-down version of the report on the five-year investigation referred to by the *Sunday Dispatch*. The anonymous Air Ministry writer had drawn upon a range of scientific data to explain visual sightings, photographs and strange echoes that had been detected by radar. The Ministry's conclusions were highly sceptical, but stressed that study of reports should continue because there was 'always the chance of observing foreign aircraft of revolutionary design', although, it added, 'As for controlled manifestations from outer space, there is no tangible evidence of their existence.'[75]

On 4 May 1955 the Conservative MP Major Patrick Wall tabled a par-liamentary question asking 'whether the Air Ministry inquiry into the existence of "flying saucers" has been completed; and whether [the Air Minister] proposes to publish a report'.[76] In his reply, Air Minister George Ward said they had been 'no formal inquiry' but that reports were investi-gated as they came in and 90 per cent were found to have ordinary explanations. 'The fact that the other 10 per cent are unexplained need be attributed to nothing more sinister than lack of data.'[77] Wall received an identical reply from the Secretary of State for Air, Julian Ridsdale, to a similar question in 1962. On both occasions the MP was assured that 'no formal inquiry' had taken place. He was misinformed. The Flying Saucer Working Party's Report No. 7 was most certainly a 'formal inquiry', even if the 1955 report was not.

If the government was prepared to mislead an MP, was it any wonder that many ordinary people had begun to accept there was a high-level conspiracy to hide UFO evidence from the public?

Chapter 7

INTERCEPT UFO!

'...they had scrambled a pair of
Javelins and as they came
hurtling down towards us the
THING shot forward and upward at
incredible speed, rapidly
disappearing from sight with the
Javelins in pursuit...'

**From a report of a UFO seen by the crew of an RAF
Shackleton near Akrotiri, Cyprus, in 1958[1]**

Throughout the Cold War official interest in UFOs rose and fell alongside growing international tensions between the West and the expanding Soviet empire. During 1956 these tensions reached a peak with the Suez crisis when the USAF was brought to a high state of readiness in case of Soviet intervention. Behind the scenes a 'secret war' was already ongoing as the US and Britain sent specially adapted aircraft on reconnaissance missions above Soviet territory. In the race to put a rocket into space, America faced humiliation when in October 1957 the Russians placed the first satellite, Sputnik, into Earth orbit, followed a month later by a second capsule carrying the dog Laika. These historic events coincided with a worldwide UFO wave which included some of the most dramatic and convincing sightings, many by military witnesses.

Running the Risk of War

The CIA's concerns about the dangers UFO reports posed to national security was spelled out during the Robertson Panel era. Surveys of the Russian media had failed to find any mention of UFOs behind the Iron Curtain, which had led the agency to ask whether the phenomena could be predicted or even controlled for use in psychological warfare. In terms of defence, the US air warning system depended upon the combination of radar and visual observation to protect it against Soviet attack. Yet according to a secret intelligence briefing:

```
'At any given moment ... there may be currently
a dozen official unidentified sightings plus
many unofficial ones [which could lead to a
situation] where we cannot distinguish
hardware from phantom, and as the tension
mounts we will run the increasing risk of
false alerts and the even greater danger of
falsely identifying the real as phantom.'²
```

This hypothetical scenario became reality on 5 October 1960 when a formation of UFOs was detected by the ballistic missile early warning system (BMEWS) radar at Thule in Greenland. The formation appeared to be heading towards North America from the direction of the Soviet Union. Within seconds Strategic Air Command HQ in Omaha scrambled bomber crews, and a Royal Canadian Air Force Marshal, Roy Slemon, had just 15 minutes to decide whether to launch a retaliatory strike. At the last moment a series of checks revealed the 'missiles' were spurious echoes. Unusual atmospheric conditions had created phantom images on the BMEWS that could not be seen by other radar. A nuclear conflagration was narrowly averted.³

Following the Thule incident Labour MPs asked the British Prime Minister, Harold Macmillan, how close the West had come to war and how easy it was for the system to be fooled. Macmillan told them that he was satisfied 'that our precautions are amply sufficient to prevent nuclear war starting as a result of accident on the part of the West' and said the arrangements for 'co-operation and co-ordination of radar warning systems between ourselves and the United States are excellent'.⁴

In 1960 the Prime Minister assured Parliament that no RAF or US aircraft based in Britain had been placed on alert as a result of this 'false alarm', but two years earlier a similar incident occurred that was equally serious. In the early hours of 19 April 1958 a group of five 'unidentified targets' was tracked over the North Sea, heading towards a complex of nuclear-armed USAF bases in East Anglia. The UFOs were picked up by radar at RAF Lakenheath and Sculthorpe and jets were scrambled to intercept. Almost an hour passed before controllers decided the blips were caused by 'freak weather conditions'. The *Sunday Express* revealed they had almost reached Lakenheath and were within 75 miles of London before the alarm was cancelled.[5]

Although both the Lakenheath and Thule incidents were played down by the government, they were just two in a whole series of frightening episodes during the Cold War when air defence radar was fooled by mysterious blips or UFOs. How many other 'false alarms' brought the world to the brink of nuclear war during this tense period? And how many were triggered by UFOs?

East Anglia, with its complex of joint RAF-USAF bases, appeared to be particularly prone to radar phantoms. During the late 1950s bases such as Lakenheath and Sculthorpe were not only home to nuclear-armed USAF bombers, but shortly before the Suez crisis they also briefly played host to the U-2 spy plane that flew high-altitude reconnaissance flights above the Soviet Union. Hundreds of flights continued in great secrecy until 1960, when US pilot Gary Powers was captured after his U-2 was shot down over Russia. Throughout this period there remained the possibility that 'UFOs' detected near Strategic Air Command bases in Europe were Russian spy planes gathering intelligence on the West's defences. It became increasingly important that efficient methods were in place to quickly identify blips on radar screens.

In Britain elaborate preparations were in place to defend against Soviet attack. These were never fully activated, although Russian 'bears' and 'badgers' – RAF jargon for enemy intruders – regularly tested radar and fighter defences. QRA squadrons held aircraft at permanent readiness and in these tense circumstances controllers had to distinguish Russian 'bears' from freak weather conditions and 'UFOs'.

Radar UFOs remained a sensitive subject for the RAF, whose responsibility it was to identify all 'unidentified' objects tracked within British airspace. The presence of an elusive aerial phenomena was a security headache for the RAF and public knowledge of the problem exposed weaknesses that could be exploited by the enemy. Air Ministry files reveal how the British government chose to say nothing of its interest in UFOs in public and increasingly relied upon the OSA to prevent news of the more worrying incidents leaking to the press. Those that caused the most concern involved the tracking of UFOs by radar.

Radar UFOs: From Angels to X-tracks

Radar – an acronym for 'radio detection and ranging' – is popularly regarded as a precision instrument that, like a camera, cannot lie. Radar in the 21st century is comprehensive in its coverage and, although not trouble-free, is operated by sophisticated automated computer technology.

Half a century ago the situation was completely different.

At the height of the flying saucer era air defence radar in Britain and America was reliant upon valve-based technology developed before World War II. For over a decade after the ending of hostilities defence radar remained basic by today's standards and was vulnerable to a range of technical problems that were not resolved until the introduction of high-powered centimetric systems. In addition, for much of the early part of the Cold War radar was manually operated and correct interpretation relied upon the skill and experience of the operator. It cannot be just a coincidence that a large proportion of the 'classic' radar reports described in the UFO literature originate from the 1950s, when the complexities of the equipment were not fully understood.

Mysterious echoes or blips were first detected by RAF radar during the tense months that followed the outbreak of World War II. Early in 1941, when the threat of German invasion was at its greatest, a CH radar on the south coast of England began to pass unusual plots to Fighter Command that caused great concern. Sir Edward Fennessy, a former managing director of Decca Radar, serving at that time with Fighter Command, was responsible for the CH chain. He said the blips appeared 'as a very large formation of aircraft flying a low speed from the Cherbourg area at about 80 knots'.[6] Their speed suggested they were towed gliders and senior RAF officers believed a German invasion had begun. Fighters were scrambled, but when they reached a position to intercept, nothing could be seen. Checks were made with the radar research station at Swanage and engineers suggested various adjustments to the CH to eliminate false plots, but the radar continued to detect waves of blips moving from the French coast before fading out in the middle of the English Channel. Sir Edward recalled:

'No explanation was ever obtained and because we were busy
fighting a war we spent no time investigating this phenomena.
So it remains a mystery. After the war and with the development
of high power radar we had more incidents of similar targets.'[7]

Unusual echoes were also reported by early radar stations in the USA and had become known as 'angels' or 'ghosts.' The echoes were detected on a wide range of equipment and their true source remained a source of controversy for decades.

Throughout this period research into the puzzling radar phenomena remained hidden behind a veil of Cold War secrecy. There were two competing theories to explain unusual echoes. One school claimed they were caused by flocks of migrating birds and even swarms of insects. Another believed they were created by the atmosphere and weather, either as pockets of 'non-standard' air or temperature inversions which trapped and reflected radar energy.[8]

In 1953 MoD scientists working at the Royal Radar Development Establishment in Worcestershire conducted trials with the first moving target indicator (MTI) radar. MTI was a filter system that used frequency stable transmitters and receivers to remove stationary blips caused by 'ground clutter' from the radar display. The operators were mystified to find the clutter had been replaced by dozens of small echoes that moved at varying speeds in the direction of the prevailing wind.

'Ring angels' were also detected by an advanced prototype MTI system developed by Marconi engineers. When observed on the screen, these appeared as wide rings that expanded outwards like the ripples on a pond. They were eventually found to have been caused by starlings swarming from their roosts at dawn.[9]

According to radar historian Jack Gough, 'angels' disappeared when a new generation of high-powered radar was developed. In more recent years new technology has removed a range of spurious echoes produced by 'noise' such as flocks of birds and weather systems. Today all large aircraft carry transponders, transmitters that respond automatically to radar pulses and broadcast a signal which identifies the flight, altitude, destination and other information to air traffic control. UFOs, by definition, do not carry transponders and are ignored by modern ATC radar unless they pose a direct threat to an aircraft.[10]

These developments have not entirely eliminated UFOs from modern systems, as NATO's network of early warning radar is continually watching for evidence of intruder aircraft and missiles.

Standard Operational Procedure

Concern about the lack of an adequate identification procedure for unknown targets detected during the 1950s led the RAF to draw up its first standard operational procedure for the reporting of UFOs. The SOP laid down procedures for the reporting of both radar and visual sightings. Radar stations were ordered to investigate all 'unusual phenomena or tracks' which should be reported immediately to HQ Fighter Command. These were defined as 'a target moving at a ground speed exceeding 700 knots [800 mph] or at an altitude exceeding 60,000 feet'. Copies of record sheets, track tracing and relevant radar films would then be examined by Operations branch 'and if an explanation cannot be found' all the data would be sent to DDI (Tech) at the Air Ministry.[11]

In the event of a visual sighting by aircrew, controllers at master radar stations were instructed to check whether the report could be correlated with a radar contact. Significantly, 'if the Station has aircraft under control in the vicinity of the reported phenomena, those aircraft are to be diverted to investigate the phenomena'.[12] In other words it was official policy to scramble RAF jets to chase UFOs. In 1996 Defence Minister Nicholas Soames confirmed these orders remain in place today.[13]

The MoD has claimed that UFOs were never covered by the OSA, but the SOPs issued in 1953 and 1960 contain direct warnings to RAF personnel not to discuss UFOs – particularly those tracked on radar – in public. The order read:

> 'The Press are never to be given information about unusual radar sightings ... unauthorised disclosures of this type will be viewed as offences under the Official Secrets Act.'[14]

Similarly, sightings by RAF personnel or reports made to them by members of the public 'are in no circumstances to be disclosed to the Press'.[15]

Orders such as these were not unusual during the Cold War, but have done much to encourage claims that the British government was involved in a conspiracy to conceal evidence of UFOs tracked by military radar.

Taking the Tracks Seriously

RAF radar technician John Bowden, who served at RAF Neatishead at the height of the Cold War, recalled how seriously radar UFOs were treated by senior officers. On one occasion in 1954 or 1955 an operator called him to one of the control cabins to witness an unknown target that was being tracked travelling at 1,725–2,300 mph 'which he thought was a fault, as he knew of no craft at that time capable of such speeds'.[16] After checking the equipment Bowden was unable to find any evidence of a fault, as the other displays were tracking aircraft in the normal manner.

On the next watch a senior officer announced that the phenomenon they had observed was 'interference on the radar', but Bowden, familiar with the range of radar problems, remained unconvinced. He said:

> 'A week or two later we were issued with a black metal hood to mount a camera onto one of the PPI displays to enable photographs to be taken by the operations staff when other similar radar contacts were received. I cannot recall for how long the camera and mounting hood remained on the selected display, but it was certainly weeks or months rather than days.'[17]

When in the summer of 1953 unidentified blips were tracked by radar high over the north Atlantic, they quickly attracted the attention of experts at the Air Ministry. Fighter Plotter J. W. Foulds recalled how the tracks he saw at RAF Bawburgh were moving at speeds of up to 1,500 mph at heights in excess of 80,000 feet. They reappeared at least twice in the days that followed. Soon afterwards a group of dark-suited 'men from the Ministry' arrived and a film camera was set up to record any further incidents. Mr Foulds said:

> 'We were all advised not to talk about it and many weeks later we learned indirectly that it had been decided that what we had witnessed were test firings of Russian missiles from beyond the Arctic Circle.'[18]

Meteorological Explanations

In 1955 the Air Ministry published a study that listed a range of meteorological phenomena that had given rise to reports of flying saucers by radar. These included echoes produced by thunderstorms, weather systems and clouds of ionised gas that appeared in the wake of meteorites.

Most important of all was anomalous propagation (AP), pockets of highly reflective air that differed in temperature, pressure and humidity from the surrounding atmosphere. A study of these phenomena was prepared by a radar meteorologist, Dr R. F. Jones, for the Air Ministry following the sightings at Washington National Airport in 1952. He concluded that reflective air could on occasions 'bounce' radar waves so that features on the ground, such as hills and even moving trains, would appear on screens as if they were in mid-air.[19] Mirages such as these could in rare circumstances be misinterpreted as unidentified blips, or UFOs, even by experienced radar operators. Eventually these atmospheric anomalies would be detected to heights of 3–6 miles and experiments revealed they were capable of trapping and reflecting radar pulses over great distances.

On rare occasions AP and other complex atmospheric phenomena could create a series of images on a radar display that rapidly appeared and disappeared as the atmospheric conditions producing them changed. Scope misinterpretation could lead radar operators to assume 'that the echo return presented on successive rotations of the antennae is derived from a single moving source when actually the returns are unrelated'. As a secret RAF study of 1955 pointed out, 'Perhaps it is this very rarity which assists in the creation of another flying saucer.'[20]

MoD scientists adopted the position that unless radar trackings could be reliably correlated with visual sightings, which was rarely the case, then unusual weather conditions were the most likely explanation. Physicist Dr David Atlas from the University of Chicago wrote in 1972 that:

'While some of the UFO observations required almost incredible atmospheric structures for their explanation on the basis of propagation phenomena, some phenomena which were incredible just a few years ago have now been accepted by the community at large.'[21]

His experiments with advanced radar in the California desert discovered layers of air just a few yards thick that were capable of creating strong reflections on radar screens. He concluded:

'There is now abundant evidence that the atmosphere will affect radar propagation in almost unbelievable ways and produce targets which have apparently fantastic manoeuvrability.'[22]

'Chaff' or 'Window'

Other 'UFOs' captured on radar can be the result of two or more systems interfering with each other and the deliberate jamming of signals to produce 'false' echoes, a technique known as electronic counter-measures (ECM). During World War II Allied planes created confusion by dropping strips of metal foil known as 'chaff' or 'window' to jam German radar. These techniques were developed in great secrecy during the Cold War for offensive use against Soviet radar defences.

The most revealing case in this category occurred in November 1954, when the *Sunday Dispatch* revealed how 'strange sights in the sky' were puzzling anti-aircraft radar operators across southeast England. The newspaper claimed that six times during the previous month at midday a pattern of blips had appeared on radar screens around London, moving west at a height of 12,000 feet. A War Office official told the paper they 'appear in a U or badly shaped hairpin formation and after a time converge into two parallel lines and then take up a Z formation before disappearing'.[23] He said the blips were invisible to the human eye 'but on the radar screen they appear as lots of dots formed by between 40 and 50 echoes covering an area in the sky miles long and wide'.[24]

When approached by the *Dispatch* the Air Ministry was evasive, suggesting that there were many natural phenomena that could form such an image on radar screens. The newspaper discovered that radar personnel had been given high-level orders to keep quiet about the subject. In recent years UFO advocates have used this story to support claims that the British government had tracked squadrons of flying saucers over London and was attempting to conceal the facts.[25]

The truth was revealed in April 1956 when journalist David Wightman questioned officials about the story. Although his question was answered, Wightman was told he 'mustn't repeat, let alone print the information', as it was covered by the OSA. Two years later restrictions were lifted and Wightman wrote:

```
'... the answer received from the Air Ministry
spokesman was that the radar returns were
caused by experiments being conduct to
"effect false returns" on radar screens.'
```
[26]

Apparently, one arm of the military (the War Office) was kept in the dark about the nature of these experiments by another (the Air Ministry), and a UFO mystery was the result.

The Bentwaters–Lakenheath Incident

Official secrecy continues to surround one of the most dramatic radar-visual UFO sightings ever made in British airspace. Whether this is a cover up of knowledge or ignorance remains unclear, but the case illustrates all the problems created by the use of radar to investigate the UFO phenomenon.

The single surviving official reference to the incident occurs in an Air Ministry briefing to the Under Secretary of State for Air, George Ward, in May 1957. Under the category of 'unexplained radar incidents' the note refers to:

```
'... a report of an unusual object on
Lakenheath Radar which at first moved at a
speed of between two and four thousand knots
[2,300-4,600 mph] and then remained stationary
at an high altitude. No visual contact was
made with this object by the Venom sent to
intercept it and other radars failed to pick
it up.'
```
[27]

The true extent and serious nature of the events were not revealed to the public until 12 years after the event and it has taken 46 years to even partially unravel the mystery.

The radar trackings were made by personnel at two airbases loaned to the USAF in East Anglia and by RAF air defence radar at Neatishead. The events began at RAF Bentwaters, near Ipswich, early on the evening of 13 August 1956 and had spread to the nuclear-armed Lakenheath, 22 miles northeast of Cambridge, by the early hours of 14 August. As a result, the sequence of radar and visual sightings is often referred to as 'the Bentwaters–Lakenheath case' within the UFO literature. Its unusual features helped to convince many formerly sceptical scientists, such as the USAF consultant astronomer Dr J. Allen Hynek, that UFOs deserved serious study.[28]

The case was effectively a NATO secret before USAF Sergeant Forrest Perkins, who had been watch supervisor at the regional ATC centre at Lakenheath during the height of the UFO scare, wrote to the Colorado University UFO project in 1968, drawing their attention to the case. Pressure from the project scientists led the USAF to release their classified file on the incident. In the project's report, published in 1969, the incident is listed as 'unexplained', with the caveat that 'the probability that at least one genuine UFO was involved appears to be fairly high'.

The evening of Monday 13 August 1956 was warm and calm in eastern England. At 9.30 p.m. a USAF airman working in runway approach (ground control approach (GCA)) radar unit at RAF Bentwaters tracked an unidentified blip on his screen. The blip appeared 25 to 30 miles east of the base and was initially believed to be an aircraft. When it disappeared to the northwest at an incredible speed of 4,000 mph, it quickly became apparent this was no ordinary aircraft. The USAF report explained:

'Some idea of the speed of the object could be computed from the fact that each time the GCA antennae completed a revolution the blip from this object moved 4 to 5 miles on the radar screen. The GCA antennae completes a revolution once every two seconds.'[29]

On a separate screen another airman was watching two formations of slow-moving blips scattered over a larger area. As they faded from the radar screen, the larger group 'appeared to converge into one very large object which appeared to be several times larger than a B-36 aircraft due to the size of the blip on the radar scope'.[30]

During the Cold War squadrons of the RAF's most advanced fighters were rotated through airfields dedicated to QRA duties. Twenty-four hours a day, 365 days a year, crews were continually at cockpit readiness. In 1956 the airfield defending the English coastline was RAF Waterbeach, near Cambridge. When an unidentified radar target was designated as an X-track, authorisation to scramble would pass to sector operations rooms and fighter controllers would guide the interceptors towards their targets. Before darkness fell on 13 August a Venom from 23 Squadron was scrambled from Waterbeach to investigate the UFO reports received from the USAF at Bentwaters.

Shortly after take-off pilot Les Arthur and navigator Grahame Scofield realised their aircraft had lost its wing-tip fuel tanks and were forced to return to base.[31] At the same time the control tower at Bentwaters made radio contact with two USAF T-33 trainer jets. Both aircraft were vectored to the area northeast of the base 'to search for unidentified flying objects which were being tracked by the Bentwaters GCA'. The pilots searched, but saw nothing unusual. The only lights visible to them were the pulsing beacon of the Orfordness lighthouse on the Suffolk coast and a bright light stationary on the southeastern horizon.

As the radar was tracking blips that were invisible to the eye, the shift sergeant at Bentwaters control tower began watching a twinkling light that rose slowly above the horizon. This 'UFO' was later identified as the planet Mars, which rose at 8.50 p.m. and was the brightest object in the sky. In 1956 the red planet was at its closest approach to the Earth for 32 years, an event that coincided with the peak of the spectacular Perseid meteor shower.[32] A bright planet, a meteor shower, a fast-moving blip and a fleet of invisible UFOs were all tracked on ATC radar. These unconnected events were soon to spark a series of more dramatic sightings that escalated into a UFO scare that spread quickly through the military grapevine in East Anglia. As the CIA had recognised in 1953, even trained military witnesses were not immune from spreading rumours and panics based upon misperceptions of aerial phenomena.

Shortly after the excitement generated by the radar trackings had passed, another fast-moving target was detected and, it is claimed, sighted visually by personnel at Bentwaters. This incident was reported in a secret USAF teletype which read:

```
'...Bentwaters GCA sighted object thirty miles
east of the station traveling westerly at
2,000-4,000 mph... Tower personnel at
Bentwaters reported to GCA a bright light
passed over the field east to west at
```

```
terrific speed and at about 4,000 feet
altitude. At same time pilot in [a C-47]
aircraft at 4,000 feet altitude over
Bentwaters reported a bright light streaked
under his aircraft traveling east to west at
terrific speed.'³³
```

Immediately Bentwaters phoned the neighbouring USAF stations at Sculthorpe and Lakenheath, requesting they watch for unusual radar returns. At this point Forrest Perkins asked his air traffic controllers to check their radar screens. Each set their surveillance scopes to a different range, from 10 miles to the maximum 200 miles radius. Perkins explained:

'We were using full MTI on our radar, which eliminated entirely all ground returns and stationary targets. One controller noticed a … target on the scopes about 20 to 25 miles southwest. This was unusual as a stationary target should have been eliminated unless it was moving at a speed of at least 40 to 45 knots [46 to 51 mph] and yet we could detect no movement at all… As we watched, the stationary target started moving at a speed of 400 to 600 mph in a north northeast direction until it reached a point about 20 miles north northwest of Lakenheath. There was no slow start or build-up to this speed – it was constant from the second it started to move until it stopped.'³⁴

Dogfight with UFO – the RAF Version

Earlier in the proceedings, Perkins had contacted the US 3rd Air Force Command to report the radar sightings. He was 'patched in' on a party line and provided a real-time description of events to his superiors as he listened 'to theories, guesses, etc., that the conference line people were saying' as the events unfolded.³⁵

Air defence within the UK was the responsibility of the RAF and it was to Fighter Command that the USAF took their concerns. The decision to scramble fighters for a second time was delegated to the Eastern Sector Operations Centre. Officers there were in telephone contact with Flight Lieutenant F. H. C. 'Freddie' Wimbledon, the chief controller at RAF Neatishead, who was responsible for defending the English coast against intruders. Shortly before midnight Wimbledon received a call from the USAF at Lakenheath reporting that something was 'buzzing' their airfield circuit in a sharp rectangular course.

Neatishead's radar had not picked up anything unusual, but was scanning outwards towards the North Sea, where Soviet intruders were expected to appear. Wimbledon recalled:

'My duties were to monitor the radar picture and to scramble the Battle Flight, who were on standby 24 hours a day, to intercept any intruder of British airspace not positively identified. When we received a call from Lakenheath we started taking notice and I realised that something really was happening, because we were following a track that travelled at tremendous speeds and then stopped.'[36]

The station's coverage overlapped the USAF's at Lakenheath, but in 1956 Neatishead's ageing radar equipment was being replaced. Its Air Ministry experimental station (AMES) Type 7 radar was of wartime vintage and had a range of 200 miles. This was supplemented by height finders calibrated to 50–55,000 feet.[37]

When Wimbledon's radar operators began to scan inland, they spotted an unidentified blip that behaved unlike any other they had seen. The controller was aware that 'phantom' radar echoes were common in East Anglia, but believed he was experienced enough to be able to distinguish a 'real' target from a radar mirage. He gave the order to scramble a Venom NF3 from the QRA squadron at Waterbeach to investigate the blip.

This is the point where established facts end and we have to rely upon memories that are at best contradictory and at worst faulty. The MoD maintains that all records of the incident were destroyed in 1961 as part of a routine clear out of old files.[38] Their justification is that had the incident constituted a defence threat the records would have been retained. In the absence of official documentation, the account that follows is based upon a mixture of secondary accounts, the USAF file and the memories of those who participated in the action.

In his letter to the Colorado project, Forrest Perkins was describing from memory events that had occurred 12 years earlier. His story has to be interpreted in the light of the report sent by Lakenheath's USAF intelligence officer, Paula Stimson, to Washington just two days afterwards. In a teletype she specifically states that the radar trackings began after midnight and continued until 3.30 a.m. on 14 August 1956. Stimson also confirms that during the latter stages two RAF Venom interceptors were scrambled from RAF Waterbeach to investigate the radar returns.[39]

The accounts of Perkins at Lakenheath and Wimbledon at Neatishead rely upon memory rather than documentary records and contradict each other in respect of who it was that guided the two aircrews towards the blip. Both Wimbledon and his opposite number at Eastern Sector HQ maintain that in no circumstances other than war would RAF aircraft be controlled by anyone other than a British controller under orders from Fighter Command.[40] Yet it is apparent that when airborne the Venom crews received orders to contact the USAF. Because of the compartmentalised nature of RAF procedure Wimbledon would not necessarily have been aware of this order, because his role was dedicated to interception control rather than intelligence. The aircrews had 22 coded frequencies available to them and Perkin's team was able provide them with information on the range and bearing of the UFO while they 'listened in' on the radio transmissions. As the target came within interception range the crews switched frequencies back to the Neatishead team, who were tracking the target's position and height. The RAF system relied upon code words that would not necessarily have been recognised by the USAF team listening in on the ground. It is this jargon that *may* have led the Americans to misinterpret coded exchanges between the aircrews and their interception controller. The confusion that followed helped to create the unusual aspects of the case in accounts published many years after the events.

To this day, Wimbledon insists the Venom was under the control of his interception team, consisting of a fighter controller, a corporal, a tracker and a height reader. As chief controller, he said he monitored the conversations between the fighter controller and the pilot of the Venom. Because of the unusual nature of the event Wimbledon ordered a second interception cabin to back up the first, making a total of eight witnesses in all. He said:

> 'After being vectored onto the tail of the object by the
> Interception Controller the pilot called, "Contact," then a short
> time later, "Judy," which meant the navigator had it fairly and
> squarely on his own radar screen and needed no further help
> from my controller. After a few seconds, in the space of one sweep
> of our screens, the object appeared behind our own fighter and
> our pilot called, "Lost contact, more help." He was told the target
> was now behind him and I scrambled a second Venom which was
> vectored towards the area.'[11]

The USAF Version

Forrest Perkins claimed his team at Lakenheath made radio and radar contact with the Venom, providing the pilot with information on the distance and bearing of the now stationary UFO. His ATC radars had no height-finding capability and the crew was not trained in the complexities of directing an interception from the ground. They were, however, able to report that the target was somewhere between 1,500 and 20,000 feet.

When the Venom was half a mile from the UFO Perkins claimed he heard the pilot call, 'Roger, Lakenheath, I've got my guns locked on him.' There followed a pause, followed by the words: 'Where did he go? Do you still have him?' Perkins claimed:

> '…the movement [of the blip] was so swift (circling behind the interceptor) [that] I missed it entirely, but it was seen by the other controllers… The fact that this had occurred was confirmed by the pilot of the interceptor [who] told us he would try to shake the UFO and would try again. He tried everything – he climbed, dived, circled, etc. – but the UFO acted like it was glued right behind him, always the same distance, very close, but we always had two distinct targets.'[42]

This extraordinary episode continued, with the pilot's tone becoming increasingly 'worried, excited and also pretty scared' until he announced he was low on fuel and would be returning to base. At this point the pilot of the second Venom made contact with Lakenheath. Perkins claimed he overheard the two RAF pilots talking to each other, the first saying: 'It was the damnest thing I ever saw.' He also claimed the first Venom pilot said his radar had 'locked onto whatever it was for just a few seconds so there was something there that was solid'.[43]

Unfortunately Perkins' recall of this episode is not supported by Wimbledon or the aircrew we have traced. The USAF teletype – produced two days after the events – does not corroborate the elaborate exchange recalled by Perkins in 1968. It simply states that the first pilot had remarked that the UFO was the 'clearest target I have ever seen on radar'.[44] The British participants maintain that radio chatter occurring on an open channel in a combat situation would be confined to code words necessary for the purposes of an interception. Careless chatter could have betrayed vital tactics to an enemy and, as Wimbledon points out, British aircrew would not use an expression such as 'the damnest thing I ever saw' because RAF pilots 'simply don't speak like that'.[45] It is equally possible that Perkins may have confused two separate incidents, one involving the RAF and the other involving USAF interceptors that occurred at a later date (see Chapter 8). Additionally, the USAF version claimed the first Venom's airborne radar had 'locked onto' the target, but according to the aircrew who flew this version of the Venom NF3 the onboard radar was not capable of gunlock.[46]

The Account of the RAF Aircrew

Wimbledon said the target had 'disappeared' before the second Venom was able carry out an interception:

'[It] appeared to "give up the chase" as though it had achieved its
objective and more or less "melted"... My own theory is that it
either went straight up at very high speed or down to ground
level under our radar cover.'[17]

He remembers the appearance of the UFO echo as strong and clear and
said the blip was similar in size to a fighter aircraft but capable of 'terrific
acceleration and apparently stopping without slowing down'[48] – behaviour
impossible for conventional aircraft in 1956 and indeed today.

What actually happened above East Anglia that night has remained a
mystery for over 40 years. In 1996 retired RAF Squadron Leader Ivan
Logan, who had served with 23 Squadron, received a call from a BBC
researcher working on a UFO documentary. Logan revealed he was the
navigator of a Venom sent to intercept a strange target detected by radar
near RAF Lakenheath in 1956.[49] Logan and his colleagues from both crews
remembered the incident because it was unusual to be scrambled to investigate a target at low altitude over land. QRA missions usually took place
over the North Sea at altitudes of up to 45,000 feet.

Grahame Scofield, who was the navigator of the Venom involved in
the aborted pre-midnight scramble, said that when he returned to the
crew room at Waterbeach later the same night he became aware that two
additional aircraft had been scrambled and were now closing on a 'UFO'.
A radio receiver had been tuned to the frequency they were using and
Scofield was able to listen to the events as they unfolded:

'We could hear the various voices and recognised the distinctive
voices of the individuals. The first crew made radar contact and
closed rapidly on to the target... They tracked it down to within
about three miles and then lost contact... Remember it was a dark
night, they had no navigation lights and the target also appeared
to be in darkness. They were called off and the second crew
instructed to make an intercept. They also reported radar contact
at about ten miles directly ahead. The navigator called off the
distance as the target rapidly closed. At one mile there was a
shout of confusion from the pilot who had seen nothing. We then
heard: "I think they are now on our tail!" '[50]

What did the aircrew remember? Flying Officer John Brady was the
navigator of the first RAF Venom scrambled. He was told the Americans
wanted them 'to go and look for something'.[51] Once airborne, orders were
received to contact the USAF and Brady made a note of the fact in his
flying log book. His pilot, David Chambers, recalls being told he was

above Lakenheath and the crew then received information on the distance and bearing of the target. '[The USAF] were directing us towards this thing at around 7,000 feet,' Brady recalled.

> 'The first run we had at it I saw nothing. The next time we turned onto a reciprocal heading and I then obtained a contact which I held 10–15 degrees off dead ahead and noticed that it raced down the tube at high speed. We were flying at around 300–350 knots [350–400 mph]. I remember saying to David, "*Contact* … there, it's out 45 starboard now at one mile"… and he kept saying to me, "Where is it? Where is it? I can't see it!" as we rushed past on each pass. And it would go down the right-hand side or the left-hand side, depending which way we went at it and it would be a little paint [on the radar screen]. Two further runs were made with the same result and it was fairly obvious that whatever it was, it was stationary. There was no movement. Dave looked out on each run but could see nothing. My radar contact was firm but messy but there *was* something there. We continued to fly around looking until returning to base.'[52]

Before deciding to return the crew was told that a second Venom was approaching Lakenheath. Pilot Ian Fraser-Ker and navigator Ivan Logan were preparing to take up where their colleagues had left off. As they approached, the blip appeared stationary and raced down Logan's radar tube as the pilot tried to turn behind it. At low altitude the radar display was flooded with ground clutter, reducing its range and reliability. 'I recall picking up a contact several times, usually at about three or four miles,' Logan told us.

> 'As it appeared to be virtually stationary we could not turn behind it as it was closing at high speed probably 300 knots [345 mph] or so. Our targets were normally travelling at our speed and when in behind we synchronised speeds at visual range. In this case it was impossible.'[53]

After several futile attempts to intercept this elusive target Logan and Fraser-Ker abandoned the mission and returned to Waterbeach. There they met up with Brady and Chambers, who had joined Scofield in the mess room. Brady recalled asking Logan, 'Did you see something?' His friend replied, 'Yes,' and Brady nodded, saying, 'So did I.'

Brady was keen to point out that although he remembered using the word 'contact', 'Never at any stage was there a visual sighting, since there was nothing to see as far as [the pilot] was concerned.' He described the radar target as 'a little, faint paint… You wouldn't call it a real, positive blip… I was incapable of carrying out an interception upon this thing, because it just wasn't there – it was ephemeral.'[54]

Both Brady and Logan said the blip they saw on the Venom's airborne radar was similar to that produced by a meteorological balloon fitted with a metal reflector. Other personnel serving with 23 Squadron recall the two aircrews returning 'with looks on their faces that told us something odd had happened before they even said a word'.[55] Both crews completed standard operations reports, Brady being debriefed by a more senior officer. 'I don't think any of us heard about other aspects of the incident until 40 years later,' he told us. 'Although we all thought it was unusual, none of us connected it with UFOs or alien visitors.'[56]

The airmen's ambivalent conclusions are confirmed by an entry in the diary kept by 23 Squadron:

> '… two aircraft were scrambled after a strange object had been picked up by Lakenheath GCA. The GCA became a GCI and several attempts were made to intercept the "object" but as it was standing [still] it was most difficult and nothing was seen by either of the crews… *It was decided that the object must have been a balloon.*'[our emphasis][57]

'A Mystery and a Challenge'

In 1969 Gordon Thayer, in his account of the Lakenheath incident for the Colorado University report, described it as:

> '… the most puzzling and unusual case in the radar-visual files… The apparently rational, intelligent behaviour of the UFO suggests a mechanical device of unknown origin as the most probable explanation of this sighting… In view of the inevitable fallibility of witnesses, more conventional explanations of this report cannot be ruled out.'[58]

The contradictions between the movement and behaviour of the UFOs described by the ground radar teams and the testimony of the aircrew are central to the interpretation of this extraordinary sequence of events. The original fast-moving target had disappeared when the first Venom reached a position where interception was possible. Both the USAF and RAF controllers agreed the UFO was *stationary* as the aircraft approached, precisely as the aircrew recalled. As the Venom closed upon the target both sets of ground radar appeared to 'see' the target 'loop behind' the aircraft as it rushed past.

This is the point where human perception, as opposed to the 'evidence' of radar becomes a factor. Firstly, the claims made by the ground radar crews were not supported by the testimony of the aircrew, who repeatedly describe overshooting a stationary target they were unable to turn behind. Secondly, scientist and astronomer Donald Menzel pointed out that the USAF team could *not* have seen the target circle behind the Venom because the scan rate of their equipment was such that the radar beam only 'looked' at the target once every 15 seconds. 'What ground radar observed was simply the disappearance of the target, followed by its reappearance behind the airplane fifteen seconds later.'[59]

Menzel concluded the 'tail chase' was an illusion, but even so it must have frightened everyone involved and contributed to the belief that this was 'the most inexplicable aspect of the case'. Furthermore, in 1959 a scientific intelligence study classified phantom echoes that 'overtake, fly parallel with, or collide with aircraft echoes' as typical of the scattering of radar energy that is associated with unusual atmospheric conditions. In cases such as these, the signal from a ground radar station bounces from the plane to a target on the ground then back to the plane. Ground radar operators then see two blips, one from the plane and one long-delayed 'phantom' echo from the plane via the ground. The two blips keep pace with each other as the plane is generating both 'targets', creating the illusion of a 'chase.'[60]

In the light of these factors, was the extraordinary encounter between radar, aircraft and UFOs over East Anglia 'the most impressive case of its kind on record', as one researcher has claimed? Or is more accurate to state, as UFO historian Jerome Clark has, that the events 'remain a mystery and a challenge to all who would seek to reduce every UFO report to a prosaic cause'.[61]

Anomalous Propagation?

The earliest surviving analysis of the Lakenheath incident is that by scientific advisors at Project Blue Book, which included Menzel. Their conclusion was anomalous propagation. Based upon a limited amount of data, Captain George Gregory said the echoes were 'characteristic of weather returns on radar':

> 'The sudden disappearance of all targets,
> observed erratic movements and tremendous
> speeds of supposed solid targets or "fade
> outs", reappearing at different locations on
> scopes, were typical of unusual atmospheric
> phenomena.'[62]

Gregory pointed to a reference in the USAF teletype to the targets disappearing from radar screens as the skies were obscured by clouds at 3.30 a.m. This confirmed his suspicion that the targets were radar mirages, created by unusual conditions in the upper atmosphere.

Lack of reliable information means this theory will ultimately remain unproven, but a meteorological solution is supported by the lack of any reliable visual sightings that could be directly linked with any of the radar trackings. The two USAF jets that searched the sky for targets reported by Bentwaters GCA radar earlier that evening found nothing. Not only were these UFOs apparently invisible, but targets tracked by radar later that night moving in excess of 4,000 mph – a speed five times the speed of sound – failed to produce a sonic boom. If a solid object had moved at such a terrific speed at low altitude – impossible for any conventional aircraft at that time – it could not have failed to produce air displacement in its wake. Yet nothing was heard or reported.

Meteorological Office records show that a temperature inversion had developed below the tropopause at 6 miles above sea level over Norfolk on the evening of 13 August.[63] In his investigation of 'angels' R. F. Jones found phantom echoes developed at altitudes below 8,000 feet and near the region of the tropopause. He also noted a tendency for the echoes to be particularly strong during summer, after sunset on warm evenings as the ground began to cool.[64] These were precisely the conditions that prevailed when the blips first began to appear on radar screens at Bentwaters and Lakenheath on the evening of 13 August 1956.

The University of Colorado's radar meteorologist, Gordon Thayer, came to believe that 'at least one genuine UFO' was probably involved in the episode. However, he accepted that the formation of slow-moving echoes tracked by the radar at Bentwaters 'tends to confirm a diagnosis of anomalous propagation', since the speed and direction of the echoes followed the upper winds recorded at the time.[65]

The Bentwaters–Lakenheath incident was neither the first nor the last time that unusual atmospheric conditions produced UFOs on radar screens in East Anglia. A DDI (Tech) briefing mentions another incident on 19 March 1957 when 'unusual responses which did not resemble those from conventional aircraft' were tracked by radar at Lakenheath and a satellite station at Bempton.[66] RAF interceptors were scrambled once again, but could find nothing in the area of the response. On this occasion the Air Ministry called in the Meteorological Office to investigate and concluded:

> 'It is possible that the response was due to a seasonal phenomena known as "angels" or "anaprop" which is a result of inversion and reflection in the ionosphere.'[67]

We have gone into great detail over the events at Bentwaters–Lakenheath in order to provide a clear understanding of the political, scientific and military background against which this incident occurred. For those seeking evidence of 'alien craft', Bentwaters–Lakenheath appeared to have everything – multiple radar trackings and visual and radar sightings from the ground and by aircrew, all concealed by a government conspiracy. However, as was the case with many other 'classic' UFO incidents, when the 'evidence' is carefully scrutinised the facts are found to be not as clear-cut as they have often been portrayed in the UFO literature. Natural phenomena, human perception and the will to believe on behalf both of witnesses and commentators have all contributed to the creation of an elaborate story from very mundane origins.

Cover Up?

One of the unanswered questions concerning the Bentwaters–Lakenheath case relates to the conclusions reached by the Air Ministry. There is no surviving evidence of any liaison between the British and the USAF during their investigation of the incident, which suggests there was official embarrassment over the RAF's failure to identify the UFO. A senior RAF officer has confirmed the radar trackings were investigated by DDI (Tech), which reported the findings to the Assistant Chief of Air Staff (Intelligence), Air Vice Marshal Bill MacDonald.[68] His conclusions have not survived.

Flight Lieutenant 'Freddie' Wimbledon describes how, throughout the action, Fighter Command was 'kept in the picture ... and a full report [was] made'.[69] Within a day, a senior officer – a group captain – travelled to

Neatishead to interview the chief controller and his men. Wimbledon said:

> "'I remember well his final words, which were, "Don't think you
> imagined this – these things are happening but you must not
> discuss this with anyone, especially the Press."'[70]

Wimbledon took this to mean the incident was covered by the OSA and told no one about the events until 1978, when, after retirement, he decided to write a letter to *The Sunday Times* newspaper. He maintains that when the officer left he took with him the station log book that contained all records of the incident. Since that time the log book and all other files relating to the case have vanished.

In 1972, three years after the case became public knowledge, an MoD official took part in a BBC TV debate on UFOs. Air Commodore Anthony Davis worked for the Ministry's UFO investigation branch, S4. Unknown to the audience he had been the commanding officer of 23 Squadron at the time of the Lakenheath incident and was presumably fully aware of the events because his own squadron supplied the intercepting Venoms. When a member of the audience questioned him about the RAF's role, Davis replied that the Ministry couldn't comment because the documents had been 'accidentally destroyed'. The question and answer were subsequently edited from the TV broadcast but Davis's own handwritten notes for the broadcast have survived. These contain the words '1956 ... vectored towards UFO'.[71]

Whatever the ultimate origin of the Bentwaters–Lakenheath phenomena, we believe there is evidence in this case for an official cover up of *something*. Files have been destroyed, removing them from public scrutiny, and this means we will never know the truth, however mysterious or mundane, about the events of 13–14 August 1956.

The lack of any official record leaves the MoD as ignorant of the facts as the UFOlogists, a situation that simply encourages suspicion. Today Whitehall maintains there are no records of UFOs tracked by RAF Neatishead at any time in the station's history. Answering a direct question concerning the incident, an official told us:

> 'We are unable to either confirm or deny Flight Lieutenant
> Wimbledon's account. Prior to 1990, the detection of unidentified
> tracks on radar and the subsequent response by air defence
> aircraft was not unusual. As is still the case, details of operations
> were recorded in operational log books but we can only assume
> that some books were not considered to be of historic value and
> were, therefore, destroyed.'[72]

Chapter 8

PHANTOM ECHOES

'There is a type of non-aircraft echo that suddenly appears, moves for a matter of minutes in a semi-straight line pal at velocities of some 600–2,000 mph, and then disappears. There are other echoes popularly termed "radar flying saucers"... Unidentified scope echoes [such as these] necessitate warnings to pilots or perhaps the dispatch of interceptors. Their elimination is very much desired.'

From a Scientific Intelligence report to the MoD
Radar and Signals Advisory Board, 1959[1]

The Lakenheath incident illustrated how poorly prepared the RAF was to respond to aerial intruders that did not follow conventional rules of engagement. For a number of hours, Britain's air defences were unable to identify a target that had evaded radar and approached a nuclear-armed airbase. Even more embarrassing, the USAF was well aware of these facts. Ralph Noyes, who at the time worked in the Air Minister's department, with high-level access to classified material, recalled the furore the incident caused at Whitehall.

Awkward Questions

During 1957 the Air Ministry found itself under the spotlight over its handling of the 'flying saucer' issue. April brought a series of parliamentary questions on UFOs, first from the Labour MP for Bristol, Stan Awbery, who asked George Ward, the Under Secretary of State for Air: 'What recent investigations have been made into unidentified flying objects; what photographs have been taken; and what reports have been made on this subject?'[2]

This triggered a flurry of internal memos between Ward's office, the Air Ministry secretariat S6 and DDI (Tech). Having received notice of Awbery's question, P. J. Hudson of S6 sought advice from Air Intelligence on two points: 'a) what should we tell the MP [and] b) what additional background information should be given to the Under Secretary of State for his information?' He was referred to the misleading reply given in response to an earlier question by Patrick Wall in 1955, when he was told that 'no formal inquiry' had been conducted by the Air Ministry.[3]

Ward's reply to Awbery was typically brief: 'Reports are continually being received, and we investigate them wherever the details are sufficient. Most of the objects turn out to be balloons or meteors.'[4]

Awbery's question was followed by another from Major Sir Patrick Wall, MP, who wanted to know how many UFOs had been detected over Great Britain during 1957, compared to earlier years.[5]

Secret Air Defence Alerts

Meanwhile George Ward was secretly briefed upon a number of reports made to the RAF in 1956–57 which the Ministry was keen to conceal both from MPs and the public. The briefing reveals the Lakenheath incident was in fact just one of a series of serious air defence alerts triggered by radar trackings of UFOs during 1956–57. On a number of occasions the cream of the RAF and USAF interceptor force had been scrambled to intercept unidentified blips.

Air Ministry records contain few details of these tense incidents that must have been terrifying for the aircrews whose duty it was to defend the British Isles from attack. One incident involved the tracking by airborne radar of a UFO for 1 minute, 15 seconds as it approached an RAF Vulcan bomber. The second came from RAF Wethersfield, Essex, a base for nuclear-armed USAF F-84 bombers. One night in 1956 a UFO was tracked on the base's defence radar and two interceptors were scrambled to make an interception. A brief report on the incident states:

'One of the two aircraft sent to intercept
made a momentary contact and the other made
no contact at all. No other ground radars ...
were able to find a trace of any object.'[6]

Completely absent from the briefings is any mention of a dramatic encounter between a UFO and F-84D Sabres belonging to the USAF's 406th Fighter Interceptor Wing based in England. Armed with Mighty Mouse rockets, the single-seater F-84D was the most advanced interceptor of its day and, unlike the RAF Venoms, was capable of automatic radar 'lock on' to targets.

In 1957 the 406th Wing was based at RAF Manston in Kent, where crews shared QRA duties with RAF squadrons. On the evening of 20 May 1957 pilots Milton Torres and Dave Robertson were ordered to intercept a 'bogey' tracked by RAF radar high above the North Sea. Lieutenant Torres was ordered to climb to a point at 32,000 feet, under the instruction of an RAF controller at Bawdsey. He recalled that as he closed, the order came from the GCI controller to fire his full salvo of 24 rockets at the UFO. Torres told air historian Duncas Curtis:

> 'I was only a lieutenant and very much aware of the gravity of the situation. To be quite candid, I almost shit my pants! ... The final turn was given, and the instructions were given to look 30 degrees to port for my bogey. I did not have a hard time at all. There it was exactly where I was told it would be ... the blip was burning a hole in the radar with its incredible intensity. It was similar to a blip I had received from B-52s and seemed to be a magnet of light.'[7]

As Torres' onboard radar locked on to the blip he called out the code word 'Judy', which meant he needed no further assistance from the ground, but with just ten seconds to go the blip started to take evasive action.

> 'The circle, which was down to about an inch and a half in diameter, started to open up rapidly... This meant that it was going away from me. I reported this to the GCI and they replied by asking, "Do you have a Tally Ho [visual sighting]?" I reported that I was still in the soup and could see nothing. By this time the UFO had broken lock and I saw him leaving my 30-mile range. Again I reported that he was gone, only to be told that he was now off their scope as well. With the loss of the blip off their scope, the mission was over.'[8]

After returning to Manston, Torres was debriefed by a civilian intelligence officer:

> 'He advised me that this would be considered highly classified and that I should not discuss it with anybody, not even my commander. He threatened me with a national security breach if I breathed a word about it to anyone… I was significantly impressed … and I have not spoken of this to anyone until recent years.'[9]

Evidence of this overriding concern for secrecy is found in orders circulated to 42 RAF stations and units in southern England in December 1956. In the accompanying letter HQ No. 11 Group said that 'recent reports on aerial phenomena' showed that some units were unaware of the orders circulated in 1953 that gave 'instructions for reporting and action to be taken in regard to the detection of unusual aerial phenomena'. Personnel were reminded that 'in no circumstances were details to be given to anyone other than official persons'.[10]

Figure 17:
Ralph Noyes.
Served with the RAF from 1940–46 before entering the Air Ministry in 1949. As head of MoD branch DS8 UFOs became one of his responsibilities before he retired at the grade of Under Secretary of State for Defence in 1977. The first senior MoD civil servant to write and lecture publicly on UFOs which he believed to be a 'paraphysical' phenomena akin to apparitions. Noyes told the authors: 'I and military colleagues had little doubt that something had taken place for which we had no explanation – not once, however, was there the faintest suggestion that extra terrestrials might be in question.'
(Courtesy of John Rimmer)

Gun-Camera Footage

Action to be taken in response to UFO trackings included interception and the gathering of intelligence by camera-guns fitted to aircraft. The existence of aircraft-mounted gun-camera film of UFOs has long been the subject of speculation. In Britain such footage would have been sent for analysis by intelligence experts at the Air Ministry, working for a branch of DDI (Tech).

We are aware of several occasions when cameras were triggered by aircrews confronted by unidentified aerial phenomena. In one incident, the captain of a Shackleton transport shot several frames from an RAF F24 camera as he was tailed by a UFO near Cyprus in 1958. After the film was sent to the squadron photographic section for development, he was told nothing was visible except 'light interference'.[11]

The MoD claims to have no knowledge of the existence of any UFO footage obtained by the RAF. Nevertheless Ralph Noyes said that he recalled seeing gun-camera film of 'aerial phenomena' taken by RAF aircrews during his time at Whitehall. He said that the films he saw were shown at an MoD briefing in 1968. The film show was arranged by the head of S4 and was attended by the Director of Air Defence, air staff personnel and a representative from the Meteorological Office. Its purpose was to inform 'those few who had a concern with these matters what the phenomena might be about'.[12]

Noyes was under the impression that the films were taken between 1956 and 1957:

> 'I [saw] very short gun-camera clips – fuzzy objects, self-luminous, rather dark against a light sky. Never anything like a structured craft. Always globular. Capable of moving very fast. Nothing more sensational than that, but puzzling.'[13]

Noyes believed that some of the footage was taken by the Venoms involved in the Lakenheath incident, but it appears that he was mistaken, as the aircraft involved were not equipped with cameras. However, interceptors attached to other squadrons, including the USAF's 406th Fighter Interceptor Wing did use camera-guns. Footage obtained during another incident such as the scramble in May 1957 may therefore be the source of the footage he saw.

Noyes' impression was that the films depicted unknown atmospheric phenomena and he assumed they had been turned over to the Meteorological Office for analysis. He said:

'The natural instinct was to hide away the stuff. To that extent you might talk about a cover up. There never was such a thing in my day, but we certainly kept as tight-lipped as we could because we didn't know what the phenomenon was. But we had come to the conclusion it was not a threat.'[11]

The 1968 date for the briefing is significant because PRO files show that the Meteorological Office had become more formally integrated into a new UFO investigation system at precisely this time.[15]

Where are these films today? Enquiries at the Meteorological Office archive drew a blank. Officials there said any footage of this nature would be preserved in MoD records. In 1993 UFO researcher Nick Redfern asked about the films and Nick Pope, then incumbent at AS 2, ordered a search of records held at the Main Building, in Records Management and at the PRO. He drew a blank, saying:

'I've no doubt [they] existed. If Ralph says he was at a briefing and he saw the footage, then [I've] absolutely no doubt that is precisely what happened. I assume that it exists no more because either it was getting unstable and it was destroyed, or simply it was lost somewhere, sent to archives without a label, misdirected somewhere.'[16]

Surviving Evidence

Gun-camera film is not the only evidence of strange aerial phenomena that has been 'destroyed' or 'lost' in the MoD archives. During a House of Lords debate in 1982 Admiral of the Fleet Lord Hill-Norton asked the government if it was true that 'all sighting reports received ... before 1962 were destroyed because they were deemed to be "of no defence interest" ... and if it is true, who was it decided they were of no interest?' In reply, Viscount Long avoided answering the second question and said: 'Since 1967 all UFO reports have been preserved [and] before that time they were generally destroyed.'[17]

Fortunately, a few records of the most puzzling unidentified radar UFOs have survived this arbitrary policy of destruction. They are the only surviving evidence of the concern about the nature of the phenomenon that existed at the highest levels of air staff and government. They also show the determined attempts that were made to prevent reports of UFOs by RAF personnel reaching the press.

The West Freugh Incident

Unbroken cloud shrouded Luce Bay, on Scotland's Galloway Peninsula, on the morning of Thursday 4 April 1957. The Ministry of Supply bomb trials unit at West Freugh used the bay there for 'blind-bombing' practice, a number of mobile trailer-mounted radar units being used to track aircraft during exercises. On this morning a group of civilian radar operators employed by the Ministry of Supply was preparing for the arrival of a bomber from Farnborough. A signal arrived to warn them the aircraft would be late, but the radar transmitters at Balscalloch, near Corsewall Point, were left revolving in readiness. Although manually operated, the equipment was capable of locking on to and following objects automatically. Glancing at the surveillance scope, the operator had to take a second look to ensure he was not hallucinating. There was no doubt about it – a large, unidentified echo was clearly visible.

The blip on Balscalloch's screen maintained its stationary position after successive sweeps of the radar transmitter. The target appeared to be large, solid and apparently hanging in the sky over the Irish Sea at 70,000 feet, 20–25 miles north of Stranraer.

West Freugh's air traffic control officer, Flight Lieutenant Ken England, received an excited phone call from Balscalloch 'to the effect that his crew were watching moving targets on their screen at speeds of seemingly thousands of miles an hour like nothing he had ever seen before'.[18]

England suggested they should call up another radar unit at Ardwell, 14 miles to the south, to confirm their sighting. This mobile radar was operated by civilians Charles Hollands and Stanley Farley. 'Anything on your screens?' they were asked. Sure enough, as soon as Hollands switched on his radar he saw the 'object' hovering at the same range and height as seen from Balscalloch.

Meanwhile, data from both radars was being fed into a plotting board which displayed the UFO's range and bearing by means of an electronically-operated pen, the height registering on a meter. After ten minutes, the pen began to move slowly in a northeasterly direction. A check found the UFO was then at 54,000 feet and was moving at a ground speed of 70 mph.

At this point a third auxiliary station equipped with the same type of radar 20 miles away was asked to search for the object and immediately locked on to a target apparently at the same range and bearing as the others.

Wing Commander Peter Whitworth, base commander at West Freugh, recalled what happened next:

> 'After remaining stationary for a short time, the UFO began to
> rise vertically with no forward movement, rising rapidly to

approximately 60,000 feet in much less than a minute. The UFO then began to move in an easterly direction, slowly at first but later accelerating very fast and travelling towards Newton Stewart, losing height on the way.'[19]

Suddenly the UFO turned to the southeast, picking up speed to 240 mph as it moved towards the Isle of Man. It was at this stage that the radar signals became contradictory. Balscalloch tracked a single 'object' at high altitude while Ardwell picked up what appeared to be four separate objects moving line astern behind each other at a height of 14,000 feet. As the echoes disappeared, all three radars fleetingly traced the four smaller UFOs 'trailing' behind the larger object. The UFO had been tracked for 36 minutes.

Twenty-five years later, Whitworth remained astonished by the UFO's performance: 'The sharp turn made near Newton Stewart would be impossible for any aircraft travelling at similar speed.'[20] He described how, acting upon instructions from London, he had submitted a full report on the events to the Air Ministry that was classified 'Secret'. He did not hear 'any mention of that report or of any action taken by anyone in connection with it' until 1971, when he was contacted by Julian Hennessey, a British UFOlogist studying radar UFO reports.[21] Prompted by Hennessey's questions, Whitworth contacted the MoD and asked for clearance to disclose all he could remember about the West Freugh event. This placed the MoD in a quandary, as the official stance was that all UFO reports before 1962 had been destroyed. Les Ackhurst of S4 advised his colleagues, 'We are therefore unable to discover from our own sources what information Wing Commander Whitworth intends to disclose.' Suddenly, some of the documents that no longer officially existed were 'found' in a DDI (Tech) folder!

The DDI (Tech) report notes that investigation had ruled out private and military aircraft movements in the area; indeed, the radar operators had reported that the echoes were 'considerably larger than would be expected from normal aircraft … in fact they considered that the size was nearer that of a ship's echo'.[22] Heavily charged rain clouds at high altitude were another theory considered and rejected, as were meteorological balloons, a possibility that was nevertheless offered to press enquirers by the Air Ministry.

The final paragraph of the report was startling:

'It is concluded that the incident was due to the presence of five reflecting objects of unidentified type and origin. It is

> considered unlikely that they were
> conventional aircraft, meteorological
> balloons or charged clouds.'[23]

Nothing could be said about the physical construction of the UFOs other than they were extremely good reflectors of radar signals and were therefore probably 'of considerable size'. One historian has concluded that DDI (Tech)'s report on the West Freugh incident 'contains ... the nearest we have so far got to an official recognition that UFOs exist'.[24]

Security Fears

Unlike the Lakenheath incident of the previous year, the incident at West Freugh was witnessed by civilian radar operators and a civil defence alert was triggered. The story leaked to the press, causing a major headache for the Air Ministry, which was doing its best to play down the UFO mystery. Whitworth suddenly found himself besieged by questions from journalists. He could only respond:

> 'I am not allowed to reveal its position, course and speed. It was no fluke or technical hitch. A double check was taken by putting on another scanner, and by switching from one to the other and the object was still there.'[25]

These public revelations caused an immense stir in the corridors of Whitehall, more so than any other UFO reported by the media to date. There were concerns that security could have been breached by the newspaper stories. In particular, the height at which the object had been tracked was at the upper limit of the capabilities of defence radar at that time. If the UFO were a Russian spy plane, the leak of the story could have inadvertently revealed the height capability of British radar. These concerns remained in 1971, as Whitworth was told he could talk about the case, but should not reveal the capabilities of West Freugh's radar and 'should say that the views expressed in the press cuttings are not necessarily supported by the Department'.[26]

These security fears resulted in formal orders being sent to the base reminding personnel of their obligations under the OSA. In June the senior security officer at the Directorate of Intelligence, Air Ministry, wrote to West Freugh's commanding officer asking him to draw up an instruction to all personnel ordering them to say nothing to the press on the subject of UFOs:

'... such instructions should convey the injunction that nothing which occurs on the station is a proper subject for conversation in public places, nor even in private should it be discussed with anybody who has no need to know about it... DDI (Tech) is of the opinion that a correct application of the Official Secrets Act should be adequate to safeguard security without any instructions specifically referring to unidentified flying objects.'[27]

Following the story, the Air Ministry press office issued an 'off the record' suggestion to journalists that the UFO was a weather balloon released from Aldergrove airfield in Northern Ireland. As more facts emerged it quickly became obvious that this theory was untenable and by 8 April the Ministry could only admit: 'We now only include that among other possibilities.'

The press lapped up the Ministry's predicament, pointing out that the official height record was almost 69,000 feet and civilian planes would normally be expected to fly at 10–20,000 feet, yet this object was stationary at a staggering height of 70,000 feet! The London *Evening Standard* revealed:

> 'Radar stations throughout Britain have been ordered by Air
> Ministry Intelligence to watch for a mysterious object which flew
> over the west coast of Scotland and has baffled experts.'[28]

Another paper suggested that the RAF was not ruling out the possibility that the 'mysterious object' was a Russian reconnaissance plane.[29] The Soviets were in fact testing the Backfire bomber which could reach an altitude of 60,000 feet but would not normally have strayed so close to the British mainland.

Another culprit remained, but only the most senior RAF officials knew of its existence. This was the Lockheed U-2, then being operated in great secrecy by the CIA. In April 1957 the high-altitude spy plane had been flying over mainland Russia from bases in Germany for 12 months. The U-2 was certainly capable of reaching the altitude reported by the West Freugh radar and it was not uncommon for the aircraft to be accompanied by smaller T33 and T38 jets, which could account for the four smaller objects following the large UFO.[30]

Writing in the CIA's historical journal in 1997, agency historian Gerald Haines claimed there was a link between the U-2 flights and the increase in UFO sightings reported during this part of the Cold War. The U-2s began flying in August 1955 at a height of 60,000 feet and their silver-coloured skins often reflected the sun's rays, giving them a 'fiery appearance'. At that time no one believed manned flight was possible above 60,000 feet and the CIA noted:

> 'Blue Book investigators regularly called on the [Central Intelligence] Agency's Project staff in Washington to check reported UFO sightings against U-2 flight logs. This enabled the investigators to eliminate the majority of UFO reports, although they could not reveal to the letter writers the true cause of the sightings.'[31]

According to CIA historians Pendlow and Welzenbach, more than half the reports made to Blue Book during the late 1950s and early 1960s were accounted for as flights by the U-2 and the subsequent SR-71 or 'Blackbird' project.[32] Haines' article maintains it was necessary for the USAF to make misleading and deceptive public statements, which added to the UFO mythology, in order to allay public fears about UFOs while keeping secret 'an extraordinarily sensitive national security project'.

Was the West Freugh UFO an American spy plane passing through UK airspace or secretly probing British defences to test the height capabilities of NATO radar? Ministry of Supply bomb trials units would have been ignorant of U-2 flights and only Fighter Command was aware of the movements of what were then referred to as 'specials'. Until CIA records are made available for scrutiny the true source of the West Freugh UFO is likely to remain a mystery.

Further Investigations

Widespread press coverage of this incident led MPs to table questions in the House of Commons and piled pressure upon the Air Ministry to make a statement on their UFO investigations. The dangers posed by this level of press interest was underlined in an 11 April briefing to S6 by A. G. Peacock of DDI (Tech). This revealed that in addition to West Freugh, the

Air Ministry was investigating two further 'unexplained' radar incidents. Peacock noted:

'It was unfortunate that the [West Freugh] radar incident fell into the hands of the Press... Two other radar incidents have not been made public and reached us by means of official secret channels.'[33]

One of these incidents was a report from a station at Church Lawford in North Yorkshire on 26 March 1957 where radar had tracked an unusual echo that first appeared stationary at great height and then accelerated to over 1,400 mph. Peacock stated:

'No explanation has been found for this, as, in view of the speed and height, it could not have been any conventional aircraft. The radar may have been at fault but this is unlikely as it performed a normal plot on a V type aircraft while it was watching the UFO.'[34]

The growing popular belief, encouraged by magazines such as *FSR*, that the government was concealing information on UFOs worried the Air Ministry, not least because it was true. By 1957 the Ministry was in possession of a collection of reliable reports from their own radar stations and aircrew that had no obvious explanation. To make such an admission in public at the height of the Cold War was unthinkable, however, as it would damage public confidence in their ability to defend Britain from air attack.

In 1987 Ralph Noyes told us that during his service with the Air Ministry he dealt with several 'high strangeness' reports from military establishments:

'I and military colleagues had little doubt that something had taken place for which we had no explanation. Not once, however, was there the faintest suggestion that extraterrestrials might be in question. We suspected the Russians, we suspected faulty radar, we wondered whether RAF personnel might be succumbing to hallucinogens. We found no evidence of any such things and in the end – and fairly swiftly – we simply forgot these uncomfortable "intrusions". We never had the smallest evidence that Brothers from Space were responsible for our transient unease – and I do believe we would have picked up anything of that kind, given our highly effective radar cover and the incessant watch kept on radio communications by GCHQ and the NSA.[35]

The Joint Intelligence Committee

As a direct result of these concerns and the questions posed by MPs and the press, the subject of UFOs was raised for the first time at a meeting of the Joint Intelligence Committee (JIC) at the Cabinet Office in London. The JIC was made up of elite representatives from the service intelligence branches, the Foreign Office, Treasury and secret intelligence services. Its function was to advise the Joint Chiefs of Staff and the Prime Minister on defence policy.

At the meeting held on 11 April 1957, the Assistant Chief of Air Staff (Intelligence), Air Vice Marshal Bill Macdonald tried to reassure the other members of the committee:

'There have recently been reports of a number of unexplained aerial phenomena. All of these phenomena have ... been satisfactorily explained through mistakes in radar interpretation, maladjustment of sets, as balloons or even as aircraft.'[36]

To expand further upon these points, the Air Ministry prepared a note for inclusion in the JIC's Weekly Digest of Intelligence, which was known informally as 'the Red Book'. This stated that UFO reports were received by the Ministry from 'official and unofficial sources' at the rate of approximately one per week. Since 1 January 1957, 16 reports had been received, of which ten had been explained as nothing more alarming than balloons, aircraft and meteorites. The Air Ministry report stated:

'Lack of evidence and a cold scent account for one of the two unexplained incidents and the other might feasibly have been a meteorological balloon but this cannot be confirmed. The remaining four incidents

still under investigation are all radar
sightings. In each, unusual behaviour of the
radar blips in terms of course, speed and
heights were reported. Attempts are being
made to trace the cause of these sightings
to aircraft known to have been near,
inexperienced operators or spurious echoes
of unexplained origin.'[37]

The Secret of Room 801

The true nature of those 'spurious echoes of unexplained origin' was known only to a privileged few among the team of technical intelligence officers attached to Air Intelligence 5, the DDI (Tech) branch responsible for UFO analysis. In 1957 they were based at offices in the Metropole Building on Northumberland Avenue, near Whitehall.

In June 1957 the Sunday newspaper *Reynolds News* ran a story which emphasised how seriously reports of flying saucers were treated. The story claimed that a 'special department' of the Air Ministry dedicated to UFO investigation operated from Room 801, a former attic room on the ninth floor of the old hotel (*see* Figure 18, page 158). An anonymous source claimed the Ministry had been investigating reports since 1947 and had up to 10,000 on file, most of which had been 'cleared up', but a number of which remained unexplained. The source also stated the department had direct links with fighter airfields, where some planes were dedicated to intercept UFOs. 'That is why nobody in the know is prepared to say that all reports of these mystery objects are nonsense.'[38]

Reynolds News' source appeared to be a Board of Trade technician, Ronald R. Russell, who had visited the DDI (Tech) offices by invitation in 1954 to report his own sightings. He was provided with a standard form and was told 15,000 similar reports had been received by the branch, all of which were carefully filed away in three large wooden cabinets situated in Room 801. Journalist John Pitt later said he was reliably informed that 'in each cabinet there were three drawers, locked by Yale-type locks and doubly secured by a hinged plate locked in turn by a large padlock'.[39] As befitting such high security, the room was heavily guarded and few were allowed access. Pitt claimed he had been reliably informed that above the filing cabinets was a huge map of the British Isles covered with thousands of coloured pins – the heaviest concentration being over the Norwich area of East Anglia!

the H-bomb had such poten-
tialities a decision to use it might
not be taken by Parliament, or
even by a Cabinet, but solely by
a Prime Minister.
PAGE 6: Macmillan is wrong

Five British MPs will be at the
Lidice anniversary ceremony today. Some child survivors of the
tragedy (the whole male population of 190 were shot) will be
present.

eroes—
l young
David

JOHN ENNIS

a time for boldness
set Square, London,
ay.

ne of the bravest men
nen of the war—British
nch cloak-and-dagger
—looked on, the Queen
unveiled a plaque out-
house which had been

-year-old David Shil-
ved. Clutching an old
era, the boy pushed
back of the crowd.

worked his way to the
d looked around. He
band of the Coldstream
and a guard of honour
sh and French para-

3ritish Prime Minister
millan, and the French
M. Bourgès-Maunoury,
an outstanding resist-
ster.

ny died . . .

red-carpeted steps of
one Dorset Square the
other spoke:

1941 this house was
as a base for special
ns work in France . . .
as no lack of volun-
r this hazardous and
vork.

this house they were
she went on, "here
ent their last hours or
fore their departure,
for the message to say
her was right.

volunteers passed this
these, 110 met violent
the enemy's hands. A
12 preferred death to

ling tried to push past
ry Policeman. "Stand
onny," the Redcap

eps of the house now
f Bertram Mills Circus
n Mother spoke to the
Men like Col. Pierre
, who still has two
bullets in his head.

he Military Policeman,
f Clarence Gate Gar-
riggled forward. He
under a rope and
boldly towards the

Mayflower flops

FLYING SAUCERS ARE NO LONGER A JOKE
THE SECRET OF ROOM 801

REYNOLDS NEWS REPORTER

IN Room 801 of what was once the Hotel Metropole,
Britain's Air Ministry is investigating Flying Saucers—
and that's official. After years of speculation it can now be
revealed that Defence Chiefs are taking the Flying Saucer
SERIOUSLY.

Not only is there this special
department for following up all
"Saucer" reports but there is
action, too.

At airfields all over Britain,
fighter planes are kept ready to
intercept, and if necessary en-
gage, any unidentified flying
object within combat range.

The heart of all this activity—
Room 801—was once an attic on
the ninth floor of the former
hotel building in London's Northumberland Avenue, off Trafalgar
Square.

Its existence was admitted last
night by an Air Ministry spokesman. He disclosed that it has
been investigating Flying Saucer
reports since 1947. "We have
something like 10,000 on our
files," he said.

Mystery remains

Many of these had been
"cleared up." But there were
some that could not be explained.

"This is why nobody in the
know is prepared to say that
ALL reports about these mystery objects are nonsense," he
added.

Earlier, I spoke to a man who
has been inside Room 801. Its
secrets are well guarded. But
hanging over three padlocked
filing cabinets is a map of the
British Isles covered with thousands of coloured pins.

"The heaviest concentration
of pins," he said, "appears to be
over the Norwich area."

Again I talked to Mr. R. R.
Russell, a Board of Trade technician, who has reported flying
saucer sightings to the Ministry
He showed me some special
forms on which these reports
have to be made.

The Ministry, he said always
insisted on the greatest secrecy

Tribute to R

CREA
LAVEN

Pirie.
"Th
sic im
this
anothe
tests."

The
the pr
big an
of peo
of 'flu

This
Britai
virus
epider

On
change
The g
1918-1
out of
land a
mild fo

Upon receiving the *Reynolds News* article Major Donald Keyhoe of NICAP (National Investigations Committee on Aerial Phenomena), then a major player in the UFO movement, wrote to the Air Ministry asking for confirmation of the claims made in the story. The Ministry's Information Division replied that they could 'definitely state that UFO investigation headquarters are not in Room 801 of the former Hotel Metropole [and] the figure quoted for the number of sightings [10,000] is rather exaggerated'.[40] The spokesman said the Ministry was not aware of any authorised interview that was the source of the story and added:

> 'We have not made and no not make categorical statements on the subject of UFOs. Our function is purely to assist the Press, in every way compatible with current security regulations, by answering such queries as they choose to make on this subject.'[41]

That the story did contain a kernel of truth was implicit from the confirmation that the Ministry did indeed operate 'a UFO investigation headquarters', only this was not located in Room 801! Its true location within the Metropole Building is revealed by an internal memo sent in 1960 from an RAF Signals branch to the UFO desk, addressed to: 'AI (Tech) 5b, Metropole, Room 800'. Equally mysterious is the fate of AI5's records. Despite searches of MoD records in recent years 'no files created by AI5 have been identified to date'.[42]

As Ralph Noyes pointed out, officials would never lie in answer to a direct question, but:

> 'When we felt it necessary to conceal something, we simply clammed up or stone-walled. We would never have been so stupid as to engage in active lying. It was simpler and safer to keep quiet.'[43]

Reorganisation

Surviving papers from this period show that steps were taken to ensure no further security breaches occurred at the UFO investigation headquarters. Until 1958 intelligence officers from DDI (Tech) continued to reply

Figure 18 (*opposite*): **In 1957 *Reynolds News* revealed that the Air Ministry operated a highly secret UFO investigation bureau from an attic room in the Metropole Hotel, central London, then headquarters for the Defence Intelligence Staff. Despite denials, files released at the PRO in 2002 reveal that Air Intelligence 5, the branch responsible for UFOs at this time, were indeed based there – in Room 800! The MoD claim that all records created by this covert investigation team have been destroyed because they were "not deemed to be of historical significance."**
(By permission of the British Library)

directly to correspondence from the public under the signature of the public relations unit of the Air Ministry. After the *Reynolds News* story efforts were made to offload that responsibility onto a civilian department. In a memo of July 1958 Flight Lieutenant Sheppard of AI5 makes it clear that the intelligence branch wished to 'disassociate itself from work on this subject for security reasons'.[44] Sheppard added that on occasions members of the public had sought interviews on the subject of UFOs with the Air Ministry, but: 'It is not acceptable for security reasons for such an interview to take place in any of the offices used by the staff of DDI (Tech).'[45]

As a direct result of further questions from both UFO believers and MPs, a decision was taken in August 1958 to ensure that all public statements on the subject were made by one central department, with DDI (Tech) personnel acting simply as technical advisors. All contact with the press and public was transferred to Secretariat 6 (or S6, as it was known), which became the immediate forerunner of all branches that were to have responsibility for UFO matters following the creation of the modern MoD in 1964. It was then that UFO responsibilities moved to S4, which became DS8 in 1972 and finally Secretariat (Air Staff) 2A in 1985.

S6 was staffed by civil servants and RAF officers who had transferred to desk duties. In 1958 an officer called D. A. J. West set the tone for future policy by writing that he would consult DDI (Tech) 'as necessary on any technical aspects arising from these letters, but for the most part we expect to be politely unhelpful'.[46]

Files created by S6 and S4 dating from 1962 were among the first official UFO records to be transferred to the PRO. The files demonstrate how, during the early 1960s, these two secretariats shared responsibility for the investigation of UFO reports and public statements on the subject.[47] In the majority of cases a mundane explanation was found, the favourites being aircraft, balloons and meteorites. From 1957, when Sputnik was launched by the Russians, the Air Ministry received an increasing number of sightings of orbital satellites which were reported as UFOs. Those reports which remained unresolved were referred to Air Intelligence 5, which had access to a other sources of information, including data from space-tracking stations.

A former member of AI5's staff, responsible for liaising with S6 during this period was retired Flight Lieutenant Anthony Bardsley, who told us:

> 'This work was a negligible part of my responsibilities. I would only have dealt with a single figure number of incidents annually. I had no direct contact with originators of reports made to the MoD and my second-hand guess would be that most reports were from supporters of, or believers in, "extra-terrestrial activity". In my opinion these people represented a cross-section of society

rather than a homogeneous group. Reports from serving personnel were subject to deeper investigation in which a variety of "Research and Development establishments" could be involved, but DDI (Tech)'s role was largely "comment, analysis and conclusions about incidents"... [That] was as far as it went. Although I cannot recall the detail of a specific investigation, I can say that every report I saw, or with which I dealt, no doubt ever entered my mind that there was any other than a rational cause for its explanation. I believe at the time the official approach to such investigations was that they should be based on inference rather than implication.'[18]

Alex Birch's Photograph

The most bizarre incident that Bardsley was asked to comment upon was a UFO photograph taken by a 14-year-old schoolboy, Alex Birch. The youngster and two schoolfriends became a media sensation in August 1962 when his photograph of five 'flying saucers' over Sheffield, Yorkshire, was published in the national press (*see* Figure 19, page 162).

When Alex's father contacted the Air Ministry and offered access to the camera and print, S6 faced a public relations dilemma. If officials rejected the offer they could be seen to be neglecting their air defence responsibilities, but if they displayed any interest this would be interpreted as evidence the Air Ministry was interested in flying saucers. In the end, young Alex and his father were invited to visit Whitehall.

Almost 40 years afterwards Alex remembered entering the MoD Main Building where 'there were some men and a doctor' who examined the photograph and the camera. The journalist who accompanied Alex and his father to London had by this stage been separated from the trio and taken to visit the public relations office. Meanwhile, Alex was carefully questioned for two hours by Flight Lieutenant Bardsley and a colleague from S6 who 'took the negative and the camera and kept them overnight, taking the camera apart. They asked me all these questions for so long I got muddled ... telling me they were not flying saucers but Russians.'[49]

Alex's father, a believer in alien visitors, claimed his son was placed under duress during the interview and emerged 'sick with fear'. But internal notes exchanged by the two officials paint a different picture, describing the atmosphere as relaxed, with 'both Mr Birch and his son prepared to talk ... at length'. The file contains evidence that the Air Ministry did not believe Alex's story but could not be seen to brand him a hoaxer in public. Bardsley concluded:

Figure 19 (*Above*): **Fleet of flying saucers over Sheffield, Yorkshire, photographed by Alex Birch in 1962 and Alex Birch in 1998 with his camera and photo** (*Left*). **In August 1962 Alex and his father were invited to visit the Air Ministry in London where the photo and camera were examined by technical intelligence experts.** (Copyright: Alex Birch)

'[It] is a relatively simple task to reproduce
an identical photograph to the one we were
shown [and] the sequence of exposures on the
two strips of negatives we saw do not
exactly fit the boy's story.'[50]

After much internal deliberation S6 decided the only solution was to write to Alex's father stating that their experts had decided the photo showed 'ice particles in the atmosphere'. As they had expected, the letter was immediately published by the newspapers and helped to encourage the belief that a cover up was underway. Mr Birch himself told *FSR* that it was the letter that had led him to conclude flying saucers were from outer space 'and what is more the Air Ministry knows also but won't admit it'.[51]

The truth did not emerge until ten years later, when a 24-year-old Alex Birch, tired of the constant ridicule, contacted the *Daily Express* to confess the saucer photo was a fake. The 'flying saucers' were simply cut-out shapes pasted onto a sheet of glass and re-photographed against a background of trees. Alex's schoolfriend David Brownlow confirmed his statement, adding: 'We were all into *Quatermass* and *War of the Worlds* at the time. It was just a hoax that snowballed and we all got swept along with it.'[52]

In cases such as this the Air Ministry was obliged to make cautious public statements so as not to impugn the integrity of witnesses. In other cases denial and subterfuge were necessary so that sensitive military information was not revealed in public.

The Aer Lingus Sighting

A classic example of this occurred in May 1962 when the crew of an Aer Lingus Viscount reported seeing a 'flying saucer' streaking beneath the airliner while at 17,000 feet above the West of England. Captain George Pendleton described the UFO as globe-shaped, 'large, brown and irregularly-shaped' without wings. The sighting was reported by a number of national newspapers and the Air Ministry would only say the case was 'under investigation'.

No formal solution was ever issued, but when S6 was pressurised for an answer by a member of the public, Flight Lieutenant Bardsley told his colleagues:

'This sighting was in fact "window" being
used in a Bomber Command exercise — the Aer

```
Lingus aircraft flew right through it, even
though they had been warned to avoid the
area. But, we do not give [the public] this
information.'⁵³
```

Continuing Questions

Absent from this mass of surviving material and testimony is any evidence of a high-level conspiracy to hide evidence of extraterrestrial craft. There is unambiguous evidence both from documents and personnel such as Anthony Bardsley, whose job it was to investigate UFOs, that this task was a minor part of their responsibilities and was regarded as an irritation. The Ministry has consistently denied that any member of the defence staff was devoted full time to the investigation and study of UFOs and the documentary evidence bears this out. The vast majority of reports were simply received by phone or post and only the most perfunctory of investigations were carried out by MoD. The only thorough investigations were those that followed questions in Parliament or pressure from MPs, and these invariably resulted in negative conclusions.

Senior RAF and MoD officials were no different from the public in that some rejected the subject as nonsense, while others nurtured a more open mind. This was certainly the case among the few who had witnessed phenomena themselves and had fallen foul of the Ministry's often clumsy attempts to warn them against speaking about their experiences in public.

The nearest S6 ever got to accepting the possibility that some 'unexplained' UFOs could be exotic phenomena appears in an internal minute sent to a sister department during the summer of 1958. This occurred at a time when a number of UFO groups whose members believed that a conspiracy of silence existed enlisted MPs to put pressure upon the Air Ministry to make a statement. The campaign culminated in a series of questions in the House of Commons and a rally in central London organised by the Aetherius Society, which demanded that the government reveal 'the facts about flying saucers'. Mr West of S6 noted:

```
'The authors of the campaign are firmly
convinced that extra terrestrial
manifestations have appeared, whereas the
Air Staff are by no means certain [our
```

emphasis]. As it is not possible to release official information about something which does not exist, it is difficult to satisfy those with preconceived ideas to the contrary...'[54]

In 1959 questions were again asked in Parliament following newspaper reports that a mysterious 'yellow disc' had been sighted hovering just 200 feet from the runway of London Airport (now Heathrow) before climbing away at speed. Suggestions were made that the 'yellow disc' was the planet Venus and the rapidly moving object a nose light on an aircraft leaving the runway, but doubts clearly remained, as the Air Ministry eventually listed the report as 'unexplained'.[55]

This case and continuing questions from MPs led to 'aerial phenomena' reappearing on the agenda at a March 1959 meeting of the JIC in Downing Street. A Foreign Office official, R. W. J. Hooper, asked the MoD's scientific advisors take a second look at the subject which the Air Ministry had assured them was nonsense in 1957. The 'Scientific and Technical Intelligence Sub-Committee' was tasked to make enquiries into recent reports 'and inform [the JIC] whether they could be explained'.[56] The conclusions are likely to remain a mystery as the Cabinet Office Historical and Records Section assures us that all Scientific and Technical Intelligence files held by the JIC were destroyed in 1973 'at the first review stage'.[57]

The JIC sub-committee was made up of experts from the DSI, the same MoD branch that produced the Working Party on UFOs that was presented to Winston Churchill in 1952. The conclusions had recommended an immediate halt to all further study of 'flying saucer' reports until new evidence emerged. The reports from RAF stations such as Lakenheath and West Freugh had led to a reversal of this policy within the space of a decade and ensured that the MoD had no option but to continue its covert surveillance of UFOs into the 1960s.

Chapter 9

THE YEAR OF THE FLYING CROSS

'The "inescapable conclusion" that
"major governments of the world are
holding back some critical
information about UFOs – especially
the United States and Great Britain"
– can be utterly repudiated.
There is no international cover-up
conspiracy.'

MoD briefing, 1968[1]

Shortly after 4 a.m. on the morning of 24 October 1967 a police car pulled up behind a Land Rover parked in a layby in rural Devon. The occupant, 29-year-old Christopher Garner, stepped out. One of the policeman pointed to the horizon, where a bright light was hovering in the sky. 'I thought I was having a nightmare when they woke me up,' Garner said later. 'They said they wanted confirmation of what they had seen. I don't know what it was, but this object was much too bright for any star.'[2]

The officers were PC Clifford Waycott and PC Roger Willey. At a press conference held at Okehampton police station they described chasing an unidentified flying object at speeds of up to 90 mph for almost an hour. PC Waycott told journalists:

> 'I am normally a bit sceptical – you get like that in the police. We were driving beside fields and trees when I saw a light in front of us. I thought what a funny place for a street lamp. It wasn't

piercing, but it was very bright. It was star spangled, just like looking through wet glass. Before I spoke, the driver saw the light and put his foot down. We reached 90 mph but the light accelerated away from us.'[3]

The policemen described the UFO as 'like a star-spangled cross radiating points of light from all angles'. PC Willey said:

'It first appeared to the left of us, then went in an arc, and dipped down and we thought it had landed. It seemed to be watching us and wouldn't let us catch up... It had terrific acceleration. It seemed to know we were chasing it.'[4]

At the press conference Inspector Frank Harding commented:

'We are mystified, but we must keep an open mind. After all there may be other planets already in advance of the satellite launchings we are beginning to make.'[5]

The press immediately dubbed the UFO the 'flying cross' and the following morning's headlines were dominated by the policemen's report: 'Z-car patrol shadows flying saucer' (The *Sun*), 'The flying thing leaves two constables baffled' (*The Times*), 'UFO – we chased it at 90 mph say PCs' (*Western Daily Press*).

A spokesman at RAF Chivenor, the nearest RAF station to the drama, said none of their aircraft were flying. The MoD had no comment to make. The UFOs were back – in force.

UFO Mania 1967

During 1967 the MoD received 362 sighting reports, the greatest number since statistics had first been preserved by the Air Ministry in 1959.[6] Of those sightings, the vast majority (150) were explained as aircraft, with satellites and space debris (57) and balloons (42) following in order of importance. A total of 46 reports remained 'unexplained', a category the MoD preferred to describe as 'insufficient information'. A detailed policy document drawn up by the head of S4, James Carruthers, explained the nature of these 'unexplained' reports:

```
'They share one common characteristic: they
lack information vital to their explanation.
From such information as these reports do
```

contain, it can be firmly stated that there
is nothing in any of them to suggest that
the incidents to which they relate are any
different in nature to those mentioned in
the reports that have been explained. There
are no "unknown" reports as defined by the
US Air Force studies as "reports which are
detailed, accurate and reliable, and which
cannot be explained".'[7]

The wave of sightings triggered a new flurry of questions from MPs. Some MPs were concerned about a potential threat to Britain's defence. Others posed questions on behalf of UFOlogists who believed the Earth was under surveillance by an alien intelligence. Ministers asked the MoD for detailed briefings and this presented an additional workload, adding to the magnitude of the 'UFO problem', as the MoD was beginning to refer to the subject. They were told that the marked increase in UFO reports during 1967 was significant only in terms of the fact that large numbers of people had been encouraged to report sightings because of the press coverage. During the month of October alone 79 reports were received, the majority following news reports of the flying cross incident. Most of these were what Carruthers called 'inferior' reports generated by people looking at the sky 'impelled either by the good weather or by Press-aroused curiosity'.[8]

During the course of 1967 the MoD received eight reports from military sources, but none of these remained unexplained. 'Three bright cones' seen in the sky over Spurn Head by the crew of an RAF Victor aircraft on 13 July were later found to have been a high-altitude balloon reflecting sunlight. Other reports had similar prosaic origins. The brilliant planet Saturn fooled the crew of a RAF helicopter above Thorney Island on 5 September and on 18 July a brilliant burning light was seen by the crews of two RAF aircraft and hundreds of other observers as it sped across the night skies. This was found to be a piece of Russian satellite burning up as it re-entered the atmosphere, one of a growing number of reports explained as sightings of man-made space junk.[9]

Several sightings by the pilots of civil aircraft did, however, give the MoD serious cause for concern. One reported to the British and Spanish authorities came from the crew of a DC6 Air Ferry *en route* from Palma to Manston in Kent on 10 September 1967. They were above the Pyrenees when a metallic object 'like an inverted cone on top of a vague streamlined shape' passed in front of the aircraft at immense speed. The UFO performed 'a supersonic turn' before decelerating to approach the DC6. This object was 'not positively identified' but nevertheless was dismissed as 'having no defence implications for the UK'.[10]

Defence Intelligence staff were asked to examine a sighting by Captain Alden and the crew of a British European airliner who saw a 'silver rocket-like vehicle' speeding over Portaferry in Northern Ireland on the morning of 1 September 1967. When the captain radioed his report to ATC he was told a member of the local aero club had reported a similar object from the ground, although nothing was captured on radar.

This was described by the MoD as 'a detailed report from a reliable source' and the head of S4 demanded a thorough inquiry. Checks ruled out the possibility of a missile fired from the Aberporth rocket range and the MoD was at a loss. It was decided that the crew had seen either a daylight meteor or the burn-up of a Thor rocket as it re-entered the atmosphere. The MoD's conclusions summed up the policy of taking investigations no further than was necessary to evaluate the defence threat:

'Positive identification is not possible in this case. We have no factual "proof" - only "most probable" conjecture.'[11]

More 'Fiery Crosses'

This policy was of limited success when it came to dealing with civilian sightings of the 'flying cross'. Initially the USAF 3rd Air Force came up with a solution for the sightings by the police officers in Devon. They said the UFOs were probably USAF tankers practising refuelling in midair over the West Country, with the lights of the aircraft and their fighter escorts appearing as a cross-shaped formation from the ground.[12] This theory was soon abandoned when it became clear that the refuelling exercises had taken place between 5 and 9 p.m., whereas the 'fiery crosses' had all been reported between midnight and dawn.

The most obvious culprit, the planet Venus, was overlooked in the press-driven mêlée. But the fact remained that the planet rose in the east between 3 and 4 a.m. and was shining brightly at precisely the time the policeman saw their UFO. Venus was also the solution put forward by the Plymouth Astronomical Society and aircrew from RAF Chivenor, who used a sextant to demonstrate that at least one 'flying cross' was the morning planet.

The Devon police chase was heavily featured in the British press and when the officers described their experience live on TV many other people began to scan the sky. On 24 October retired RAF Wing Commander Eric Cox reported a V-shaped formation of seven bright white lights hovering in the night sky above the New Forest. As Cox and his wife watched, three of the lights faded and the remaining four formed into 'a perfect formation of a cross or a plus sign'. The pair saw their UFO minutes after they had watched an interview with the two police officers on a TV news bulletin.

As the contagion spread, police officers in Sussex, Hampshire, Derbyshire and Oxfordshire all reported seeing 'fiery crosses'. A Sussex police motorcycle patrol first radioed news of a sighting to colleagues shortly after 4 a.m. on 25 October. Within minutes the crews of four police cars in other parts of the county had reported the same UFO. Acting swiftly, the Chief Constable of Sussex, George Terry, called a press conference at Lewes where he said he was satisfied that there was 'nothing sinister' going on and the UFO was 'probably Venus'.[13]

It was the Cox sighting, however, reported by a credible and trained observer, that led the MoD to order a field investigation by a team of hand-picked defence staff. This three-man team interviewed Cox and took him to the scene of his sighting, where he pointed out where the lights had appeared. When plotted on a map, his line of sight was found to point directly towards the airfield at Boscombe Down and slightly to the left of the army artillery range at Larkhill.

In the MoD file Leslie Ackhurst notes that by making detailed checks on air activity they had been able to put forward 'a strong probability' that Cox had seen either illuminated flares from Larkhill, or, less likely, an aircraft landing at Boscombe Down viewed from an unusual angle. Both were in use on the night the UFO was seen and were in Cox's direct line of sight. One of the investigators added: 'The case of Wing Commander Cox could be used as a copybook example of how people are misled by ordinary mundane events.'[14]

The Cox case was important because as a retired RAF technical officer Cox's testimony carried more weight than that of an ordinary member of the public. But, as W. Cassells of S4 pointed out in a note to Merlyn Rees, the Under Secretary of State for the RAF, 'Even experienced aircrew have been known to mistake objects they should have been familiar with.'[15]

The Psychological Angle

The MoD was now beginning to fully appreciate the role mass suggestion played in creating UFO scares. 'The number of other reports show that it is becoming fashionable for people to see UFOs,' James Carruthers noted in a briefing to Merlyn Rees on 30 October.[16]

The use of psychologists in the questioning of UFO witnesses was mentioned in the House of Commons on 8 November by Rees in a reply to a parliamentary question on the 'flying cross' sightings. Asked if he could reassure MPs that he had received scientific advice on the recent sightings in Devon and Sussex, the Under Secretary of State replied:

> 'I can give that assurance. This not just an air defence matter. We have access to scientists of high repute – they have been consulted on all these matters – and also to psychologists.'[17]

Advice was also sought from psychologists on plans to improve the lines of communication between the MoD and the public 'in order to discourage the type of speculative reports that one sees in the newspapers on UFOs'. The MoD was aware that the USAF had included specialists in their investigation teams for some years and S4 commented, 'Psychology is in a great many ways a highly relevant science [in the study of UFO reports].'[18]

The MoD approached RAF psychologist Alex Cassie to act as an advisor on UFO psychology. Cassie was a former prisoner of war whose experiences were the basis for actor Donald Pleasance's character in the classic film *The Great Escape*. He became the first RAF psychologist brought in to advise air staff on the perceptual aspects of UFO reports and the people who made them.[19]

Eventually Cassie would join Leslie Ackhurst and members of the Defence Intelligence staff in field investigations of the more important reports made during the flap of 1967–68. He told us that he looked into the background and interests of those who made reports and often found they had a prior interest and a will to believe in UFOs:

> 'For two years I was asked to advise on sightings reported to the Air Department of the MoD. I came to the conclusion that the people who reported sightings of UFOs were far worthier of research than the reports themselves.'[20]

The Venus Solution

With the new investigation team assembled, the MoD moved quickly to investigate the sightings in Devon and satisfied themselves that the brilliant morning planet Venus was the true source of the 'flying cross'. In a ministerial briefing, James Carruthers explained:

> 'I have arranged with the Deputy Chief
> Constable of Devon and Cornwall for "an MoD

officer" [actually a member of DSTI's staff]
to interview in Exeter the policemen who saw
a UFO. I have also arranged for RAF Chivenor
to keep an eye open for any unusual
celestial phenomena. I have stressed that no
special action should be taken but that
night duty personnel should be asked to
report anything unusual and, for example, if
anyone is on duty in the tower, he should
have handy such basic equipment as a
sextant, compass and camera.'[21]

The 'MoD officer' was Dr John Dickison, a space weapons expert who had been assigned in May 1967 to assist Ackhurst and Cassie in the investigation of the more interesting UFO reports. Dickison worked for a Defence Intelligence branch of the MoD known as DI55 and was a member of the team that visited Wing Commander Cox.

After quizzing Waycott and Willey at Okehampton police station on 27 October, Dickison sent a report to Leslie Ackhurst. It concluded:

'When questioned ... one of the police
constables indicated that ... he had decided
that the light came from a spaceship. They
did not see a spaceship but only saw a light
and his conclusion appears to have no
factual basis.'[22]

By the end of that year the conclusion that the policemen had chased the planet Venus had become widely accepted by the MoD, but a thorny problem remained: how could the government announce in Parliament that two police officers, trained observers, had been fooled by a planet?

The senior MoD officer W. P. Cassell commented, in a minute to Merlyn Rees:

'Some doubt can reasonably be expressed about
the absolute reliability and accuracy of

> their account. It was apparent that the
> policemen had rehearsed their story several
> times as a result of interviews with the
> Press before they were interviewed by an
> officer of DI55. By this time they had drawn
> certain conclusions from their observations
> that they had seen a spaceship, which were
> quite unsupported by their factual account
> of events.'[23]

Cassell added that in the light of the conflict of opinion between the police and the MoD it would be 'most unfortunate' if any 'on the record' statement was made 'which appeared to brand the policemen as liars or exaggerators'. He suggested that Merlyn Rees might have a quiet word with the Okehampton MP, Peter Mills, to explain that 'off the record Venus remains the most likely explanation and that there are some grounds for believing that the policemen's account of what they saw was not 100 percent accurate'.[24]

UFOs and the Ministry of Defence 1967–68

The years 1967 and 1968 saw a significant change in the methodology by which the MoD investigated reports of unidentified flying objects. A more proactive stance was demanded by politicians, but at the same time the MoD was acutely aware that its first priority lay with the defence of the country, not with chasing phantoms in the sky. A radical rethink of responsibilities was necessary.

Hundreds of pages of MoD files relating to policy on UFOs were released to the PRO in 1998 and 1999.[25] They reveal that with continuing pressure on resources, the Ministry was only able to undertake the most basic investigations into the vast majority of the reports received. In public, officials were forced to pay lip service to the demands of those MPs who wanted a full investigation, while hiding the Ministry's own shortcomings behind a veil of official secrecy.

Following the 'flying cross' sightings a detailed briefing outlining the methods used by the MoD to investigate UFOs was drawn up by James Carruthers. This document was circulated to Directorate of Scientific and Technical Intelligence (DSTI) and the RAF in preparation for a meeting with Merlyn Rees, who was to answer questions in Parliament. Under the heading 'Causes of UFO Reports' the head of S4 listed man-made and natural objects, and lesser known meteorological phenomena such as ball lightning and plasma. 'By and large,' he observed, 'reports originate from someone who has seen some unfamiliar phenomenon or from someone who has seen something well known in an unfamiliar situation.' Reports from untrained observers could not be trusted – police files, Carruthers noted, were full of accident reports 'where ordinary unbiased spectators fail to agree in their accounts of what they witnessed'.[26]

Carruthers also pointed out that the role of the media and 'psychological factors' in the creation of UFO reports had to be taken into account:

'There are two aspects to this which should be mentioned. The first is a crowd psychology effect. When popular interest is stimulated in UFOs, as in the recent press flurry, people look for UFOs: indeed they wish to see them... The other psychological aspect is almost a religious desire to believe in UFOs. People become depressed about the troubled state of the world with its threats of nuclear, bacteriological and chemical warfare. They find it comforting to believe that superior beings exist whose technology must have triumphed over the same sort of vicissitudes as we are now undergoing; and they regard it as a sign of hope for the world.'[27]

The briefing continued by addressing the possibility that alien visitors or 'clandestine terrestrial activity' could lie behind the small number of unexplained UFOs:

'There is no evidence from our reports to show there is any extraterrestrial activity ... and this is a conclusion that the Americans draw about their reports, even taking into account their unknown reports.'[28]

Carruthers was careful to add that this conclusion did not completely deny the possibility that life did exist on other planets:

> '... indeed, it would be foolish even to think of doing so since we are already reconnoitring our planetary neighbours but there is no evidence that anyone is taking an interest in us, despite UFO reports going back for centuries.'[29]

Drawing upon over 500 reports made to the MoD since 1959, Carruthers said it was tempting to believe UFO reports could be explained 'in terms of some scientific phenomenon of which we are still unaware'. He thought this was unlikely, however, because of the very high proportion of reports that had been accounted for in mundane terms. Echoing the conclusions of R. V. Jones, he added:

> 'The only conclusion which holds water is that UFO reports are explicable in terms of man-made and natural phenomena. Nevertheless, UFO reports are certainly interesting in their own right and may have air defence implications; hence it is worthwhile continuing to examine each carefully and with an open mind.'[30]

S4's thorough assessment of the UFO 'problem' set the tone for a new approach to handling the subject in public. This resulted in the production of a 'comprehensive questionnaire' for the reporting of sightings. Standard operational procedures aimed at speeding up the process whereby reports of UFOs reached the MoD were formalised in January 1968 and circulated to police forces, civil airports and RAF stations.[31] Versions of these remain in use today.

A member of S4's staff summarised their public policy in an internal memo:

> 'At present we have a fairly clear line in not getting embroiled in UFO matters.

> Members of the public who write to us get
> brief and polite replies to their reports
> and, beyond that, we take the line that we
> cannot justify defence effort in collating
> and analysing reports and cannot release to
> other members of the public reports which
> have been sent privately to the Ministry of
> Defence.'[32]

Despite this low-key approach, during 1967 S4 was forced to respond to a series of parliamentary questions from Sir John Langford-Holt, who had been briefed by a 'well-known correspondent' of the MoD, Julian Hennessey. Using his position as a representative of the US group NICAP, Hennessey sent a stream of letters to the MoD, MPs and the Prime Minister, requesting access to government UFO files. The MoD believed that Langford-Holt's questions were part of a campaign by Hennessey and UFO 'believers' to force them into undertaking a full study of UFOs similar to that underway in the USA.[33] They were determined to resist any such moves in Britain and Carruthers assured Merlyn Rees that a new study by the MoD 'would not produce results to justify the expenditure, time, effort and money involved'.

Furthermore, what knowledge the MoD had of the progress achieved by the University of Colorado team led them to believe their study was:

> '...unlikely to reveal any significant new
> facts about UFOs of scientific or defence
> importance and ... unlikely to resolve the
> public relations problems associated with
> UFOs. This view is based on a full study of
> reports and careful comparison with data
> available from defence sources and other
> scientific and technical advice.'[34]

In a briefing to Rees, Leslie Ackhurst outlined the responsibilities of his branch in UFO matters. 'S4 (Air),' Ackhurst wrote, 'is responsible for correspondence with the public on this subject' and for providing advice for Ministers on parliamentary questions. He noted: 'We are the only

Department with a *recognised* interest in UFOs (albeit a strictly limited one).[35] In his summary Ackhurst revealed that S4f (Air) was not directly responsible for checking UFO reports for 'possible air defence implications', as this was the duty of a Defence Intelligence branch at the DSTI. In 1967 this was known by the title DI61e (Air) and had inherited the responsibility from an Air Intelligence branch at DDI (Tech) that was part of the old Air Ministry structure.

The MoD's UFO investigation system worked as follows. All sightings received – both from the services and the public – were channelled through S4 at the MoD Main Building. This branch then worked with the Air Force Operations Room (AFOR) to carry out a range of initial checks on aircraft movements and exercises. Other MoD agencies such as the Meteorological Office provided information about balloon launches and aircraft movements and the space tracking station at Fylingdales and the radio and space research station at Slough checked satellites and space debris. When no 'immediate satisfactory explanation' could be determined, 'ie they are truly unidentified flying objects', DSTI was 'required by MoD to carry out further investigations'.[36]

Defence Intelligence 55 (DISS)

In 1967 Defence Intelligence was digesting a report by a senior RAF intelligence officer, Wing Commander S. A. E. Munns, entitled: 'A Review of the Duties of the Free World Section of DI61 (Air)'. With the outbreak of the Six-Day War in June, Munn's branch was short-staffed and a major review of duties was necessary. Three sections of DI61 were 'primarily responsible for all Free World Air Technical Intelligence' but a number of other duties, some of which were deemed to have few intelligence connections, had become part of their remit. UFOs were one of these, but work on the subject could only occur 'at the expense of the primary intelligence activities'. It was imperative to reduce the workload and UFOs were deemed to be one responsibility DSTI could do without.

Investigation of UFOs, Munns said:

> '... has ... been the responsibility of Technical
> Intelligence (Air) staff for at least 10
> years ... It is not proposed to enter into any
> detailed discussion of the reasons for this
> but undoubtedly it was originally assumed
> that the characteristics of UFOs were akin
> to aerodynamic vehicles which travelled in

> the atmosphere and could, therefore, pose a
> threat similar to aircraft.'[37]

The vast majority of sightings reported to DI61 had been explained as either satellites in orbit or space debris and Munns proposed that as part of the major review DI61 should cease all work on UFOs and, 'if a watching brief is required ... this in future be carried out by the space cell of DI55'.[38]

The involvement of DI55 in UFO investigations dated from the early months of 1967. In February the MoD recommended the transfer of UFO duties from DI61 to 'the space desks in DI55 [who] are better qualified for [studying] this activity, particularly in view of their scientific context'.[39] Scientific Officer A. O. Hunter added: 'The few [UFOs] which are not satellites or space debris are almost certainly manifestations of meteorological or other natural phenomena.'[40] Hunter thought such matters clearly fell within DI55's remit, 'But I feel they must be regarded as of so low priority as not to justify any expenditure of effort in categorising them.'[41]

In a note to the Director of Scientific Intelligence, Archie Potts, Hunter labelled UFOs 'a problem' and said if he had any influence upon policy he would ensure that they received the lowest priority of all the current tasks of the Space Section. He added:

> 'When we are so short of staff for tasks of
> much higher priority it is clear that we
> cannot contemplate a special appointment for
> the investigation of UFOs and we must
> therefore always fall short of what is
> required to implement the stated official
> policy.'[42]

Neither was the movement of responsibility welcomed by the staff of the Space Section themselves. The DI55 space weapons systems officer, Squadron Leader Eric Humpston, said that after receiving UFO reports from Leslie Ackhurst for one month his staff had assessed the size of the task that faced them:

> 'It is apparent that investigations into UFOs
> cannot be regarded as a part-time or
> secondary task ... and it is completely beyond

> inclusion in the work schedule of the
> already overworked and undermanned Space
> Section of DI55. Under these circumstances
> it is recommended that it be recognised that
> DSTI cannot undertake the investigation of
> UFOs to the standard required by the stated
> policy on the subject, or, alternatively, an
> officer and transport be established in DSTI
> specifically for this purpose.'[43]

As a result, Archie Potts of DSTI wrote to the Director General of Intelligence (DGI), Sir Alfred Earle, outlining the public relations problems posed by an official policy that was impossible to fully carry out:

> 'I feel I ought to bring this to your
> attention, because it is a subject that is
> always liable to involve newspaper
> sensationalism or parliamentary questions.'[44]

The Deputy Director of Intelligence, Air Commodore J. A. C. Aitken, agreed that it was 'outside the scope of current resources' to investigate UFOs in any depth:

> 'In the United States, to allay public
> concern, the Department of Defence has been
> forced to delegate detailed investigation to
> the Universities on a substantial research
> contract. In our case, we have tailored our
> efforts to meet the minimum requirement of
> protecting UK airspace from any incursions
> which might pose a threat or a hazard.'[45]

Aitken felt it would be illogical, despite pressure from MPs, 'to give higher priority or devote more effort than we do now to such a nebulous subject'.[46]

Air Cdre (Int)/ 217

<u>DGI</u>

UNIDENTIFIED FLYING OBJECTS

Reference : DSTI/126/6 dated 19th June 1967

1.   Having examined the attached minute from DSTI, I have the following comments to make.

2.   I agree with DSTI that, if UFO are to be investigated in any depth, the task would be formidable and entirely outside the scope of current resources.   In the United States, to allay public concern, the Department of Defence has been forced to delegate detailed investigation to Universities on a substantial research contract .   In our case, we have tailored our efforts to meet the minimum requirement of protecting UK airspace from any incursions which might pose a threat or a hazard.

3.   Since investigations began no positive evidence has come to light which would indicate activity other than that associated with known phenomena. Most reported sightings in recent years have been traced to satellites in orbit, space debris, or meteorological sources.   In no case has a report been received which would indicate a real or potential hazard to UK air space. Prima facie as this is a problem connected with the integrity of our air space, it is arguable that the Air Staff should have full responsibility for it. However, because of the high percentage of UFO reports which have space or scientific connotation it is inevitable that DSTI staff will be consulted and become involved in the major part of any investigation.   There is no one else capable of doing this.   They should therefore continue to hold responsibility for advising S.4(Air) and other sections of the Air Staff as a direct extension of the work done on a single service basis by the former DDI(Tech). In fact I can think of no better place in which to undertake this work than DI 55 with its breadth of scientific and technical knowledge in space study. In the future they will be helped in this task by the presentation of detail of space, missile and aircraft events in the STCIC.

4.   In my view the case for deeper investigation into UFOs to meet public and House of Commons demands has been overstated.   Our questioners have appeared satisfied with the service given over ten years and I believe it would be illogical to give higher priority or devote more effort than we do now to such a nebulous subject.

5.   I therefore recommend that DI 55 should retain responsibility for UFOs and attach a minute to DSTI for your consideration.   I also attach a Daily Telegraph cutting of 23rd June which epitomises the medium in which we are dealing.

27th June 1967

(J.A.C. AIKEN)
Air Commodore (Intelligence)

In order to give the DGI some idea 'of the medium in which we are dealing', Aitken attached a cutting from the *Daily Telegraph* that described how 'saucer-sighters' from Britain and America were arriving in New York for the 1967 Congress of Scientific UFOlogists to mark the 30th anniversary of the first recorded sighting by Kenneth Arnold. He highlighted part of one paragraph which read:

> '...there will be talks by delegates who are convinced that they have travelled "to other planets" and some who say they have talked with men from outer space.'

This tactic worked well, for on 29 June Earle replied to the DSTI, noting that the only reason for the MoD undertaking investigations at all was to protect UK airspace. Earle said intelligence investigations of UFOs began 'over ten years ago' but that 'in no case that I am aware of has a report been received which would support a real or potential hazard to UK airspace'. It followed that: 'Until there is a clear case for treating UFOs with more concern than at present, I accept the way in which the problem is being dealt with.'[47]

S4 (Air) staff continued to remind their scientific advisors in DI55 of the importance of dealing swiftly with UFO reports they received from the general public. As a civil servant wrote to Mr Hunter of the DSTI:

```
'If we do not do this, and if we are not seen
doing this, we could give the unfortunate
and damaging impression to the public at
large that we, the Department concerned with
defence, did not care whether there were any
defence implications or not.'[48]
```

A compromise was eventually reached whereby S4 agreed to take over the lead responsibility for UFO investigations, only referring to DI55 those which 'seem so unusual that they justify the immediate attention of the Defence Intelligence Staff'. In essence this was an arrangement that continued until the DIS discontinued their interest in UFOs in the year 2000.

Figure 20 (*opposite*): **Confidential memo from Air Commodore J.A.C. Aitken, MoD (Intelligence), to Director General of Intelligence Sir Alfred Earle, 27 June 1967** (Crown copyright: MoD)

Extraterrestrial Life?

From May 1967 responsibility for the investigation of reports in DI55 fell upon two scientists. One of these, Dr John Dickison, was described as being 'concerned with the military aspects of space and with giving general scientific advice on the physical and technical aspects of UFO reports'.[49]

An insight into the internal workings of DI55's attitude to UFOs is provided by an exchange of internal notes between the branch and S4 during September 1967, which the latter described as 'a mind-sorting exercise'. After reviewing a file containing summaries of some of the more unusual reports submitted for assessment, DI55 arrived at two mutually exclusive hypotheses. The first was startling:

> 'Hypothesis 1: Extra-terrestrial life (or a foreign nation with a vastly superior technology) is capable of guiding objects over UK without the knowledge of ATC and defence radars.'

The second was more to their liking:

> 'Hypothesis 2: Hypothesis 1 is false and all reports are based on observations of natural phenomena ... or due in whole or part to the limitations of the visual process.'[50]

As the reports received did not include any from groups of independent, reliable observers of a UFO witnessed from different locations or supported by radar returns and photographs, DI55 felt the only effective method of proving or disproving Hypothesis 1 was to 'ignore as far as public relations allows' the less interesting reports 'and concentrate efforts on investigating in detail and in-depth those few reports that do tend to support Hypothesis 1'.[51] This statement appears to be the closest Defence Intelligence scientists came to considering the possibility that extraterrestrial visitations might lie behind some of the stranger UFO reports.

The vast majority of the reports received by the MoD in 1967 were of 'lights in the sky' that could be accounted for by a range of well-known natural and man-made phenomena. Unlike private UFO investigators, the

Ministry was not receiving the detailed accounts of structured objects seen at close range by reliable observers. For example hundreds of reports had reached the press and UFOlogists during a UFO flap in 1964–65 at Warminster in Wiltshire. The town and surrounding countryside became a place of pilgrimage for UFO believers. A public meeting was held in the town and for more than a year UFO spotters gathered on hills around Warminster to watch the skies. UFOs were captured on film and dozens of local residents and visitors claimed to have experienced strange aerial phenomena. But despite the huge media attention and the public concern which followed, *not one single report* was submitted to or investigated by the MoD.[52]

Gathering Information

Throughout 1967 folders bulging with newspaper cuttings and sighting reports continued to pile up on the on the desk of Leslie Ackhurst in S4 at Whitehall. It was primarily Ackhurst, a higher executive officer, who had the job of supervising MoD investigations of UFO reports. Dealing with the investigations, correspondence and briefings should have taken up a small percentage of his time, but it was rapidly becoming a full-time task. For the first time the MoD would have to consider the appointment of a full-time advisor to deal with the growing public relations headache that UFOs posed.

Again it was the Defence Intelligence Staff and the Director of Scientific Intelligence, Archie Potts, who were at the forefront of decision and policy-making on UFOs. During the UFO wave of 1967 DSTI was busy gathering information on studies of the phenomenon undertaken by the air force and intelligence agencies in the US, Russia and Sweden. The MoD was taken by surprise in November when Russian television announced that a Soviet air force commission had been set up to investigate UFOs. Britain's scientific attaché in Moscow was asked 'to make discreet enquiries' into the announcement.[53]

DSTI had more success in the USA, where the Colorado University UFO project led by physicist Dr Edward Condon was nearing the completion of its study. The British air attaché in Washington was asked to obtain an advance copy of the team's final report. An MoD briefing claimed that Condon's overtly sceptical stance had led to the study being denigrated as 'an elaborate plot to give an air of impartiality to the biased attitude of the USAF towards these reports'. Neverthless, the USAF hoped the final report would confirm the negative findings of Project Blue Book and 'that it would vindicate them in the face of growing public belief that the USAF was concealing the truth'.[54]

In August 1967 Dr Robert Low, a senior scientist from the Colorado University project, flew to London to discuss MoD policy with DSTI

Director Archie Potts, who was introduced as the most senior official responsible for UFO investigations. Low did not ask to see any UFO files and appeared more interested in paying a visit to Loch Ness to investigate the famous monster. After the meeting Potts wrote to Air Commodore C. T. Nance at the British Embassy in Washington:

> 'I half expected Dr Low to be a crank with a vested interest in believing in visitors from Outer Space. This, however, proved not to be the case; he was a rational, sensible scientist doing his best to apply some sort of scientific judgement to a mass of unscientific data. I doubt if his final report will conclude that the earth is now under observation by creatures from outer space.'[55]

A bland one-paragraph statement on British policy produced by Low for inclusion in Condon's final report was carefully edited by the MoD to remove all mention of Potts and the leading role of the Scientific and Technical Division of the MoD in UFO investigation.[56]

Potts told Dr Low the MoD had a similar public relations dilemma to the Americans in terms of dealing with pressure to investigate UFOs in more depth. While they wished to avoid wasting public money, they recognised 'that it would require only one sensational unexplained and much publicised incident to bring down a shower of public criticism on Government for failing to give proper attention to such matters'.[57]

The DSTI Calls in an Old Friend

During the last three months of 1967 the Ministry faced not one but a whole series of sensational and unexplained incidents. By November, Potts was advising the DGI (Air) that if the high level of public interest in UFOs did not recede, S4 might be prepared 'to sponsor and pay for a scientific post with DSTI for UFO investigations'.[58] The advisor, Potts suggested, could work 'on our space problems under [Defence Intelligence] direction', as well as providing a UFO investigation service for S4.

Although these remarks were underlined as 'largely hypothetical', overtures were made to a scientist who had long experience of dealing with UFOs within the context of Scientific Intelligence, R. V. Jones, who was then Professor of Natural Philosophy at the University of Aberdeen. 'If we should ever need an outside consultant,' Potts wrote in a minute to S4, 'he would be a very good choice.'[59]

In retirement from defence duties, Jones maintained the highly sceptical attitude towards aerial phenomena that he had adopted during his time as the wartime head of Scientific Intelligence for the Air Ministry. In reaching his conclusions, Jones employed Occam's Razor, the approach which had been adopted by the Flying Saucer Working Party during 1950–51 under Jones' predecessor, Dr Bertie Blount. Jones continued to believe this was the only logical way of approaching the UFO conundrum 'otherwise one lives in a fearsomely imaginative world in which rational conduct becomes impossible'.[60]

At the height of the 1967 UFO wave Jones delivered a lecture to the Newcastle Astronomical Society and northeast branch of the Institute of Physics. The paper he presented, 'The Natural Philosophy of Flying Saucers', eventually formed an appendix to the Colorado University study in 1969.[61] Jones said that if at any point in the last 20 years he had been forced to make a decision on whether flying saucers were fact or fantasy, he would have fallen back upon his critical assessment of intelligence during the war. His experiences had led him to be sceptical of eyewitness testimony unless it was supported by independent evidence, such as photographs or artefacts. As a result Jones was in no doubt that the evidence was heavily stacked against UFOs being 'intelligently controlled vehicles', although he felt it was possible that some reports might be 'an incorrect identification of a rare and unrecognised phenomenon'. Nothing short of a 'tangible relic' from a flying saucer would dispel his scepticism, but he knew that:

> '…even if the current American and Russian investigations come to the same conclusion … it will not discourage the flying saucer believers. For these investigations are faced with an impossible job, if flying saucers do not exist, of proving a completely negative case.'[62]

Such a task was one of the most difficult intelligence tasks of all, for 'the flying saucer exponents will always be able to conjure new hypotheses that have not been considered'.[63]

Jones received assistance in his research for the paper from his colleagues at DSTI and he told them: 'I am no less sceptical now than I was 20 years ago.' Potts, busy managing the media frenzy following the police chase of the flying cross, replied that his major concern was 'to keep all of this in perspective, and avoid pressures that would tend to force us into diverting too much effort to the pursuit of these objects'.[64]

Carruthers, the head of S4, was equally pessimistic. He told Jones in a private letter:

> 'I too felt that a rare natural phenomenon was a reasonable alternative to fantasy [but] in the last few months my soul has hardened and I now feel that the only possible answer must be fantasy. Like you, I am ready to change my mind when I find a specimen on public exhibition.'[65]

If the most senior members of staff at the MoD really did possess solid evidence of 'the ultimate secret', they were doing a very effective job of concealing that fact even in their own private correspondence.

Chapter 10

THEY KNEW TOO MUCH...

'My new job was rather
disappointing. There were no
flying saucers, no aliens and
there was no dark and mysterious
Government involvement.
Try as I might, I could not see
a Man in Black anywhere.'

Nick Pope, 1997[1]

A major theme in contemporary UFO lore claims that besides taking a keen interest in UFO phenomena, governments frequently send out agents to interview civilian witnesses. In Britain officials from the MoD and RAF police officers have occasionally paid visits to witnesses, most notably during the 1967 UFO wave. Documentary evidence of these visits exists in PRO documents such as the report by an officer from DI61 who interviewed a police constable, Colin Perks, who had reported a UFO sighting in Cheshire in March 1966.[2] On each of these occasions the men from the Ministry made no secret of who they were and may be regarded as civil servants carrying out one of the more unusual jobs the MoD has to tackle.

Rumours of these field investigations have been mythologised to such an extent, however, that an alternate, unsubstantiated history of government UFO involvement has evolved. Some versions of the legend allege the government agents have been dressed entirely in black, acted strangely and flashed official-looking identity cards. In contemporary legend this scenario is known as the Men In Black, or MIB, phenomenon.

It was made famous by the film of the same name starring Will Smith.[3] It is further claimed that the MIB belong to lavishly funded and highly secretive government UFO investigation branches whose brief is to remove evidence and silence witnesses. In popular legend MIB also demand that witnesses do not reveal further details of their sighting, publish it in any way or even mention they have been visited.

While some may dismiss these stories as fantasy, the development of the MIB legend deserves to be examined. Careful study of those instances where there is unambiguous evidence that MoD officials have visited civilian UFO witnesses can tell us much about official attitudes and provide clues towards the ultimate origin of the MIB mythology.

The Wardle Case

One of the first occasions that an MoD official visited civilians was during the UFO flap of 1957. Following a multi-witness sighting which gripped the village of Wardle in Lancashire it was alleged that a series of newspaper articles about the case was halted on the direct orders of the Air Ministry. The sighting itself was unremarkable, but the events surrounding it have been used to support the allegation that the MoD occasionally sends officials to silence both journalists and witnesses who delve too deeply into the UFO mystery.

On the night of 15 February 1957 Gwynneth Fitton rushed indoors and insisted that her mother come outside. Mrs Fitton senior was sceptical, but once outdoors she could clearly see a white 'disc' in the sky from which hung a smaller 'sphere' that changed colour from red to white. As the object floated toward them at treetop level, fear gripped Mrs Fitton and she ran inside shouting, 'Good God, they're here!' She emerged again to watch as the UFO moved over the town of Littleborough and drifted over the Pennine moors.

Newspaper records show the UFO was seen by several other local residents for approximately 15 minutes as it moved smoothly and noiselessly across the moors. The *Rochdale Observer* commented, 'None of the witnesses were believers in "flying saucers" before, but after seeing such a strange sight their disbelief has been badly shaken.'[4]

Shortly afterwards it was claimed that a laundry worker had sent up a balloon attached to a small light and this was responsible for the 'UFO' scare.[5] Could Mrs Fitton have mistaken a small poorly-illuminated balloon for a UFO? Both she and the local paper thought not.

The situation was further confused when a walker discovered a strange metallic contraption on the moors beneath the path of the UFO. The object had a label attached inviting the finder to contact the Air Ministry and on further inspection the object was found to be a radio transmitter which had been attached to a meteorological balloon. Was this the mysterious UFO?

The local newspaper remained sceptical of this explanation and Alan Fitzsimmons, the journalist responsible for the UFO stories, was highly suspicious, writing:

> 'The transmitter was found nearly two weeks after the sighting of the "saucer", during which time there have been considerable snowfalls, yet the cardboard cylinder is perfectly dry and unmarked except for being slightly battered.'[6]

The implication was that not only was the Air Ministry balloon not responsible for the sighting, but that it had actually been 'planted' as a cover explanation for the 'real' UFO.

Parliament became involved when a question about the UFO was tabled in the House of Commons on 30 March 1957 by the Rochdale MP, J. A. Leavey, who asked for a declaration 'that the Air Ministry is not involved in releasing objects which are normally described as flying saucers'. The response from Secretary of State for Air, Charles Orr-Ewing, was that the UFO was merely an illuminated balloon sent up by a local man. He added: 'We have not been launching any flying saucers.'[7] The balloon explanation had been taken straight from the Rochdale Observer, bringing speculation about the UFO full circle without any resolution.

Newspaper speculation continued for a few more weeks then suddenly stopped. The reason? According to Fitzsimmons, who worked on the case:

> '....the very top man from the Ministry of Defence called at our office personally, took us into a private back room, and read the Official Secrets Act to us with the warning to discontinue reporting further on that strange occurrence.'[8]

In 1957 a UFOlogist, Clifford Thornton, also alleged that the Air Ministry official had called upon some of the witnesses, warning them to keep quiet about his visit.[9] However, when questioned by a national newspaper, the Ministry made no secret of its inquiries, stating, 'It is quite true that an official went up to Wardle to investigate.'[10]

A Ministry briefing classifies what is called the 'Wardle apparition' under the heading 'Private Experiments' and journalist Geoffrey Norris was told: 'After [the official's] researches the Air Ministry still maintain it was a balloon.'[11]

The Wardle incident is intriguing and has been thrust into the forefront of speculation that the MoD 'silenced' journalists who published sensitive stories about UFOs. Unfortunately the ministerial briefing on the case, which is referred to in another Air Ministry file, has not survived.[12] As a result the evidence for the 'silencing' is entirely dependent on a contemporary article by a UFO writer and the testimony of a journalist.[13]

An alternative and equally plausible reason for the visit to the newspaper is that the Air Ministry did not take kindly to a provincial journalist making allegations that it had covered up a UFO sighting by 'planting' one of its own balloons and wished to put the record straight.

'D' Notices

In the 21st century it is difficult to imagine a newspaper taking seriously an MoD demand not to publish such a minor UFO sighting. Today such a request would make sensational headlines. Yet the idea of journalists being silenced has persisted for over 50 years.

In an effort to justify this unfounded belief some UFOlogists have suggested that 'D' Notices (now Defence Advisory Notices) have been slapped on media coverage of certain UFO cases to prevent the truth reaching the public. But D Notices are not absolute bans on publication. They are merely requests that editors should voluntarily contact the D Notice secretary for advice if they intend to publish certain types of story. D Notices are rarely invoked and then only in matters where public disclosure of information could damage national security.[14] While the idea of D Notices being applied to UFO stories appeals to conspiracy buffs, such an action would be the surest way of drawing attention to something the government wished to conceal. While no responsible journalist wishes to compromise national security, we believe it would be very difficult for the government to convince editors that any UFO story could have implications which would outweigh its worth as a news item.

The best argument against the use of D Notices to stifle UFO information comes from the advocates of a cover up themselves. Author Tim Good, a committed believer in the alien visitation of Earth, conducted a study of D Notices and contacted several national newspapers and the MoD to ask if they had ever been used to stifle a UFO story. All the responses from journalists were negative and the MoD commented: '[We] can find no evidence in our records that UFO sighting reports have been the subject of D-Notice attention.'[15] Despite this definitive evidence, Good allowed his beliefs to override the facts, concluding:

> '...although we have as yet only circumstantial evidence for the application of the D-Notice system and the Official Secrets Act where some reports of UFOs are concerned, I am confident that documentary evidence for this will be forthcoming.'[16]

Good wrote those words in 1983. As of 2002 no such evidence has been located.

Rudloe Manor

Alongside belief about government agencies silencing civilians, a mythology has grown up about how the MoD carries out its UFO investigations. Some have claimed that millions of pounds are allocated for UFO research, but cannot explain how the Treasury can hide the expenditure from MPs and the press.

As we have painstakingly detailed in this book, UFO reports are initially dealt with by a department situated at the MoD in London. This department may ask other, specialist, departments if additional information is required to resolve more puzzling reports. However, there has been considerable speculation that the MoD maintains a super-secret UFO research establishment at RAF Rudloe Manor, deep in the Wiltshire countryside.

In reality Rudloe Manor has played a vital role in the defence of Britain, first as a radar station and later as home to a number of signals and communications units. In UFO mythology Rudloe Manor is known as 'UFO HQ' and rumours proliferate about its connections with covert UFO research.[17] We queried the exact role of Rudloe Manor in UFO investigation and received this detailed reply:

> 'Until 1992 the Flying Complaints Flight (FCF), part of the HQ Provost and Security Services (UK) based at RAF Rudloe Manor, was the central co-ordination point for UFO reports made to RAF stations (from whatever source, ie members of the public or service personnel). Its function was simply to record the details and pass the reports directly to Sec(AS)2 in the Ministry of Defence. Sec(AS)2 desk officers then examined the reports and decided, with other experts as necessary, whether what was seen had any defence implications. No action was taken on the reports by staff in the FCF. The FCF no longer have any involvement in the central collection of "UFO" reports. All reports by airforce stations are now forwarded directly to DAS (formely Sec(AS)2) for consideration. The extent now of Rudloe Manor's involvement in the "UFO" reporting process, in common with all other RAF stations, is to take down the details of any reports made in the local area and pass the details to DAS.'[18]

This indicates that the sum total of Rudloe Manor's involvement in UFO matters has been to act as a conduit for UFO reports reported to RAF bases – part of an administrative process which leads to the reports arriving at the usual desk in Whitehall. Until someone comes forward with documentary evidence that Rudloe Manor performs a more sinister role in government UFO research, we must take this statement as definitive.

The Solway Spaceman

On the far fringes of speculation into British military involvement in UFO-related phenomena is the 'Solway spaceman' photograph (*see* Figure 21). Although the photo depicts a strange space-suited entity rather than a UFO, it nevertheless remains one of the most puzzling images ever taken. Although the photo itself is often dismissed as a hoax, the circumstances that surround it are frequently used to justify the existence of shadowy MIB-like government agents.

Carlisle fireman Jim Templeton had a passion for photography and on 24 May 1964 took a photograph of his eldest daughter on the Solway marshes. When he collected the processed film the shop assistant said, 'That's a marvellous colour film, but who's the big fellow?'[19] Jim was baffled until he took a close look at the photographs. On one print, apparently standing just behind his daughter's head, was a large figure dressed in a 'spaceman' suit. Jim knew there had been no one else around at the time he took the photograph and immediately had the negative tested by contacts in the police force and by the film's manufacturers, Kodak. Both said the image had not been tampered with and neither could account for the 'Solway spaceman'.

The photograph was soon on the front page of the local newspaper and within days Jim and his daughter had become media celebrities as the photograph was flashed round the world. But the price of this involuntary fame and attention was high, and Jim had to take his daughter out of school because her nerves were suffering.[20]

The MoD showed no interest in the case until the *Cumberland News* asked for their opinion. Officials said they would be pleased to analyse the photograph, but when Jim discovered they required the original film and camera for analysis, he refused and no official file exists to show they pursued the matter further.

A strange event then took place which has convinced many UFOlogists that the MoD was interested enough to send a pair of secret agents to investigate the bizarre photograph. Later that summer Jim was visited at work by two men. They were dressed entirely in black and drove a brand new black Jaguar car. They asked to be taken to the site of the photograph. Jim queried their identity and was shown a card bearing an official crest and the word 'Security'. They told him, 'We're from the Ministry, but you don't need to know who we are. We go by numbers.' Jim noticed the pair

Figure 21: **This strange 'spaceman' appeared on a photograph taken by fireman Jim Templeton of his daughter Elizabeth on the Solway Marshes near Carlisle in May 1964. Shortly afterwards Templeton was visited by two 'men in black' who he believed were agents of the British Government.** (Courtesy of Jim Templeton)

referred to each other as 'Nine' and 'Eleven'. Their lack of knowledge of the area and inability to pronounce local place names led Jim to conclude they weren't local people.

Once they reached the marshes Jim said the following exchange occurred:

'"Pull up on here. This is where the photograph was taken." They asked, "Can you take us to the exact spot?" I said, "Yes." So we walked across, and I said, "This is where the photograph was taken." One looked at the other, and the other looked at him and said, "This is where you saw the large man, the alien?" I said, "No, we didn't see anybody... I never saw anybody." "Thank you very much," he said, and he walked away.'[21]

The men drove off, abandoning Jim to walk a mile to the nearest garage for a lift to Carlisle. He never saw the mysterious MIB again.

This case has become a cause célèbre and has featured in a number of books and articles within the context of a government cover up. Analysis of documentation surrounding the case demonstrates how fact has become entangled with fantasy, with the result that another layer has been added to the MIB mythology.

When we questioned Jim Templeton in 2001 he told us he firmly believed the mystery visitors were sent by the British government. He had also made this statement to UFO writers in recent years and his mysterious visitors have been tied in with all kinds of spurious events in an attempt to keep the idea of government MIB-type agents alive. Jim's photograph has been linked to a figure which allegedly appeared on a Blue Streak missile firing range at Woomera in Australia at the same time.[22] It has also been linked to the testing of similar missiles several miles away across the Solway Firth. No real evidence of any connection between these events, or indeed proof that a similar 'figure' was ever seen at Woomera, exists. Even so, the story would bear some serious examination if it could be proven that Jim Templeton's visitors belonged to an official agency.

As it is, Air Ministry records from 1964 contain only passing references to the photograph.[23] In other instances where a field investigation was ordered the witnesses were contacted by letter or phone and the MoD officers identified themselves by name.

Furthermore, newspaper records from 1964 reveal that Jim Templeton took a very different view of the matter. In September that year he told a reporter from the *Cumberland News*:

'It all looks like a leg-pull to me. I'm sure the men were not security agents and I have no idea why they should want to pass themselves off as such.'[24]

Jim Templeton is a very sincere man, but it seems that his interpretation of what took place on the lonely Solway marshes in 1964 has, like so many elements of the UFO mystery, been coloured by what the media and UFO writers have wished to be the truth. However the photograph was produced, a detailed photographic analysis carried out in 1997 by Roger Green of Bradford University concluded that the image was 'a composite made using some superimposition technique'.[25] We do not believe that Jim Templeton faked the photograph himself, but he certainly enjoyed playing practical jokes. For example, he told us that he had created a fake five pound note for amusement only weeks before taking the photograph to demonstrate his photographic skills. Templeton took the film for processing locally, where, he said, 'Everybody in the developing department knew me.' It is not inconceivable that someone in the processing labs tampered with the film to create the 'alien' image. Within days the image was world famous. That, coupled with the fact that Jim's daughter became ill because of all the attention she attracted, would make it impossible for someone to say, 'Sorry, Jim, it was just a joke.'

So who were the Jim Templeton's mystery MIB visitors? Former incumbent of the British government's UFO desk Nick Pope believes that there may be 'Walter Mitty' types among the civilian population who are prepared to impersonate MoD officials in order to speak to UFO witnesses for their own ends.[26]

Evidence of such individuals is well documented in the MoD's files. One relates the experiences of a Mrs Bowley, who was one of several people who reported seeing a light in the sky over Walton-on-Thames in August 1969. She reported her sighting to the MoD and specifically requested they reply to her. It came, therefore, as no surprise when she was telephoned by a Sergeant Horne who claimed he was investigating UFOs on behalf of the MoD and asked for further details. When Mrs Bowley later checked with the Air Force Operations Room she was assured that no such officer existed. The PRO file on the matter ends with the suggestion that '"Sergeant Horne" be investigated by civilian police and be at least "warned off" impersonating MoD personnel'.[27]

The 'Alien Craft'

Files released at the PRO indicate that the MoD ended its policy of sending officers to investigate the more impressive UFO sightings in 1968, after once again reaching the conclusion that misperception was at the root of the UFO experiences.

This policy was tested later that same year, when a handwritten letter arrived at Whitehall offering the MoD the chance to investigate a UFO seen on a remote Northumbrian moor. It began:

'I know you will not believe me when I tell you that I know the whereabouts of an Alien Craft which crashed about a fortnight ago.'

Volunteer National Trust warden D. Robson went on to describe how while on patrol on 29 December 1968 he:

> '...glanced up at a sparrow-hawk which was hovering above me, and in a break in the clouds there appeared a silvery disc which was coming down very fast but with no noise. It was spinning very fast, trailing smoke. At first I thought it was a plane. But when it was about 1,000 ft from the ground it levelled off and went away north. I must have followed it for about 12 miles when it suddenly just nose-dived out of sight.'

Darkness was only a few hours away, so Robson waited until the following Saturday before trekking ten miles into the wilderness to search for the object:

> '...there it was, a silver disc sticking half out of the bog, half in ... it must have been 100 ft in diameter. It was just like a huge spinning top. I noticed a doorway which was open so I walked in. And what a fantastic sight. All the walls were a mass of equipment. Everything was working, lights flashing and weird noises, but not a sign of life... That is the end of my account and I swear it is the truth.'[28]

Robson's amazing letter was received at the MoD by Leslie Ackhurst of S4. Ackhurst immediately:

> '...phoned P.C. Milburn, the senior officer at Haltwhistle Police station, to discuss the matter, later writing:
>
>> "Dear Mr Milburn,
>> We spoke on the telephone today about the enclosed copy of a letter we have received from Mr Robson of Haltwhistle. We both agreed that the contents of the letter about an alien craft seemed a little far fetched and you very kindly offered to talk to Mr Robson about it. I should be most grateful if you would let me know the outcome of your enquiry.
>>
>> Yours sincerely,
>>
>> L. W. Ackhurst" '[29]

On 23 January 1969 PC Milburn interviewed the witness, but a search for the UFO was cancelled due to bad weather. PC Milburn interviewed

Robson again on 29 January 1969 and told him he intended to mount another search to locate the UFO. Robson then made a remarkable statement:

> '[I want to] admit that I haven't been to the place where I saw the object land, nor have I been in it, but I did see it in the sky and it came down.'[30]

Robson then made a statement, under caution, which makes fascinating and disturbing reading:

> 'On 12th January 1969 I wrote a letter to the War Office, London, regarding that I had been out on Sunday, 29th December, 1968, when I saw something in the sky. It looked like a disc to me with vapour coming from it... This object I saw in the sky seemed to come into land to the north-east of where I was sitting. In my letter I said I had gone to this object and had been in it. I also told P.C. Milburn of Haltwhistle that I had been in this object and that I would take him to it... I now want to admit that I did not go to where I thought this object landed, nor have I been in an object such as I describe. I don't know why I said I had been up to this object or why I had been in it. It just came over me when I was writing to the War Office in London. I am sorry I have told these lies and I apologise for any inconvenience I may have caused.
>
> Signed: D. W. D. Robson'[31]

PC Milburn forwarded these details to Ackhurst at the MoD, who commented, 'In the light of your report we do not propose to take any further action.' And there the matter ended.

This case is highly instructive for a number of reasons. Having received a letter claiming a UFO had crashed, what did the MoD do? Rather than send a covert team of UFO investigators they simply got in touch with the local police and asked them to look into it. Obviously Ackhurst and his colleagues had no way of knowing what, if any, truth lay behind the initial claim, yet they still chose to take no direct action. Had the MoD believed there was the slightest possibility a genuine alien craft had crashed, their course of action would surely have been different. Yet there is no evidence in the file of anything other than one civil servant contacting another. Clearly the man tasked by Her Majesty's Government to deal with the UFO problem was not unduly worried by civilians reporting crashed UFOs, his comments that claims of an 'alien' craft were 'a little far fetched' seeming to indicate that the MoD had no time for such frivolities.

It's possible that Robson did see an ambiguous phenomenon which he could not identify and – rightly – termed 'a UFO'. If he had stopped there his report would have been just another of the 228 reports the MoD received in 1969. But 'just another' UFO report wasn't good enough, so Robson invented a story. This was strung together in a coherent letter and sent to the MoD. Hardly the spur of the moment act as he claimed, it seems to have involved a degree of premeditation. Even when initially questioned by the police Robson stuck to his story and was prepared to lead a wild goose chase in pursuit of the non-existent 'craft'. What made him confess we shall probably never know.

It would be easy to dismiss Robson as deluded, but he was more likely to have been just an ordinary person with an interest in UFOs who decided one day to concoct a crashed saucer yarn. It must be remembered that in 1969 UFO crash stories were rare in the USA and almost unknown in Britain. Yet stories just like Robson's, in fact stories with much less internal logic than his, are today frequently admitted as 'evidence' for crashed UFOs across the world by proponents of the extraterrestrial theory.

The Role of the Military Intelligence Agencies

It is abundantly clear that neither the British nor any other government appears to be covering up any information pertaining to physical aliens and UFOs. However, it would be wrong to confuse disbelief and lack of evidence for extraterrestrials with ignorance of the power of UFO beliefs, when harnessed, for offensive and defensive purposes. Proponents of a cover up by world governments have claimed that Britain's secret military intelligence agencies such as MI5, MI6 and GCHQ have played a hidden but crucial role in the investigation of UFO cases.[32] As the files of these agencies are currently closed to the public, evidence of their involvement in UFO matters is impossible to establish. There are rumours galore, but few outright admissions from named sources.

Peter Cribb, Deputy Director of Technical Intelligence at the Air Ministry from June 1952 to June 1953, recalled receiving numerous reports of UFO sightings:

> 'In the few cases that seemed to have substance we initiated
> further investigation by whatever agency seemed appropriate –
> e.g. technical investigation of material, police, MI5, MI6,
> psychopathic or super-natural experts etc.'[33]

Cribb's statement seems to allude to a general procedure for dealing with UFO reports and it would have been logical rather than sinister for MI5 and MI6 to become involved when it was thought necessary. But exactly what logic could justify military intelligence taking an interest in UFO cases?

During the Cold War, while the military was concerned about the 'hard' threat from Soviet aggression and weaponry, the security agencies were equally worried about the ways capitalist societies could be infiltrated. The 1950s and 1960s were the era of the 'contactees', high-profile individuals who believed they had met and communicated with aliens, often from Venus and Mars. Many contactees had been warned that the Earth would be destroyed if mankind did not stop testing nuclear weapons, 'ban the bomb' and adopt a more peaceful attitude toward its fellow citizens. Within the context of the Cold War, the security services would have regarded those broadcasting this type of message as potential subversives or communist sympathisers. Indeed, a Defence Intelligence memo released in 2002 contains the following statement:

> '...it is not impossible that UFO
> organisations might be used by communist
> cells...UFO devotees usually combine a
> crusading fervour with a convinced mysticism
> that would make them easy to exploit in
> arguments for investigation of UFOs on an
> international scale...'[34]

This was certainly the case in the USA, where Nick Redfern's research revealed how the FBI maintained a hefty file on the flying saucer contactee George Adamski, among others, for these very reasons.[35] Although there is no reference in the file to intelligence sharing with foreign governments, Adamksi visited Britain in 1959 and, given the popularity of his writings with certain officials at Buckingham Palace, it would seem logical for MI5 to have picked up where the FBI left off. As ex-MI5 chief Stella Rimmington's memoirs have revealed, the British intelligence services have always kept a close eye on any subculture they consider to be outside the norm.[36]

Every year new books are produced by authors who held highly sensitive positions in agencies such as MI5 and MI6. Publication is always bitterly contested by the Establishment, who fear political secrets could be revealed, but the resulting furore only adds to the sales figures and attendant publicity circus. If the secret intelligence agencies were involved in UFO investigation, such a book would be an ideal forum in which to reveal the 'ultimate secret'. No such secret has been forthcoming, but hints have been made that the intelligence services had another use for the UFO phenomenon – that of psychological warfare. This area of study has long been ignored by UFOlogists because it does not fit their central argument that knowledge of alien craft is being concealed. It is a far more real, and possibly chilling, scenario.

Psy-ops and 'Black Projects'

One of the first intimations for the use of UFOs as a psy-ops weapon comes from the USA in a 1952 memorandum from Walter B. Smith, CIA Director, to the Director of the Psychological Strategy Board at the CIA. Smith wrote:

> 'I suggest that we discuss at an early board meeting the possible offensive or defensive utilisation of these phenomena for psychological warfare purposes.'[37]

Although unpalatable, it appears that certain world governments are participating in a genuine cover up of their psychological use of or interest in the UFO mythology for intelligence purposes (see Figure 22).

If documents unearthed by William L. Moore from the Cold War era are to be believed, the US military was prepared to spread 'crashed UFO' stories as a screen for covert activities. Following the collapse of Nazi Germany, several of Hungary's national treasures, including the fabled Crown of St Stephen, were handed over to the US military, who decided they should be smuggled to America for 'safekeeping'. They were duly delivered to Fort Knox in an elaborate operation code-named 'Klondike'. The treasure was eventually returned to Hungary in 1978. This would be just another story of political intrigue were it not for one strange fact: according to a memorandum in the US State Department, the soldiers designated to guard the treasure were told the boxes contained 'the wings and engine of a flying saucer'. This type of misinformation may well have been common and, as Bill Moore says:

'Is it effective? Certainly in the Klondike situation it was, because

Figure 22 (*opposite*): **Memo from CIA Director Walter D. Smith to Director, Psychological Strategy Board, 1952** (Copyright: Central Intelligence Agency)

CENTRAL INTELLIGENCE AGENCY

WASHINGTON 25. D. C.

OFFICE OF THE DIRECTOR

MEMORANDUM TO: Director, Psychological Strategy Board

SUBJECT: Flying Saucers

1. I am today transmitting to the National Security Council a proposal (TAB A) in which it is concluded that the problems connected with unidentified flying objects appear to have implications for psychological warfare as well as for intelligence and operations.

2. The background for this view is presented in some detail in TAB B.

3. I suggest that we discuss at an early board meeting the possible offensive or defensive utilization of these phenomena for psychological warfare purposes.

                              Walter B. Smith
                                 Director

Enclosure

unsubstantiated stories about parts of a flying saucer being stored at Fort Knox continue to be part of the UFO crash/retrieval rumour mill to this very day. How many other similar rumours have a similar origin is anybody's guess.'[38]

In his book *The Super Spies: A history of the CIA and the DIA*, Andrew Tully has a chapter intriguingly titled 'Saucers with Ears' that lends credence to the idea that the intelligence agencies are content to allow prototype aircraft to be reported as UFOs. Governments can then truthfully deny that they have any knowledge or interest in the subject and tests of secret aircraft such as the Stealth or Aurora can continue undisturbed. Tully writes:

> 'When an official report reached the Pentagon one day in September 1965 that a resident of Exeter, New Hampshire, has encountered a brilliantly glowing "flying saucer", an officer in Army Intelligence turned to a colleague with a remark familiar to one who has known battlefield action. "I hope it's one of ours, " said the officer."[39]

Using UFO mythology as a psy-ops tool to cover up secret operations and 'black projects' is just one example of how intelligence services have manipulated popular belief to their advantage. Another claim, again ignored by the UFOlogists, was put forward in a book by ex-MI5 agent Richard Tomlinson in 2001. Tomlinson's book was banned in Britain, but copies circulate on the Internet, from where this extract was drawn:

> '...during the run-up to the 1992 UN Secretary General elections, [MI6] mounted a smear operation against the Egyptian candidate, Boutros Boutros-Ghali, who was regarded as dangerously Francophile by the CIA. The CIA are constitutionally prevented from manipulating the press so they asked MI6 to help. Using their contacts in the British and American media, I/OPS planted a series of stories to portray Boutros-Ghali as unbalanced, claiming that he was a believer in the existence of UFOs and extra-terrestrial life. The operation was eventually unsuccessful, however, and Boutros-Ghali was elected.'[10]

The advantage of government agencies using UFOs in this way is that the majority of the work is already done for them. No separate agencies or expensively staffed departments are required, just a rumour planted here and there. The public and media are sensitised to UFO imagery, and belief in the physical existence of UFOs is so strong that the rumour mill will nurture and disseminate stories automatically. Although it is a contentious topic, investigators may find this aspect of government interest in the UFO phenomenon a more fruitful avenue of research than chasing physical craft and alien cadavers.

The incidents related here argue that while the MoD has had a watching brief on the UFO enigma, officials have remained unconvinced of any alien intrusion into Britain's airspace. The incidents also strongly suggest that the MoD has played no part in 'silencing' witnesses or media. Nor do there appear to be any 'hidden' repositories of information where 'the truth' about the alien reality of UFOs is located.

Chapter 11

CLOSER ENCOUNTERS

'Our policy is to play down the subject of UFOs and to avoid attaching undue attention or publicity to it. As a result, we have never had any serious political pressure to mount a large-scale investigation such as Project Blue Book.'

MoD response to USAF questionnaire
on UFO policy, 1965[1]

The great wave of sightings in 1967–68 led the British Defence Ministry to take a serious view of the increasingly weird UFO reports it was receiving from the public. In the USA, opinion poll surveys showed the number of people claiming a personal UFO sighting had doubled between 1966 and 1973, to 11 per cent of the population or 15 million Americans.[2] In the same poll, approximately half of those interviewed believed UFOs were 'real', not figments of the imagination. What was implied by 'real' could be judged by the similar percentage who said they believed there was intelligent life in outer space.

Dramatic changes had taken place in public perception since 1947, when imagination, hoax and US and Soviet secret weapons were the popular explanations for flying saucers. In the intervening years rapid technological progress had placed a man on the moon and opened up the possibility that life could soon be discovered in outer space. Belief in aliens was now an acceptable part of modern life. If it was possible for humans to visit other worlds, then surely aliens might want to travel to Earth?

The release of Steven Spielberg's movie *Close Encounters of the Third Kind* in 1978 marked the high water mark of popular belief in UFOs as extraterrestrial spacecraft. The storyline revolves around an elaborate military/government plot to conceal the first contact between humanity and alien visitors. As the film reaches its dramatic climax, the conspiracy of silence is partly foiled by a courageous scientist and a group of ordinary folk who have been selected by the aliens for contact. Millions saw the film and the semi-religious theme of contact with god-like beings from the sky had a deep resonance in popular belief. The subplot of government cover up reinforced the pervasive UFO conspiracy mythology which had undergone dramatic changes since the first flying saucer wave.

Many UFO clubs, societies and magazines dedicated to investigation and speculation had appeared by the late 1960s. A substantial number of UFOlogists believed the government was concealing evidence and in Britain pressure from sympathetic MPs such as Major Sir Patrick Wall and Sir John Langford-Holt helped to bring about subtle changes in government policy.[3]

In January 1968 S4 took the lead in the production of a formal UFO investigation procedure which allowed staff to draw upon the expertise of a wide range of special consultants:

> 'At the request of S4f (Air), Ops(GE)2 RAF [air defence radar], DI55 [scientific intelligence] and Science 4 [psychology] will join to form an investigating group to deal with cases of exceptional interest or difficulty and carry out field investigations where appropriate.'[4]

Under the new procedure, DI55 was to take a lead role in field investigations and specialise in those cases that involved 'electromagnetic effects' while RAF psychologist Alex Cassie was to be sent those reports 'which contained unusual elements'.[5]

The Brooks Case

One of the first reports to receive a full field investigation was also one of the strangest ever to reach the MoD. Angus Brooks, a retired BOAC Comet flight administration officer, claimed he had a 'close encounter' – a term originally coined by USAF astronomer Dr J. Allen Hynek, who acted as a consultant to Spielberg's film – with a flying object as it hovered above the Dorset coast in broad daylight. This took place on 26 October 1967, at the height of the 'flying cross' wave, but an investigation did not begin until almost four months afterwards.

Brooks was exercising his two dogs during a fierce gale on the deserted Moigne Downs when he decided to take shelter by lying flat on his back in a hollow:

> 'Almost immediately I observed a fine contrail [that] could have been a reflection of a "craft" very high in the sky over the Portland area. This disappeared and into my view, descending at lightning speed, came the "craft", which decelerated with what appeared to be immensely powerful reverse thrust to level out at approximately a quarter of a mile to the south of my position at 2–300 feet height.'[6]

This UFO was unlike any hitherto reported to the Ministry. It was 150 feet in length and had a central circular chamber, from the front of which extended a long 'fuselage'. Three more long fuselages extended from the rear and these moved to positions equidistant around the centre of the craft, so that it took the shape of a giant cross.

Brooks said he remained rooted to the spot for 20 minutes, fearing that he might be 'captured' if he moved. He noticed that the silent object appeared to be constructed from some translucent material, as it 'took on the colour of the sky above it and changed with clouds passing over it'. Finally, the two central fuselages suddenly folded back to their original position and the UFO sped off in the direction of the Winfrith atomic research station.

During the sighting Brooks' Alsatian returned to his side and appeared to be 'very distraught'. He believed that she might have been distressed by a VHF sound emitted by the UFO, although he had heard nothing himself.[7]

Fearing the object may have been interested in the power station or a nearby US naval base, Brooks reported his sighting to the police and the MoD. When the MoD team of Leslie Ackhurst, Dr John Dickison and Alex Cassie arrived at his home they were taken to the spot where the UFO had hovered and Brooks described his sighting in great detail. In what became a replay of the deliberations made by the Flying Saucer Working Party in 1951, all three men were immediately suspicious that such a large object could have hovered for the length of time claimed without anyone else having reported it. Ackhurst's scepticism increased when he discovered that Brooks was a subscriber to the magazine *FSR*. He concluded that the witness had not seen a 'craft' but rather something ordinary, such as a kite or a hawk, that had become transformed into a UFO 'whilst he was in a dream or a near sleep state'.[8]

Alex Cassie agreed that Brooks must have experienced a vivid daydream when he lay down to shelter from the wind. He suggested the dream had been influenced by the news reports of the 'flying cross' or triggered by a 'floater', a collection of dead cells moving in the fluid of his eyeball. The psychologist discovered that Brooks had lost the sight in his right eye in an accident but this had been restored by a corneal graft. An RAF ophthalmologist said an operation of this kind would make Brooks more prone to seeing elaborate floaters, but admitted these would not have remained visible for 20 minutes. The total experience could only be accounted for by the 'daydream' theory and Cassie said Brooks' 'instant knowledge and certainty of the size and distance [of the UFO] and its intent are all suggestive of the immediate and inexplicable awareness which are characteristic of many dreams'.[9] Although he could not prove his theory was the correct one, Cassie thought it 'possible, even likely'. In his report on the visit he could not resist adding, tongue-in-cheek, 'If his experience can't be explained in some such way, then maybe he saw an extra-terrestrial object!'[10]

Scientists at DI55 agreed with Cassie, but added, '[We] think that the probability of there being an E.T.O. [extraterrestrial object] is of a very low order.'[11]

Before the MoD team reached their conclusion, however, Brooks had circulated his report to UFO magazines and newspapers. The Ministry was acutely aware from past experience that any statements made in writing would receive maximum publicity. So, in the letter sent to Brooks, Ackhurst explained their theory carefully and told him the team did not doubt that he had had an experience 'for which no proven explanation can be given', even though: 'We have concluded that you did not see a "craft", either man-made or from outer space.'[12] Not wishing to imply the MoD entirely dismissed the possibility of alien visitors, he concluded:

> 'While it would be intellectually arrogant to dispute the
> hypothesis that in the infinity of space there could be other
> intelligent life ... we have no proof of this [and] our radar cover is
> such that we are also quite satisfied that there is no clandestine
> aerial activity over the United Kingdom under terrestrial control.
> Your report does not give us cause to alter or amend these
> conclusions.'[13]

When the letter Brooks received was quoted in *The Times*, the Under Secretary of State for Air asked the new head of S4, M. D. Hobkirk, for a briefing on the case. Hobkirk said he had considered whether the MoD had been wise to suggest Brooks had been daydreaming, but had decided that it was the right decision because the team had conducted a thorough investigation.[14]

Thirty years later Brooks, then aged 83, was interviewed by UFOlogist

John Spencer. He found Brooks' story had not altered, but he no longer believed that he had seen an 'extraterrestrial object'. He did, however, remain adamant that the UFO was 'real' and not a daydream. Echoing the preoccupations of the 1990s, he now believed that he had seen a secret prototype aircraft and said: 'If you had seen Stealth years ago you would have thought you were crazy…'[15]

'High Strangeness'

In February 1968 S4 investigated the first 'close encounter of the third kind' – a sighting of a UFO with alien occupants – reported to the MoD. A lorry driver claimed a brilliant object had appeared above a road in Devon. He said the UFO landed and disgorged 'five or six figures about four foot in height' before taking off with a brilliant blast of light.[16]

MoD advisors pointed out that stories such as these always depended upon the testimony of a single witness and were never supported by independent evidence. S4 was of the opinion that:

> 'Some must be hoaxes; in other cases [we] would be prepared to accept that the people concerned believe they have seen something; but [we] are convinced that they were victims of some form of hallucination.'[17]

One 'high strangeness' report that was taken seriously occurred in June 1969, when police in Norfolk forwarded two independent reports to Whitehall. The first came from an electrical engineer, Robin Peck, who was described as 'a very level-headed person who has been genuinely frightened by [the] experience'. Peck made the following statement concerning his sighting on 19 June:

> 'I was passing through Bircham when the lights on my vehicle started to dim. Within a few moments they had dimmed to such an extent that I was unable to see, and pulled up on my nearside. As I did this the engine also cut out and I could get no ignition light. Suspecting a fault with the battery, I got out and went to the bonnet. It was then that I experienced a feeling that the air was full of static, and my hair felt to be standing on end. I then saw an object in the sky about 100 feet from the ground. This object appeared to be like an inverted mushroom, approximately the size of a row of several cottages. It was of a very pale blue colour

surrounded by a golden glow. The object emitted no sound whatsoever and remained in this position for a least a minute. It then moved off towards King's Lynn, still without a sound. When it moved off the blue colour appeared to leave a haze trail following the object. I went back and sat in my vehicle for some minutes rather shaken, then by reflex rather than anything else I tried to start the engine and found that everything worked perfectly again.'[18]

Peck's testimony was supported by that of a trainee carpenter who lived in the same village. Near midnight on 20 June he was about to cycle home when he heard a strange whistling noise from above, but could see nothing. In a statement to police he said the noise became louder and grew to an intense throbbing:

'I suddenly felt as if every muscle in my body locked, and I was unable to release my grip on my cycle. After a few seconds the noise disappeared and I felt almost normal again ... it had felt as if I was receiving a severe electric shock and electricity was passing through my body from my head to my feet.'[19]

A police officer testified that the carpenter had burst into tears and 'was genuinely very frightened' when he returned home.

MoD scientists suspected that ball lightning might have been responsible for the two experiences but enquiries found that the skies over Norfolk had been clear at the time, with no evidence of thunderstorms. Unable to explain the electromagnetic effects, the MoD concluded: 'This sounds like a genuine UFO' – whatever one of those may have been![20]

The Condon Report

MoD policy on UFOs was heavily influenced by the conclusions reached by USAF-sponsored University of Colorado study that was published early in 1969. A copy of the project report, *The Scientific Study of UFOs*, is among the reference books on file at the MoD Library in Whitehall.[21] Its main findings were that 90 per cent of all UFOs could be explained as mundane phenomena and little had been added to scientific knowledge by the USAF study of the subject since 1947. The project leader, Dr Edward Condon, found there was no evidence that UFOs 'may represent a defence hazard' and that further expenditure on the study of the subject could not be justified.[22] His conclusions sat uneasily alongside the 30 per cent of cases studied by the project scientists that remained 'unknown' – a figure that was higher than the USAF's own statistics. Nevertheless, the project's findings were endorsed by a panel of the National Academy of Sciences and in December 1969 the USAF announced the termination of Project Blue Book, marking an end to all official investigation of UFOs.[23] The study was widely vilified by UFOlogists, who continue to believe that Condon's agenda was far from impartial.

The Colorado project findings were presented to the British MoD in a briefing paper by Air Commodore Anthony Davis of S4 in March 1970. This concluded that although 'no evidence had been found to suggest that reports represent a threat, either terrestrial or extra terrestrial to the United Kingdom', Britain's policy of low-key investigation should continue.

Davis explained this policy should remain not because the MoD was concerned about a potential threat, but because 'of the need to answer questions from the public which might arise from a real anxiety about national security'.[24] He emphasised that the Condon study's conclusions had made no impact upon the public's 'willingness to believe' in UFOs, noting, 'Recent publicity given to UFOs by the press and television has resulted in an increased volume of reports from the public.'

These exceeded even the great wave of 1967. In 1971 379 UFO reports were received, of which 46 (12.7 per cent) remained 'unexplained', the highest proportion to fall into this category since 1965. More than 100 were received in three months during the summer of 1971, double the total during the same period of 1970[25]. Twenty-three were made within three days of the screening of film depicting a 'UFO' captured by a TV crew in Oxfordshire. The footage was later identified as a USAF F-111 dumping fuel after leaving RAF Upper Heyford.[26]

MoD Official in a TV Debate

Pressure was growing for a 'responsible MoD official' to publicly present the origins and causes of UFO reports, and in January 1972 Anthony Davis became the first MoD spokesperson to appear on British TV and explain government policy to a live audience.

The programme took the form of a pre-recorded public debate, with a panel of experts answering questions from an invited audience.[27] It was recorded in Banbury, Oxfordshire, a town that had become the centre of a 'flap' of sightings over the winter of 1971–2. Initially, MoD staff were concerned that 'Mr Davis could well be a target [for hostile UFOlogists] who profess to believe in little green men.' After much debate, they accepted the more enlightened views of the public relations officers, who maintained that the only alternative was to pull out of the show and run 'the risk of leaving the field to the [UFOlogists], [thereby] giving the impression that we are afraid to stand up to questions'.[28]

The programme began with a film illustrating a range of 'natural phenomena' that often gave rise to UFO reports. RAF Lightnings were filmed flying in low cloud and rain at dusk 'to show the fire-cones of their jet effluxes in re-heat, apparently hovering and then moving sharply away [as] often described in UFO sightings'. An officer from the space-tracking station at RAF Fylingdales appeared on the film to deny that any radar recordings of UFOs existed.

The panel debate was chaired by Desmond Wilcox and included Anthony Davis, *FSR* editor Charles Bowen and a psychologist. In a minute to the Under Secretary of State for Air, Davis said that he found the producer and interviewer 'fully in sympathy with the MoD point of view [as] they have probably had their fill of the UFOlogists'.[29] He added that the official view was similar to that expressed by the psychologist in terms of 'the need felt by many people for a new mythology and hence their willingness to believe that natural things or events may have mysterious or extra-terrestrial origins'.[30]

Captain Schaffner's Tragedy

Davis' comments could easily be applied to an incident that took place 17 months earlier, on 8 September 1970, in which USAF Captain William Schaffner died when his Lightning jet crashed into the North Sea. This tragic fact is the lynchpin around which claims have been spun that suggest Schaffner lost his life while pursuing a UFO. Veteran researcher Tony Dodd has given this case great publicity, based on information received from aviation writer Barry Halpenny and assistant newspaper editor Pat Otter.[31] Yet, although featured extensively in books and magazines, no evidence has been offered in support of Dodd's allegations. They are detailed here as they demonstrate how a dramatic UFO story can arise from UFO researchers' eagerness to 'believe'.

According to Dodd, a dramatic increase in radar trackings of UFOs over the North Sea led the RAF to mount a special operation to track the intruders. Operation Aenid involved 37 observation sites, all in contact with RAF High Wycombe and RAF Rudloe Manor. The information gathered was then forwarded to the USAF.

Dodd relates how at 8.17 p.m. on 8 September Saxa Vord radar station in the Shetland Islands tracked an unidentified target travelling over the North Sea, accelerating from 630 mph to 900 mph. Lightning interceptors were scrambled from RAF Leuchars, but before they could carry out the intercept the UFO turned sharply, increased its speed to a fantastic 17,400 mph and vanished from the radar screens.

Higher command levels within NATO were now alerted and aircraft from three QRA squadrons were ordered to remain on combat air patrol in case the 'thing' returned. It did, and several unidentified radar targets were picked up over the next hour, each shooting away at high speed before interception could take place.[32]

In his book *Alien Investigator* Tony Dodd alleges that several early warning systems and tracking stations were put on full alert, including RAF Fylingdales in the UK and NORAD HQ at Cheyenne Mountain in the USA, and that it was 'almost certain' that President Nixon was closely involved.[33]

Dodd claims that NORAD contacted RAF Binbrook to request specifically that Captain Schaffner – on an exchange posting to the RAF – should be scrambled. Schaffner took off in Lightning XS 894 at 10.06 p.m., not long after he had returned from a training mission. The UFO was now being tracked on radar about 90 miles east of Whitby and Schaffner was quickly vectored onto it.

The information about what followed came from a radio interchange between Schaffner and Staxton Wold GCI station on the Yorkshire coast. According to this information, which Dodd claims was from a 'reliable source', Schaffner could see a conical shape which was so bright he could hardly bear to look at it. This UFO was accompanied by an object resembling a large glass football. As Schaffner closed in, describing the object before him, he suddenly said, 'Wait a second, it's turning … coming straight for me … am taking evasive action…'[34]

At that point the radio operator lost contact and Schaffner's radar plot merged with that of the UFO for a while before losing altitude and disappearing from the scope. Schaffner's plane was found a month later, on the bed of the North Sea, with the cockpit still closed. There was no sign of Captain Schaffner's body.

This is a literally fantastic case and one with massive political implications if any of it is true. But, as with most UFO cases, things are rarely as they first appear. Our research has indicated that the more sensational version of the incident, with its tragic end, seems to have been the product of poor investigation and wishful thinking rather than hard fact. Dodd's story, exciting though it sounds, has little evidence to support it other than the fact that Captain Schaffner did exist and was killed in an aircraft accident in the North Sea.

The factual information available about the last flight of Captain Schaffner tells a completely different story. ORB records released in 2001 show that Schaffner was taking part in a TACEVAL (tactical evaluation) exercise, called without warning, on the night he died.[35] The object of this exercise was initially to locate and identify a target that was unknown to the participants and then to shadow it. Schaffner's 'unknown target' was an Avro Shackleton which 'entered the UK airspace during daylight and remained on station through dusk and into darkness', a time period which matches Dodd's general outline of the events. Pilots from 5 Squadron at RAF Binbrook were scrambled one by one to intercept, identify and shadow the intruder. Dodd claims Schaffner was scrambled at 22.06 hrs, the MoD claim it was 20.25 hrs. Schaffner quickly located the target, travelling at mach 0.95, and confirmed he 'was in contact with the lights but would have to manoeuvre to slow down'. The Lightning pilot who had completed the previous interception and the Shackleton crew saw Schaffner flying very low in a port turn, after which contact was lost. The Lightning was later discovered on the sea bed five miles off Flamborough Head, intact and with the canopy closed. Schaffner's body was never found. The official accident report explains that the canopy mechanism had malfunctioned at the time of the crash and would not operate automatically, resulting in Schaffner having to open it manually. He apparently did so, but never reached the surface and his body was lost at sea. The cockpit closed of its own accord before the plane was retrieved, as the hydraulic pressure decayed.[36]

The MoD accepts that Schaffner ditched his jet in the North Sea, but refuses to discuss any alleged connection with UFOs. M. L. Hatch at the Air Historical Branch stressed that Schaffner died during a tactical evaluation exercise involving the interception, shadowing and shepherding of a low-speed target. He told us:

'The target aircraft in this case was a Shackleton Maritime Reconnaissance aircraft flying at 1,500 feet off the northeast coast. Capt. Schaffner was vectored onto the target and reported he was in visual contact, but no further messages were received, and it was subsequently established that he had crashed into the sea. Captain Schaffner apparently abandoned the aircraft after it had hit the sea, but despite a prolonged search he was never found and is presumed to have drowned.'[37]

This particular story seems to have arisen entirely as a result of UFOlogists believing rumours in preference to official sources. It will be claimed that the official sources are lies and that Schaffner was killed while pursuing a UFO, but this would mean the MoD has openly lied. If this is the case, then the lie will be exposed sooner or later. In the meantime the case serves to demonstrate how layer upon layer of UFOlogical folklore can be easily and uncritically attached to the most mundane of incidents.

'Phantom Helicopters'

The mid-1970s also saw a wave of UFO reports from the north of England which demonstrated how anomalous aerial phenomena were treated by an authority rarely connected with UFO research – the Metropolitan Police Special Branch.

In this case the UFOs were termed 'phantom helicopters' by both witnesses and the media (*see* Figure 23). Helicopters were very much in the news at the time of the sightings, from autumn 1973 to early spring 1974. Special Branch became interested because Britain was under siege by IRA terrorists, who were pursuing an active bombing campaign and had used helicopters for gun-running activities. Several of the 'phantom helicopter' sightings took place in the vicinity of quarries where high explosives were being stored, which only added to the tension. In addition fears were being expressed in the media about drugs and illegal immigrants being brought into Britain by helicopter.[38]

'Phantom helicopters' did not on the whole resemble helicopters but were typical of more traditional UFOs – unusual stationary and moving lights. As with the 1967 'flying cross' wave, the 'phantom helicopters' were seen and chased by the police, who were convinced that they were real flying machines.[39] Yet no photographs were taken and physical evidence of any genuine helicopters was conspicuous by its absence.

The *Daily Mail* quoted Professor John Cohen of the Department of Psychology at Manchester University, who cast doubts on any real helicopter being the cause of the sightings: 'The first reports of the helicopter may have started a rash of them. It is contagious – plant an idea and you get a kind of visual epidemic.'[40]

This kind of psycho-social theorising didn't impress Special Branch. Because of the possible terrorist connections they decided to conduct a thorough investigation. Their hitherto secret file reveals a top-level meeting was called to discuss the matter in London on 21 March 1974[41] (*see* Figure 24). Attendees included three visitors from the Home Office, two assistant chief constables, a superintendent and two MoD representatives. The meeting questioned the authenticity of the numerous helicopter sightings and a small number of radar trackings from late 1973 to January 1974, using information provided by the Civil Aviation Authority and ATC at Preston. Out of the hundreds of sightings received, only three were believed to relate to 'real' helicopters and no terrorist or 'subversive' activity was thought to be taking place. A Special Branch superintendent described the sightings as being 'only loosely connected and may in fact simply be a random amalgam of the frequent sighting reports which are made to one authority or another on a daily basis'.[42]

Whatever its findings, the fact that a high-level investigation took place serves to demonstrate that the authorities were not afraid to look closely

Figure 23 (*opposite*): **Unidentified helicopter sighted in Derbyshire. Metropolitan Police Special Branch report, 22 November 1973** (Copyright: Home Office)

METROPOLITAN POLICE

SPECIAL BRANCH

......22nd..day of.......November.................................19.73..

No. 1 (Plain)

Special Report }

SUBJECT ....
...ntified
...copter/sighted
...rbyshire.

...rence to Papers

....
....

1.   With reference to a report dated 15th November 1973 ▮▮▮▮▮▮▮▮▮▮▮ which includes a list of owners of Augusta Bell 206A Jet Ranger helicopters in the U.K, a type of machine recently seen flying at night in the Derbyshire area; I have made enquiries to ascertain the validity of the circumstances surrounding these incidents.

2.   On Wednesday 21st November 1973 I contacted ▮▮▮▮▮▮ ▮ Derby County and Borough Constabulary who stated that a positive identification of an Augusta Bell 206A Jet Ranger helicopter has been made by a number of individual witnesses including two police officers. The machine was observed on a number of occasions over a period of two weeks to be apparently practicing landings in the vicinity of the sites of quarries and explosives stores in the Derbyshire countryside. The helicopter was last seen on the 3rd September 1973.

3.   ▮▮▮▮▮▮▮▮▮▮▮ has made numerous enquiries to discover the ownership and reasons for the flights from various sources but has as yet failed to establish any positive facts. He has contacted an experienced R.A.F. helicopter pilot with night flying experience who explained that night flying in the Derbyshire area would be extremely dangerous due to the nature of the terrain and to the number of overhead pylons in that area. There is therefore a strong possibility of these flights being of an illegal nature.

4.   I have been requested ▮▮▮▮▮▮▮▮▮▮ that the list of owners of the Bell Augusta helicopters be forwarded to Derby County and Borough Constabulary in order that they may make further enquiries regarding this matter.

▮▮▮▮▮▮▮▮▮▮

Constable

Submitted:

▮▮▮▮▮▮▮▮▮▮

Chief Inspector

S. 698.
-87728/20M (2)

22 March 1974

MEMORANDUM

CHIEF SUPT. 'B' SQUAD

1.   At 2 pm today, 21 March 1974, a meeting was held at
Horseferry House with D H J Hilary in the Chair to discuss
a number of unexplained helicopter sightings at night,
mainly reported to the police in Derbyshire.

2.   Present were Messrs Clayton, McQueen and Montgomery-Pott
of Home Office, Assistant Chief Constable Bowers (Derby
County and Borough Constabulary), Assistant Chief Constable
Laugharne and Superintendent Dean (Cheshire Constabulary),
and two Ministry of Defence representatives. ▅▅▅▅▅▅▅
▅▅▅▅▅▅▅▅▅▅

3.   The meeting discussed the authenticity of the numerous
sightings reported during the end of 1973 and January 1974,
together with some allegedly corroborative reports available
through the Civil Aviation Authority, from the Air Traffic
Control Centre at Preston and Manchester Air Traffic Control.

4.   In the event there were found to be only three 'hard'
sightings and no useful pattern of timing or positioning
was discernible; in addition, no crimes were reported at the
times of the alleged flights. I was able to report that the
Metropolitan Police Special Branch had no hard information
to place potential subversive activities in the area.

5.   However, it was agreed that the sightings could not be
ignored and MOD were asked what facilities they could provide
to assist with identifying the helicopter. The use of
searchlights, radar, MOD helicopters, and the Harrier Jump Jet
were discussed but considered either impractical or too
expensive.

6.   The meeting concluded with agreement that MOD would
prepare a paper on the services they could provide should further
sightings be made, the costs involved, and to which authority
they would be attributed. Furthermore, the police forces
involved were to keep in touch to co-ordinate any further
useful information coming to hand.

7.   No further action is required from Metropolitan Police
Special Branch.

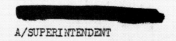

A/SUPERINTENDENT

into any kind of UFO phenomenon and to report their findings accurately and truthfully.

The meeting ended with an agreement that the MoD would prepare a list of facilities they could provide to help the police capture the phantom helicopters. According to the report, 'The use of searchlights, radar, MoD helicopters and the Harrier Jump Jet were discussed but considered impractical or too expensive.'[43]

The 'flap' of sightings ended before any further action was taken and no 'phantom helicopter' was ever identified.

The Berwyn Mountain UFO Crash

In popular UFO lore the phantom helicopter wave has blended into another UFO event, known as the Berwyn Mountain UFO crash. A widespread belief has arisen that the phantom helicopters were real and operated by a secret military UFO retrieval team who had advance knowledge that an alien craft was going to land or crash in the north of England or Wales.

The alleged crash took place on 24 January 1974 just after 8.30 p.m. People across the north of England and Wales saw brilliant lights streaking across the sky, followed by a huge explosion on a mountain, Cader Bronwen. A nurse went looking for survivors from what she thought was a plane crash and saw an unusual series of lights on the mountain. Search parties were sent out, but nothing was found.

The event received a great deal of media coverage and in the 1990s UFOlogists resurrected it and interpreted it as a possible UFO crash. It was at this point that the phantom helicopter sightings were woven into the story, adding another layer and intimating government knowledge and cover up of the event.[44] As with Roswell, anonymous witnesses were quoted years after the actual event as saying alien bodies had been retrieved and there were stories about police and military teams combing the mountainside.

The Berwyn Mountain case is a complex one, but among the claim and counter-claim no factual evidence has yet been presented that a UFO crashed and the documentary evidence that does exist has been ignored in favour of rumour and anecdote.[45] The case speaks volumes for the human ability to make connections between disparate events and create complicated mysteries from rare natural phenomena.

The MoD allowed us access to the UFO reports they received for January 1974. These consist of accounts of lights seen streaking through

Figure 24 (*opposite*): **Special Branch memo, 22 March 1974, re: MoD/Home Office meeting to discuss unidentified helicopter sightings** (Copyright: Home Office)

the night sky from east to west, at times exactly matching the 'UFOs' seen over the Berwyn Mountains.[46] University astronomy records reveal these lights were bolides, bright meteors which fly close to the Earth's atmosphere and often explode in vivid bursts of colour. The bolides were seen from 7.30 p.m. to 8.00 p.m., during which time a localised earth tremor was experienced in North Wales.[47] But for many who experienced the bolides and the tremor, not knowing their source, it *appeared* that something, perhaps a plane, had crashed. Police switchboards were jammed as a result and as the Berwyns had been the scene of several military jet crashes over the years, police and military mountain rescue teams were sent out in case a crash had taken place.

Like so many UFO mysteries the Berwyn Mountain case stems from radical misperception of natural phenomena complicated by the need to believe in the mysterious. These factors, together with a refusal on the part of UFOlogists to make use of all available sources of documentary evidence, have encouraged the development of an alleged government cover up of an alien crash-landing.

The Berwyn case became part of a growing mythology, centred upon the revived Roswell incident, that would become the basis of UFOlogical speculation and belief in the closing decades of the 20th century.

Until 1980 Britain had nothing to compare with the claims that the US government had captured a flying saucer, but a dramatic incident was to occur that would soon become known as 'Britain's Roswell'.

Chapter 12

LIGHTS THROUGH
THE TREES

'I hope that Bentwaters does not
become East Anglia's answer to
Warminster...'

Peter Watkins of DS8, MoD, November 1982[1]

The extent of the MoD's interest in the UFO phenomenon was brought into focus by the sightings of US servicemen in Rendlesham Forest, Suffolk, late in December 1980. The MoD first learned of these events from a memo written in January 1981 by a USAF Lieutenant Colonel (later full Colonel) Charles Halt, who was the deputy commander of a NATO airbase. The incredible events described in Halt's memo were soon to become a *cause célèbre* in the folklore of UFOlogy second only to the Roswell incident (*see* Figure 25).

Until 1993 the twin airbase complex of Bentwaters–Woodbridge, 30 miles east of Ipswich, was loaned to the USAF by the MoD. Woodbridge's runway was circled by the pine plantations of Rendlesham Forest which helped to conceal a highly sensitive storage area for nuclear weapons. The base perimeter was patrolled by armed US airmen from the 81st Tactical Fighter Wing Security Police who would become central witnesses to the UFO incident.

Rumours of a confrontation between military personnel and UFOs near a NATO complex in East Anglia first leaked to the outside world in early 1981.[2] Two local women, Brenda Butler and Dot Street, heard stories both from off-duty USAF personnel and local people who had seen strange lights and objects over the Christmas period. Other rumours came from Forestry Commission workers who discovered an area of the forest cordoned off and heard rumours about an aircraft accident. The mystery deepened when an area of the forest where the incident had reportedly occurred was suddenly felled. The wildest story of all came from an

DEPARTMENT OF THE AIR FORCE
HEADQUARTERS 81ST COMBAT SUPPORT GROUP (USAFE)
APO NEW YORK 09755

REPLY TO
ATTN OF. CD

13 Jan 81

SUBJECT: Unexplained Lights

TO: RAF/CC

1. Early in the morning of 27 Dec 80 (approximately 0300L), two USAF
security police patrolmen saw unusual lights outside the back gate at
RAF Woodbridge. Thinking an aircraft might have crashed or been forced
down, they called for permission to go outside the gate to investigate.
The on-duty flight chief responded and allowed three patrolmen to proceed on foot. The individuals reported seeing a strange glowing object
in the forest. The object was described as being metalic in appearance
and triangular in shape, approximately two to three meters across the
base and approximately two meters high. It illuminated the entire forest
with a white light. The object itself had a pulsing red light on top and
a bank(s) of blue lights underneath. The object was hovering or on legs.
As the patrolmen approached the object, it maneuvered through the trees
and disappeared. At this time the animals on a nearby farm went into a
frenzy. The object was briefly sighted approximately an hour later near
the back gate.

2. The next day, three depressions 1 1/2" deep and 7" in diameter were
found where the object had been sighted on the ground. The following
night (29 Dec 80) the area was checked for radiation. Beta/gamma readings
of 0.1 milliroentgens were recorded with peak readings in the three depressions and near the center of the triangle formed by the depressions.
A nearby tree had moderate (.05-.07) readings on the side of the tree
toward the depressions.

3. Later in the night a red sun-like light was seen through the trees.
It moved about and pulsed. At one point it appeared to throw off glowing
particles and then broke into five separate white objects and then disappeared. Immediately thereafter, three star-like objects were noticed
in the sky, two objects to the north and one to the south, all of which
were about 10° off the horizon. The objects moved rapidly in sharp angular
movements and displayed red, green and blue lights. The objects to the
north appeared to be elliptical through an 8-12 power lens. They then
turned to full circles. The objects to the north remained in the sky for
an hour or more. The object to the south was visible for two or three
hours and beamed down a stream of light from time to time. Numerous individuals, including the undersigned, witnessed the activities in paragraphs
2 and 3.

CHARLES I. HALT, Lt Col, USAF
Deputy Base Commander

airman who insisted that his identity should not be revealed. He claimed a disc-shaped object had landed in the woods and disgorged alien beings suspended in shafts of light. The creatures had communicated with the airbase commander, Wing Commander Gordon Williams, as the craft underwent repairs.[3]

UFOlogist Jenny Randles received a similar story alleging the UFO had been detected by radar before the 'landing'. She concluded that the authorities were going to great lengths to hide the truth about some mysterious incident. This was the period when there was a great deal of speculation concerning the Stealth fighter and rumours spread that it was operating secretly from USAF bases in East Anglia. Some UFOlogists believed stories had been deliberately spread about a UFO landing to distract attention from the crash or malfunction of a Stealth prototype, or an accident involving a nuclear missile.

Ralph Noyes, who had close knowledge of the workings of the military, assured us in 1989, 'Major military mishaps can't be concealed in this country, and not even the stupidest of officials would attempt concealment by seeking to over-excite local UFOlogists.'[4]

In fact a series of nuclear mishaps on British territory were effectively concealed by the MoD throughout the Cold War. The most serious happened in July 1956 when a USAF B-47 bomber laden with nuclear weapons crashed while leaving the runway at RAF Lakenheath. The bomber demolished a weapons store, setting fire to three nuclear bombs. If the bombs had exploded, there could have been widespread contamination, but disaster was averted by swift action by fire crews. This accident occurred during the Suez crisis and just a month before a dramatic UFO incident occurred at the base (*see* pages 130–143). The facts were concealed from the public for 23 years until a retired USAF general admitted there had been a near disaster.[5]

In a magazine article Jenny Randles drew parallels between this cover up and the official silence that surrounded the sightings at Bentwaters–Woodbridge.[6] An MoD letter that emerged in 2001 revealed that Jenny's public speculation had caused far more concern at Whitehall than the rumours about a UFO landing. The letter warned the RAF base commander at Bentwaters:

'[We] would not expect "UFOlogists" to pursue either of these angles any further; if they do, I suggest you refer them to us.'[7]

When challenged directly in 1981–82 the MoD denied knowledge of any

Figure 25 (*opposite*): **Memo from Lieutenant Col Charles Halt, USAF, Deputy Base Commander, RAF Woodbridge, to DS8, MoD, 13 January 1981** (Crown copyright: MoD)

UFO incident at or near the airbase complex. It was not until 1983 that an official of DS8 admitted:

> '...USAF personnel did see unusual lights outside the boundary fence in the morning of 27 December 1980 but no explanation for the occurrence was ever forthcoming. There was, however, no question of the account being a cover-up for a crashed aircraft or testing of secret devices as you suggest, nor was there any contact with "alien beings".'[8]

Colonel Halt's Memo

What began as a rumour became an overnight sensation in 1983 when Halt's memo was splashed across the front page of the *News of the World* (see Figure 18). The headline screamed: 'UFO lands in Suffolk – and that's official.'[9] The paper claimed that 200 military personnel had witnessed the 'astonishing event' but the story was based entirely upon the contents of the memo and the testimony of an airman who claimed he had witnessed one of the UFO landings. He said the CIA had warned him to keep quiet about the events and that 'bullets were cheap'.

Halt's memo was described as a 'confidential' report to the MoD. In fact it was unclassified, but was certainly never intended for public release. It would not have surfaced for 30 years under Britain's then existing secrecy laws. That it entered the public domain was due to American researcher Robert Todd, who obtained a copy under the US FOIA.[10] The covering letter said the memo had been made available courtesy of the British government – the same government that had denied all knowledge of its existence to its own citizens!

Halt's report was not just another case of lights in the sky. Three USAF security policemen reported approaching 'a strange glowing object' that illuminated the trees outside the perimeter of the base in British territory. The UFO was triangular and metallic and it appeared to hover inside the forest before zig-zagging through the trees. It left indentations on the ground and the next morning traces of radiation allegedly higher than normal background levels were found in the forest

The following night, according to Halt's memo, a security patrol again spotted lights in the forest and the rumour spread that the UFO had returned. When the story reached Halt he interrupted a Christmas party

Figure 26 (*opposite*): ***News of the World*, 2 October 1983. "UFO Lands in Suffolk." This was how the Sunday tabloid broke the story of the best known UFO incident investigated by the MoD. Today the Rendlesham Forest incident is second only to Roswell in the UFO mythology.**
(By permission of News International.)

● **Colonel's top secret report tells the facts**   ● **Mystery craft in exploding wall of colour**   ● **Animals flee from strange glowing object**

UFO LANDS IN SUFFOLK

And that's OFFICIAL

...FO has landed in Britain ...d that staggering fact has ... officially confirmed. ...espite a massive cover-up, ...s of the World investigators ... proof that the mysterious ... came to earth in a red ball of ... at 3 a.m. on December 27,

... happened in a pine forest ...e d Tangham ... just half a ... from the United ...s Air Force ... at RAF Wood-...e, in Suffolk. ... American airman ... was a ... s there were three ... in silver space ... aboard the craft. ... cattle and forest ...s ran beneath as the ... aft, a sloping silver ... about 20ft across ... silently glided to ... a blinding explo-... lights. ...t 200 military and ... personnel. British ... American, witnessed ... onishing event. The ... said the visitors ... to earth in the ... se Encounters, but ... OOF that an uni-...ed flying object ... in Britain is ... able.

... key witness is Lt. ... Charles I. Halt, ... commander of the

NEWS OF THE WORLD INVESTIGATES
By KEITH BEABEY

USAF 81st Tactical Flying Wing stationed alongside the RAF at Woodbridge.

With the help of UFO experts in Britain and the U.S. we have obtained a copy of his official report on the incident, part of which is reproduced on the right.

On official USAF note-paper and headed "Unexplained Light," Colonel Halt wrote:

"Early in the morning two USAF security police patrolmen saw unusual lights outside the back gate at RAF Woodbridge.

"Thinking an aircraft might have crashed or been forced down they called for permission to go outside the gate to investigate.

"The on-duty flight chief responded and allowed three patrolmen to proceed on foot.

"The individuals reported seeing a strange glowing object in the forest.

PULSED

"The object was described as being metallic in appearance and triangular in shape, approximately two to three metres across the base and approximately two metres high. It illuminated the entire

inches deep and seven inches in diameter were found where the object had been sighted on the ground.

"The following night, the colonel reported, the area was checked for radiation and readings were found in the depressions and on a tree.

His report goes on:

"Later in the night a red sun-like light was seen through the trees It moved about and pulsed. At one point it appeared to throw off glowing particles and then broke into five separate white objects and disappeared.

WORRIED

"Immediately thereafter three star-like objects were noted in the sky. Two objects to the North and one to the South, all of which were about 10 degrees off the horizon.

"The objects moved rapidly in sharp angular movements and displayed green and blue lights. The objects to the North appeared elliptical through an 8-12 power lens.

"They then turned to full circles.

"The object' to the North remained in the sky for an hour or more.

report was intended to be confidential.

"I have been told very clearly that I would jeopardise my career if I talk to you about it."

But before filing his report Colonel Halt sought advice from the RAF base commander, Squadron Leader Donald Morland, who told me:

"The Colonel sat in my office and was a very worried man.

"The first I knew of these events was when he came to me and related what he had seen. I know Col. Halt well and respect him and fully believe he was telling me the truth.

"In 30 years of service in the RAF that must have been the nearest I have ever been to a UFO. Until that day the colonel came to my office I would have scoffed, but not now.

"I have a completely open mind. It was never seriously thought to be an aircraft in difficulty otherwise the whole rescue fleet would have been put into operation. That did not happen.

"But, whatever it was, it was able to perform feats in the air which no known aircraft is capable of doing.

CONVOY

"I am a Christian and believe that certain things can happen which we are unable to explain. Such as the birth of Jesus Christ. I put the events the colonel related to me down to an inexplicable phenomena.

"He asked me what he

EVIDENCE

DETAIL from Lt.-Col. Charles Halt's confidential report about the sighting of "unexplained lights" and a strange glowing object that lit up the forest.

No HOAX: Brig. Gen. Williams

NO HOAX SAYS THE AIR CHIEF

THERE has been no hoax, says the man who was in charge of the USAF base at Woodbridge at the time the UFO came down.

The wing commander, now Brigadier General, Gordon Williams, said back home in America: "I recall Lt-Colonel Halt's report.

Silence

"I don't know exactly what happened. It is all there.

"He is not a man who would hoax the British Ministry of Defence or the American Air Force Department."

At Woodbridge, all enquiries ran into a wall of silence.

USAF Capt. Kathleen McCollon, chief of the public affairs division at the base told solicitor Harry Harris, a UFO investigator from Manchester, in a letter:

"I was not an eyewitness to the events

and led a group of airmen to investigate, armed with a Geiger counter and a tape recorder. As the team checked trees with the Geiger counter, a red, pulsing light appeared above the trees and animals on a nearby farm fled in panic.[11]

As both incidents were centred upon Rendlesham Forest, outside the jurisdiction of the USAF, Halt reported them to the RAF base commander, Squadron Leader Donald Moreland. He acted as a liaison officer between the Americans and Whitehall but was away on Christmas leave when the sightings occurred. It was not until he returned to the base at the beginning of January 1981 that he asked Halt to produce a report for the MoD. This was sent, with a covering letter from Moreland, to Whitehall.[12] Although Halt may have provided more details to his superiors, he maintains that his memo was never followed up by the MoD. This has remained, until 2001, one of the most puzzling aspects of the whole mystery.

Silence, Confusion and Hypnotic Regression...

More than 20 years after these events the stories of Colonel Halt and the other major participants have been picked apart in magazines, books and Internet publications. Some of the airmen involved have resorted to hypnotic regression to recall details and as a result the stories have grown more fantastic and contradictory. Others who claim to have played a peripheral role in the later events in and around the airbase have come forward offering their own 'experiences' and further muddied the waters. One person has claimed that some airmen were warned to keep quiet while others were drugged and brainwashed in an underground complex beneath the base.[13]

Reconstructing an objective account from the layers of rumour and exaggeration has been made more difficult because of the official silence that has surrounded the events. This has been further compounded by confusion over the dates upon which the incidents occurred, as those that appear in Halt's memo contradict independent evidence both from the local police and the RAF.

The Rendlesham Forest UFO case has spawned five books whose authors have tried to divine the truth from a mass of conflicting testimony. For those who wish to pursue the minutiae we recommend Jenny Randles' *UFO Crash Landing?*[14] and Georgina Bruni's *You Can't Tell the People*.[15] Sceptical interpretations have been put forward by Ian Ridpath[16] and James Easton, who edits an Internet website dedicated to the incident.[17] Despite a wealth of testimony, hard evidence is lacking and the truth no nearer resolution. Although a much clearer picture of the events has now emerged, the debate has become polarised between those who believe there is a conspiracy to hide a UFO landing and those who have decided the airmen were the victims of a complex misperception.

The following account uses original, contemporary material to cut through the mythology. The release of the MoD file on the case in 2001, along with other new evidence, has revealed how the personnel who were responsible for Britain's air defences responded to Halt's sensational report. This has allowed us to assess the reliability of the more recent claims that have been made about 'Britain's Roswell'.

The MoD and Rendlesham Incident

Since 1983, when questions were first asked about the Rendlesham case in Parliament, the MoD has relied upon a standard statement in response to questions from MPs and members of the public.[18] The public stance remains that Halt's report was examined by specialist air defence staff who decided the contents were 'of no defence significance'. This was repeated in a 1994 briefing prepared by Nick Pope during his posting to AS2, the successor to DS8.[19] Pope claims that he was obliged to follow the party line even though he privately believed that Rendlesham had 'an extraterrestrial explanation'. He continues to maintain that there was no cover up but rather 'a lack of action'.[20]

A number of retired MoD officials with an interest in UFOs, including Ralph Noyes and the former Chief of Defence Staff Lord Hill-Norton, have been less charitable. They felt that out of all the UFO incidents reported to the MoD, the USAF report must have been regarded as a potential threat to Britain's defences. Lord Hill-Norton has questioned the MoD about the case on numerous occasions in the House of Lords, while Ralph Noyes summed up his attitude in a 1984 letter to his former department:

> 'The report either implies that Halt was the subject of
> hallucinations or that something not explained in the report
> intruded into British airspace and "landed" in British territory.'[21]

Given the nuclear capability of the airbase, it was apparent that whatever option was chosen the incident could not be dismissed as being of 'no defence significance'. After repeatedly failing to obtain a clear statement from his former colleagues, Noyes concluded the MoD had 'played a thoroughly dishonest game over the Rendlesham affair'.[22]

For those who claim there was a conspiracy of silence, the Ministry's refusal to elaborate upon their bland denials for 20 years was proof of a cover up. Secrecy has been a long tradition within the British Establishment and has encouraged suspicion that conspiracies exist to conceal facts across a whole range of subjects. Although UFOs were never specifically covered by a ruling under the OSA, investigations into sightings often have touched upon areas that remained sensitive. These include the accuracy and performance of radar, as in the West Freugh case of 1957, and the possibility that in certain circumstances even highly trained personnel could radically misperceive mundane phenomena. Both could be deemed as potential weaknesses that could be exploited by an enemy, hence the need for silence.

The basis for the MoD's conclusions was unclear until the release of their file on the Rendlesham forest sightings.[23] We obtained a copy under the Code of Practice for Access to Government Information – a precursor of the British FOIA – early in 2001. The file included documents created from 1981 to 1983 by specialist MoD branches including RAF radar and members of DSTI who had received copies of Halt's memo. Three documents were withheld on the grounds they contain confidential briefings to Ministers that form the basis for the MoD's conclusions.[24] Under current legislation, these briefings will not be released until 30 years after the date they were created.

Nick Pope said the file he saw while serving with AS2 from 1991 to 1994 opened with Halt's memo and consisted largely of correspondence with members of the public.[25] Before the release of the complete file Pope said he had not seen any evidence that Halt's report had been investigated at the time, but in 2001 his story changed. He now claimed that he was aware of the DSTI's involvement all along but had been unable to mention the fact before because of his obligations under the OSA.[26]

These developments have failed to bring an end to claims that the MoD still has something to hide about the Rendlesham incident. It is apparent from the contents of the file that the Ministry was anxious to avoid accusations of 'concealing the truth'. One enclosure contains a 'defensive press briefing' to help officials deal with media calls in the aftermath of the *News of the World* story. This dismisses the more sensational claims and says the article 'appears to be one fabrication after another'. Ironically, the briefing notes that the most unfortunate aspect of the story was 'the fact that MoD refused to comment on the grounds that it was a matter for the USAF while the USAF were saying it was a matter for MoD'. This, it comments, 'will have done nothing but confirm suspicions widely held in UFO circles that we are engaged in a cover-up!'[27]

Figure 27 (*opposite*): **Cover sheet of MoD file D/Sec(AS)12/2/1: 'Unidentified Flying Objects (UFOs); Report of Sighting, Rendlesham Forest, December 1980', released to the authors under to Code of Practice for Access to Government Information in May 2001** (Crown copyright: MoD)

RESTRICTED/UNCLASSIFIED

MINISTRY OF DEFENCE

MOD Form 329D
(Revised 3/83)

S/R
2025

82.

File number

Sec (AS) 12/2/1

Part No. ___ A

1. Attention is drawn to the notes on the inside flap

2. Enter notes of related files on page 2 of this jacket.

DIVISION/ESTABLISHMENT/UNIT/BRANCH

Sec (AS) 2a

SUBJECT Unidentified Flying Objects (U.F.O's) Report of Sighting, Rendlesham Forest December 1980

Date	Min/Encl	Referred to	Date	Min/Encl	Referred to	Date	Min/Encl	Referred to	Date	Min/Encl

Sent Out Date: ▬▬▬▬ 1 - 11 - 00
Ext 344
From DR2e2
Bourne Ave. Hayes, Middx, UB3 1RF.

Debra Bere

3A 3 - 8 - 4

Figure 28:

Nick Pope.
Pope was Executive Officer at Sec (AS) 2A, MoD, 1991–94, during which time he became convinced that some UFOs were alien visitors. After leaving the post he wrote *Open Skies, Closed Minds* and a number of science fiction novels.
(Authors' collection)

Radiation at Rendlesham

Documents in the file reveal that Halt's memo failed to raise the alarm at Whitehall, even though it claimed that radiation readings had been detected both in three depressions left by the UFO on the forest floor and on nearby trees. If the readings were correct there was a possibility that the radiation could have posed a hazard to the public.

Two months passed before Defence Intelligence responded to a request from DS8 for advice on the significance of the information in Halt's memo. DSTI and DI55 both scrutinised Halt's report but said they could not 'offer any explanation for the phenomena'.[28] A note from a scientific officer at DI52 said the readings appeared to be 'significantly higher than the average background' but his conclusions were based entirely upon the content of Halt's memo.[29] There is no evidence that further enquiries were made to obtain more accurate, or independent, confirmation of Halt's claims. The conclusion is obvious – the MoD believed the alleged radiation traces were meaningless.

Figure 29 (*opposite*): **'Defensive Press Line' – UFO Incident at RAF Woodbridge, 27 December 1980; prepared by Pam Titchmarsh of DS8 following the *News of the World* story, 3 October 1983** (Crown copyright: MoD)

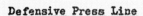

Defensive Press Line

I can confirm that the Ministry of Defence did receive a report from base personnel of a UFO sighting near RAF Woodbridge on 27 December 1980. (This was the report published by the News of the World on 2 October 1983). The report was dealt with in accordance with normal procedures ie. it was passed to staff concerned with air defence matters who examine such reports to satisfy themselves that there are no defence implications. In this instance MOD was satisfied that there was nothing of defence interest in the alleged sightings. There was no question of any contact with "alien beings".

Q1.   Did the US authorities investigate the incident?

A1.   No. Once the report had been sent to the Ministry of Defence the US authorities carried out no further investigations. /Investigations of UFO reports in the UK are carried out by the Ministry of Defence; the USAF has no responsibility in such matters/.

Q2.   Was Col Halt told to keep quiet?

A2.   No. Lt Col Halt has not been told to keep quiet about the incident nor has he been informed that his career could be in jeopardy.

Q3.   Was the object tracked on radar?

A3.   No. No unidentified object was seen on any radar recordings during the period in question.

In 1994 Nick Pope, while serving in AS2, decided to make his own enquiries with the Defence Radiological Protection Service (DRPS). Pope's notes of his discussion with Giles Cowling at the DRPS form the last enclosure in the MoD file.[30] Cowling told Pope the readings appeared to be ten times higher than normal background levels but even this level was 'completely harmless'. He also urged caution because the model of Geiger counter used by Halt's men was not known. Geiger counters used by the USAF were generally designed to monitor the workplace or radiation levels after nuclear accidents. They were not suitable for environmental monitoring of low-level background radiation in the environment as was clearly described in Halt's memo.

In 1998 science writer Ian Ridpath made his own enquiries with the UK Radiological Protection Board (NRPB) and established that the Geiger counter used by Halt's men was not calibrated for monitoring background levels. When presented with these facts Cowling said:

> 'In my original discussions with Mr Pope I did indeed state that the readings were around 10 times normal background levels, provided that the instrument was appropriate for measuring background radiation, calibrated and being used correctly... The use of a high range survey instrument to measure accurately environmental levels of radiation is somewhat questionable and this must throw some doubt on the validity of the data reported.'[31]

Cowling's conclusions were confirmed by the physicist Professor Frank Close during a TV debate with Pope and Colonel Halt in 1997. Enquiries with the US manufacturers of the instrument found that Halt's peak measurement of 0.1 mR/h was the 'bottom reading on the lowest range' of the monitor and was 'of little or no significance'.[32]

Despite these conclusions, Nick Pope claimed in his book *Open Skies, Closed Minds* that the radiation readings are 'the most tangible proof that something extraordinary happened' in Rendlesham Forest.[33] He continued to justify his stance in 2001 by claiming those who dismissed the significance of the readings had missed the point. Although he accepted they were 'quite normal [and] very, very low', he continued:

> 'The point as far as I'm concerned is that they peaked where they peaked, exactly in the indentations and exactly at the tree damage. That to me implies the presence of something that affected the environment.'[34]

Unfortunately, the 'tree damage' at the alleged landing site was not connected with the UFO but was in fact created by Forestry Commission workers in preparation for a felling operation. As for the levels of background radiation found inside the 'indentations', a plant biologist said these could just as easily have been generated by the pine needles which blanketed the forest floor. Ian Ridpath also pointed out that a tape recording made by Halt at the scene confirmed that the readings quoted in his memo were not detected at a steady level and for much of the time hardly any readings were detected at all.[35]

It is odd that Pope, as a former official at the MoD's UFO branch, continues to make speculative statements concerning the significance of the alleged radiation traces at Rendlesham. As Ian Ridpath has pointed out, in order to justify such claims, it is essential that the readings are shown to be beyond reproach.[36] They are in fact baseless and the MoD file indicates this was also the conclusion reached by Scientific Intelligence in 1981. Nick Pope's continued support for these claims can only be explained by his own personal belief that an alien spaceship landed near RAF Woodbridge. In a 1996 interview he stated his conviction that 'on the first night of the activity a small remote craft was seen by the guard patrol [and] trace evidence was found'.[37] Five years later he amplified this statement when we asked what he now believed about the incident:

> 'Despite the fact that I am a non-conspiracy theorist and a
> rational guy, you know that I am a believer in the Extra Terrestrial
> Hypothesis and I will go with the ETH on this one.'[38]

The Rendlesham UFOs on Radar?

Some of the earliest rumours claimed that the Rendlesham UFOs had been detected by radar, but these have never been substantiated. The MoD file reveals that by 1980 a UFO had 'defence significance' only if a visual report could be correlated with a unidentified blip on the radar picture. A 1983 briefing on the case states that the RAF had consulted NATO and been told informally that 'nothing was seen on any radar recordings' for the period of the sightings.[39] When Jenny Randles visited Whitehall with the newly-released Halt memo in August 1983 an official revealed that DS8 staff had recently received a briefing on radar UFO reports by RAF specialists. One of the incidents selected as an example of visual sightings which lacked radar confirmation was that reported by Colonel Halt![40]

Upon receiving Halt's memo in January 1981, DS8 circulated its contents to a number of MoD branches. Action was taken immediately, for within days a team from Military Air Traffic Operations (MATO) at Uxbridge visited Eastern Radar at RAF Watton in Norfolk to check their radar tapes.[41] The MoD's concern was whether Halt's report could be correlated with any unidentified targets captured on radar. The outcome of those checks would be dependent upon the accuracy of the information provided by Halt, a fact that would soon become crucial to the course of events.

In his memo Halt described several sightings of unexplained lights at shortly after 3 a.m., during his expedition into Rendlesham Forest. In 1997 he described how he had 'called the command post, asked them to call Eastern Radar, responsible for air defence of the sector... Twice they reported that they didn't see anything.'[42] These checks were repeated days later because Halt recalled being 'questioned specifically on times and areas of the sky and so on', in contradiction to his earlier claim that he never received any follow-up after his memo was sent to Whitehall.[43]

The involvement of RAF Watton came to light in February 1981 when a story from a civilian radar operator reached Jenny Randles.[44] Although he was not on duty at the time, the man heard the story from a colleague present on the night of 27–28 December 1980. He claimed an unidentified blip was tracked travelling towards Suffolk from the North Sea, disappearing in the vicinity of Rendlesham Forest. Shortly afterwards RAF Watton was visited by intelligence officers from the USAF who confiscated the radar tapes. The man believed this was unusual, but far stranger was the story the USAF men casually told the civilian operators. This was to the effect that they wanted the tapes because a UFO had landed in the forest and the base commander had communicated with aliens – the basis of the story would soon become part of UFO mythology!

Why would USAF officers be so talkative about an incident if it was subject to a high level of secrecy? Was this evidence of a disinformation campaign or simply a rumour that had begun to snowball? Whatever the truth of the matter, it is a fact that although some aspects of the story, such as the meeting with aliens, would later be confirmed as false, others would prove to be accurate. For instance, the radar personnel were told that Bentwaters had called Watton asking for radar confirmation of the UFO sightings made by Halt's team *as they were taking place*. This was confirmed when a radar operator present on the night of 27–28 December contacted Nick Pope. Nigel Kerr remembered a telephone call from Bentwaters reporting 'a flashing light in the sky'. He claimed that upon checking his scope there was a blip hovering above the runway which remained stationary for three or four sweeps of the radar before 'fading out'.[45]

Further information on Watton's role emerged in 1988 when UFO researcher Nick Redfern asked Eastern Radar for confirmation of the story. Squadron Leader Eric Webster told Redfern that all tape recordings from the period in question had been 'routinely disposed of' but he provided a transcript of the relevant entry from the base log. This timed the call from Bentwaters at 03.25a.m. on 28 December 1980 and read:

```
'Bentwaters Command Post contacted Eastern
Radar and requested information of aircraft
in the area - UA37 traffic southbound FL370
- UFO sightings at Bentwaters. They are
taking reporting action.'⁴⁶
```

UA37 was the code for an air corridor used by civilian aircraft which ran north/south approximately 40 miles east of Bentwaters. FL370 signified 'traffic' at 37,000 feet in altitude.

Eastern Radar's commanding officer, Squadron Leader Derek Coumbe, provided the final piece of the jigsaw. It was Coumbe who took the call from Bentwaters, who were in contact with Halt's patrol in Rendlesham Forest. In 2001 he told us:

> 'I recall the incident well, [as] I was on duty at the time it occurred. As far as I can recall there was only one report. I can confirm the report that the call came from Bentwaters RAPcom. They requested that we scan the radars for any radar targets in their area; there were *none*. They reported flashing lights in the Rendlesham Forest area, outside the airfield runway [and that] the base police were investigating the incident.'[17]

Coumbe suggested that if Nigel Kerr saw a blip on the radar this was never reported officially and 'could well have been spurious'. The equipment in use was subject to 'all sorts of spurious returns which dissipated after a few sweeps'.

Following the report Coumbe ordered that all the radar tapes should be impounded for examination. In January they were removed for analysis by the team from MATO that included RAF intelligence and USAF liaison officers. This must be the basis of the rumour that the radar tapes had been 'confiscated' that reached Jenny Randles in February 1981.

Coumbe's story is confirmed by a memo which reports how one film 'of the reported sighting' was at fault. Coumbe added:

> 'On the night of the reported sighting our controller on duty was requested to view the radar; nothing was observed. The facts are recorded in our log book of that night.'[18]

If UFOs had penetrated UK air defences over the Christmas period, they should have been detected by the military radar at RAF Neatishead. The equipment there was linked by computer with the ATC radar at Watton and gave excellent coverage of the Bentwaters area. Checks on Neatishead's tapes were carried out and resulted in the following conclusion:

> `'Neatishead, which is the Sector Ops Centre`
> `responsible for that area, had nothing`
> `unusual to report, and nothing more`
> `substantive has come to light. I have`
> `received no evidence that any radar reported`
> `unusual tracks.'`[49]

This definitive evidence provided the basis for the MoD's conclusion that the Rendlesham incident was 'of no defence significance'. But one problem remained. During their checks on radar in 1981 and again in 1983, the MoD was relying upon the major UFO incident dates supplied by Halt – 27 and 29 December. Unfortunately, his memo contained a number of errors and omissions, the most serious of which was that both dates were wrong! It was another two years before the MoD was made aware of this fact when Ian Ridpath obtained confirmation of the date of the first incident from the duty log at Woodbridge police station.[50] This revealed that two British police constables had paid a visit to Rendlesham Forest in the early hours following a call from the USAF at Bentwaters–Woodbridge. Suffolk Police told Ridpath that the call was logged at 4.11 a.m. on 26 December 1980:

> 'The first visit followed immediately the reported incident and the two officers who attended made a search of the area with a negative result. A note on the log indicates that Air Traffic Control at West Drayton was contacted and that there was no known knowledge of aircraft in that area to coincide with the time of the sighting. The only lights visible to the officers visiting the incident were those from Orford Light House. A further report was received at 10.30 a.m. on 26 December from a staff member at RAF Bentwaters indicating that a place had been found where a craft of some sort could have landed. An officer attended and the area involved did bear three marks of an indeterminate pattern. The marks were apparently of no depth and the officer attending thought they could have been made by an animal.'[51]

When presented with this new information the MoD continued to maintain that the dates in Halt's memo *were* correct, but they must have realised a huge mistake had been made when the case was first investigated. The MoD rechecked the dates with RAF Woodbridge in 1983, but was told: 'The incident is now almost three years old and no one here remembers it clearly. All we have is Lieutenant Colonel Halt's letter.'[52]

The Halt Tape and the Flying Lighthouse

Several references have been made to the 'live' taped commentary of events in Rendlesham Forest on the night of 27–28 December 1980 recorded by Halt on a micro-cassette recorder. In 1984 an 18-minute version of the tape containing Halt's voice and those of a number of other airmen was released.[53] The commentary on the tape is broken, as Halt switched the machine on and off during the expedition.

The MoD file notes that 'tape recordings of the evidence' were handed to USAF General Charles Gabriel, who 'happened to be visiting the station' in January 1981.[54] Gabriel was commander of USAF forces in Europe and a member of the US Joint Chiefs of Staff, who advised the US President. He had flown to the airbase from his HQ at Ramstein air force base in Germany to attend a staff meeting of the 3rd Air Force in England shortly after the sightings in Rendlesham Forest.

In 1997 Halt described how he had played the tape to the base commander, Wing Commander Gordon Williams:

> 'He said: "May I take this to the Third Air Force, to the staff meeting?" I said, "Certainly." Well, I couldn't tell him no. And he took it down and played it to the staff and the General looked at the staff and said, "Is he a credible witness?" and the answer was, "Yes." So he turned to the staff and said, "What do we do now?" and nobody knew what to do. So there was some chuckling in the room and I understand the comment was, "Well, it's a British affair. Let's give it to them…" I was told when he came back, he gave me the tape, thanked me and said, "Get with Don Moreland. Let the British handle this." '[55]

What has become known as 'the Halt tape' is now one of the central pieces of evidence for UFOs in Rendlesham Forest, but rather than providing a resolution, it has added to the confusion. Although the MoD initially felt it may contain further evidence, their file reveals that by 1983 'it was considered that the tapes would reveal no better report than that already received'.[56] Sceptics who have carefully analysed the tape note that Halt's description of the flashing light that 'looks like it's clear off to the coast

... right on the horizon' is consistent with the pulse and sweep of the Orfordness lighthouse five miles away on the coast.

When the *News of the World* broke the story Ian Ridpath became the champion of the lighthouse theory when a film he made was broadcast on British television. Ridpath had visited the forest to investigate the newspaper claims and interviewed forestry worker Vince Thurkettle, who lived close to the alleged landing site. He believed the pulsating beacon of the lighthouse was the basis of the story and pointed out that the airmen would have been walking directly towards Orfordness as they pursued the UFO. The pair returned to the forest with a camera crew at night and saw the unusual effects produced by the lighthouse. Ridpath wrote:

> '...the area had by now been cleared of trees as part of normal
> forest operations, but enough pines remained at the edge to give
> us a realistic idea of what the airmen saw that night. Sure enough,
> the lighthouse beam seemed to hover a few feet above ground
> level, because Rendlesham Forest is higher than the coastline.
> The light seemed to move around as we moved. And it looked
> close – only a few hundred yards away among the trees.'[57]

Halt claims the lighthouse was visible the whole time his team was in the forest and could not have been confused with the UFO.[58] But on his tape Halt gives a bearing for the flashing light of 110 degrees – just 11 degrees away from the true compass position of the lighthouse. In addition, in 1980 the Shipwash lightship buoy was visible from the forest to the right of the lighthouse but was not mentioned either by Halt or the other airmen. Ridpath said it was suspicious that:

> '...at no stage does anyone on the tape mention seeing a
> lighthouse. Halt's own words undermine his claim that he knew
> and recognised the Orfordness lighthouse and make it more
> likely, rather than less, that he mistook it for the UFO.'[59]

Promoters of the UFO case scoffed at Ridpath's conclusion and argued that trained airmen could not have been misled by a landmark that should have been a familiar sight to them. But as the MoD had concluded in a ministerial briefing in 1967:

> '...by and large [UFO] reports originate from
> someone who has seen some unfamiliar phenomenon
> or from someone who has seen something well
> known in an unfamiliar situation.'[60]

The lighthouse theory appeared even more likely when in 1998 the statements made by the security police who witnessed the first UFO 'landing' in the early hours of 26 December 1980 were revealed. It then became clear that the lighthouse had indeed played an important role in the original sightings, even if it could not explain every aspect of the experiences. The statements make it clear that the lighthouse was just one of a series of alternate and conflicting stimuli for the lights seen in and around Rendlesham Forest.

Ridpath's theory can be dismissed only if the claims in Halt's memo are taken at face value. Researcher James Easton found that not everyone on the base accepted Halt's claims that the lighthouse could not have been mistaken for a UFO. He interviewed a USAF security policeman, Chris Armold, who had called the local police after the first UFO reports and had gone to the East Gate of RAF Woodbridge to see what all the fuss was about. He told Easton:

> 'We could see lights in the distance and it appeared unusual as it was a sweeping light... Contrary to what some people assert, at the time almost none of us knew there was a lighthouse at Orfordness. That's one reason the lights appeared interesting or out of the ordinary to some people. After it was discovered that a light was out there the "strangeness" of the lights evaporated.'[61]

In reality, the lighthouse beacon played just one small part in a complex chain of events that began several hours before the first UFO sightings. Shortly after 9 p.m. on 25 December hundreds of people in Europe and southeastern England saw the blazing trail left in the sky by the re-entry into Earth's atmosphere of part of a Russian satellite, Cosmos 749. This spectacular sight was followed, at 2.50 a.m. on 26 December, by the appearance of a brilliant fireball meteor, a bolide, over eastern England.[62] Bolides are frequently misinterpreted by 'credible witnesses', as in the 1974 Berwyn Mountain incident (see page 218), either as burning aircraft falling from the sky or as UFOs.

The original statements made by the USAF security police to Halt on 2 January 1981 all give the time of the first UFO incident as around 3 a.m. on 26 December, within ten minutes of the fireball.[63] Sceptics have pointed out that the chances of the two incidents being entirely unrelated are remote. The MoD would also have been aware of this information when their defence experts assessed the incident.

The Airmen's Statements

As the statements were completed a week after the reported events, they are of vital importance in any assessment of what really happened in Rendlesham Forest. They reveal that two members of a security patrol, Airman First Class John Burroughs and Sergeant Bud Steffens, were the first to see strange coloured lights in the woods beyond the East Gate of RAF Woodbridge. Soon afterwards, they were joined by Sergeant Jim Penniston and his driver, Ed Cabansag. They both saw a bank of yellow, red and blue lights apparently hovering within the forest. Fearing they could have witnessed the crash landing of a light aircraft, the men contacted base security for authorisation to investigate. When this was received, Steffens remained at the East Gate and the other airmen entered the forest, eventually proceeding on foot. It is at this point that events became confused, possibly because the men had become disorientated. Although disregarded by the UFO proponents, the statements imply the three men were wandering through the dark forest in a state of confusion similar to that depicted in the fictional film *The Blair Witch Project*.

Airman Ed Cabansag originally believed he was looking at an aircraft accident and headed towards the light. In his 1981 statement he said: 'We could see a glowing near the beacon light, but as we got closer we found it to be a lit-up farmhouse.'[64] John Burroughs has also revealed confusion about his sighting, saying in 2001 that: 'We did follow a light, not knowing what it was, but at no time did we feel that it was the object we first saw.'[65] This seems to imply that their search of the woods was triggered by an initially unknown, but not necessarily anomalous, light source and then continued in the investigation of another equally unknown light.

In 1981 Burroughs wrote that they wanted to identify what that 'flashing light in the distance was' and 'followed it for about 2 miles before we could see it was coming from a lighthouse'.[66] Why should it have taken a two-mile walk to identify the lighthouse as the source of the strange lights? If the men could misperceive the lighthouse to such an extent this must cast doubt upon the validity of other 'lights' they could not identify.

The existence of these and similar misperceptions of light sources in Rendlesham Forest do not completely negate the possibility that a genuine UFO was present. However, they amplify the fact that both Halt and the airmen, on both nights of the major 'UFO' events, were confused about what they were seeing. The fact that they were fooled to some degree or another by lighthouses, farmhouses and other light sources opens a wider argument as to whether or not the whole Rendlesham case is based entirely on misperception and uncertainty. It is not an argument the UFO believers wish to see developed further.

When interviewed by Georgina Bruni, Cabansag claimed the UFO he saw was to the right of lighthouse and therefore could not have been the lighthouse. However, the position of the light he saw was consistent with the position of the Shipwash lightship! The former airman claimed he did not recall chasing the beacon for two miles or writing a statement at the time, but simply signed a document he was given by Halt. The limited memory he has of the incident was interpreted by Bruni as evidence that he had experienced a period of 'missing time'. UFO proponents believe such episodes indicate that witnesses have been abducted by aliens who have 'erased' their memory of the experience, and often encourage their informants to accept this interpretation.[67] In this instance faulty memory combined with disorientation seems a far simpler and likelier explanation for Cabansag's confusion.

Similarly, Jim Penniston claimed the team had lost contact with security control for three hours during their expedition,[68] but a statement made at the time by their commander Fred Buran states that radio contact with the men was monitored unbroken for the *hour* they spent in the forest. It was at the end of this hour, when it became clear that the men had been chasing a lighthouse, that Buran said he 'terminated the investigation and ordered all units back to their normal duties'.[69]

In the 1981 statements Jim Penniston is the only member of the three-man patrol to claim the lights he saw were attached to a structured object that was 'definitely mechanical in nature'. Both Halt and Bruni claim this statement is a 'watered down version' of the experience. Penniston maintains that the object he saw was not a conventional aircraft, implying that it must have been extraterrestrial in origin. The retired Sergeant has since elaborated on his 1981 statement, claiming he approached a structured 'craft' as it sat in a clearing inside the forest and found himself surrounded by a stultifying wave of static electricity. Although he saw no sign of occupants he said the craft had a smooth shell engraved with symbols that he was able to touch. After a period 'of what seemed like hours but was in fact only minutes' the UFO suddenly lifted off the ground. 'There was a momentary pause – and then literally with the blink of an eye it was gone. All with no sound. That still boggles my mind.'[70] Penniston has subsequently undergone regression hypnosis and now suspects that he too experienced a period of 'missing time' while in the forest.[71]

The story told by Penniston is not confirmed by either Burroughs or Cabansag, who give contradictory versions of their experiences. For instance Burroughs claims he saw lights only. This means that the evidence for the presence of a 'structured craft of unknown origin' in Rendlesham Forest rests entirely upon the testimony of a single witness,

D/S of S/210/83   ∫ November 1983

[signature]

    Thank you for your letter of 19th October enclosing the
one attached from your constituent, Mr Philip Mantle.

    I can assure you that there is not a grain of truth in the
allegation that there has been a "cover up" about alleged UFO
sightings.

    As you will recall from your time as Minister for the Royal Air
Force, reports of alleged sightings are examined by operations staff
to see whether there is any interest from a defence point of view.
No such interest was found in the case of the incident reported in
the "News of the World" of 2nd October, or in any of the other
sightings reported in the UK. In the "News of the World" incident
there was in fact no question of any contact with "alien beings",
nor was any unidentified object seen on radar.

    My Department's interest remains solely in the implications
for the air defence of the UK, as you may have seen in John Stanley's
answer in the House on 24th October (copy attached) to a question
about the "News of the World" report.

[signature]

Michael Heseltine

The Rt Hon Merlyn Rees MP

whose recall has been influenced by the use of hypnotic regression.

The events described by Halt's expedition into Rendlesham Forest on the night of 27–28 December 1980 were influenced by what he described as 'the rumours about what Jim Penniston and John Burroughs had seen' which were 'beginning to circulate out of control'.[72] Given the levels of excitement and anticipation that were generated, it is hardly surprising that a range of mundane phenomena were misinterpreted as something far stranger. In the absence of confirmation by radar or independent witnesses, the claimed UFO landing in Rendlesham Forest ultimately rests entirely upon witness testimony. Investigations into the events at RAF Bentwaters–Woodbridge in 1980 are unlikely to progress further until Charles Halt and the other major participants present more conclusive evidence. In the meantime, the debate between the believers and sceptics looks set to continue.

The case left the MoD with yet another public relations dilemma. Ralph Noyes summarised their predicament when he said:

> 'They have resisted all attempts to obtain a sensible statement, even under sustained pressure. Why? Simply, I think, because it embarrasses them. Either they must admit that a senior USAF officer at a highly sensitive base in the UK went out of his mind in December 1980 – with unthinkable potential consequences in defence terms – or they must acknowledge publicly that weird things occur for which no explanation is at present possible.'[73]

Figure 30 (*opposite*): **Letter from Michael Heseltine, Secretary of State for Defence, to Merlyn Rees, MP, 3 November 1983** (Copyright: Philip Mantle)

Chapter 13

UFOs: No Defence Significance?

'UFOs, the saucer-shaped craft bringing visitors from distant planets, have been with us since shortly after the Bomb was tested in 1945. The sense that the world had lost its cosmic innocence found bizarre expression when mysterious craft appeared in the skies. As extraterrestrial sightings gathered pace (earning the name "flying saucers" in 1947) the craft seemed to carry a religious cargo, offering either guidance, or retribution for human folly. George Adamski, a hamburger chef, was invited by the Space Brothers from Venus to jaunt around the solar system... They wanted to warn humanity of the dangers of its behaviour. Later aliens, sighted when Cold War fears were most acute, were less friendly... modern aliens have been portrayed as Satanists rather than red invaders. Now, after half a century of upheaval, belief in UFOs is declining.'

The Times, 23 April 2001[1]

Signs and omens in the sky have always formed part of human belief and tradition. Sightings of mysterious lights and strange flying objects are recorded in the history of every society, particularly at times of social tension and war. However, it was not until the end of World War II, when the terms 'flying saucer' and later 'UFO' were coined that the mass media began to transmit the *idea* of visitors from space to mass audiences across the world. The invention of the atomic bomb, the guided missile and the jet fighter meant the science-fiction fantasies of H. G. Wells and Jules Verne had become science fact, bringing the dream of space travel one step nearer to reality. In 1954 one London newspaper told its readers:

> '...in an age when the wartime Spitfire is now just an old-
> fashioned flying machine, a Flying Saucer could so easily be just
> the newest prototype out on its test flight.'[2]

The saucer sightings were soon followed by the contactees who claimed to have met benevolent aliens from Venus and Saturn. The beautiful telepathic space people promised their advanced technology could teach us how to live in harmony. Salvation from the space people brought hope to a world living in fear of nuclear destruction. The atomic sword of Damocles meant the optimism of the post-war world was short-lived and Western governments remained fearful of the threat posed by communism.

Fear and suspicion of Soviet Russia's intentions formed the backdrop of the first 'flying saucer' flap and guaranteed that UFOs would be treated as a real threat to national security throughout the Cold War. These fears reached their peak in the feverish summer of 1952 when the UFO invasion of Washington, DC,. brought UFOs to the attention of President Truman and ultimately the CIA, who decided the best form of defence was denial.

Donald Keyhoe's writings were typical Cold War texts which placed great emphasis upon 'official sightings' and the military credentials of those who saw 'flying saucers'. A naval graduate himself, Keyhoe found witnesses who were not hamburger chefs but highly trained observers – air force personnel, scientists and civil airline pilots. Although his belief in extraterrestrials was dismissed by the authorities in public, his contention that the saucers were real, not imaginary, was secretly shared by some of the highest military minds in the USA. For example, a secret briefing prepared by a USAF Air Intelligence special study group in 1952 underlined how seriously governments viewed the threat posed by UFOs: 'The Air Force cannot assume that flying saucers are of non-terrestrial origin, and hence, they could be Soviet.'[3]

The Culture of Silence

The pervasive culture of official silence that grew out of World War II flourished during the Cold War and ensured that all government studies of UFOs would become military secrets. As tension grew and one flashpoint followed another, from the Korean War to the Cuban missile crisis to Vietnam, UFOs could at any moment be transformed from flying saucers to guided missiles or advanced enemy aircraft. It was for this reason that secrecy continued to surround all government UFO investigations until the fall of the Berlin wall ended half a century of mutual paranoia. Despite denials, military intelligence agencies both in the West and behind the Iron Curtain have always collected information on UFOs, while publicly downplaying both the subject and their own interest.

Judging from the official files released so far, very little was done with the material collected by the intelligence agencies. Very few of the more impressive reports were followed up and little if any meaningful analysis of the data was made, despite the protests of a few enlightened defence scientists. As the perceptive UFO historian Peter Brookesmith concluded:

> '...there seems to have been no cover-up of cosmic secrets, or of any specifically UFO-related research project. What was being hidden was the existence of the interest itself.'[1]

CIA historian Gerald Haines notes how during the Robertson Panel era, officials were paranoid about any public leak of agency interest in flying saucers. The policy of secrecy directly encouraged those who believed in a government conspiracy and 'would later cause the [CIA] major problems relating to its credibility'.[5] Alternatively, there is evidence that the CIA's Psychological Strategy Board was secretly encouraging rumours that the US Air Force had captured an alien craft as part of a deliberate psy-ops strategy to spread disinformation to 'the enemy'.

One outcome of what Brookesmith has dubbed 'the overblown habit of secrecy and a culture of arrogance' was a tradition of deep distrust of government that slowly fermented within the American psyche. Distrust of all government statements soon became endemic within UFOlogy. Cries of 'Cover up!' and 'Conspiracy!' remain a staple ingredient of discourse in an increasingly paranoid subject, with the contents of all official documents regarded as possible disinformation or worse. This mindset has been reflected in popular culture in TV series such as *The X-Files*. One 1998 opinion survey found that 86 per cent of the public – including a large percentage of those who said they did not believe in

UFOs – 'expected the Government to lie' or conceal evidence if life was discovered in outer space.[6]

Where Have All the UFOs Gone?

By the end of the 20th century, dramatic military encounters with UFOs, radar trackings and air defence alerts were just a memory. British newspapers began to ask: 'Why does no one see UFOs anymore?'

Fleet Street columnist Andrew Brown has linked the decline in sightings with the more cynical world that emerged from the space race that placed a man on the moon. 'It's difficult for space to be the home of benevolent and wise strangers when we have been there ourselves,' he concluded.[7]

Fashions change both in terms of UFOs and aliens. As future threats grew darker and more sinister, so the benevolent space people of the more innocent 1950s were replaced by the cold and sinister 'greys' who kidnapped helpless humans for horrific medical experiments. And just as phantom planes and rockets had been replaced by flying saucers, so the UFOs of the Cold War era were in turn replaced by 'black triangles', reflecting the hi-tech and dehumanised weaponry employed in modern computerised warfare.

In the 1990s sightings of these sleek Stealth-like UFOs became commonplace in the USA, Britain and many other countries. They led to claims that governments were using the belief in 'alien' UFOs as a clever cover for the testing of advanced prototype aircraft and secret 'black projects' outside restricted military zones. In some cases the huge, menacing aerial apparitions have been associated with sonic booms indicative of aircraft moving at supersonic speeds. In March 1990 F-16 fighters were scrambled by the Belgian air force after dozens of witnesses reported a silent triangular-shaped UFO. In this case the Belgian government suspected the flying objects were Stealth aircraft on a secret mission, an allegation that was twice rejected by the US government.[8]

On occasions during the 1990s the British MoD took steps to check upon the whereabouts of the USAF's Stealth squadrons and the super-secret Aurora hypersonic spy plane during their UFO investigations. In 1996 Defence Minister Nicholas Soames revealed that RAF Tornado interceptors were scrambled on two occasions to investigate 'uncorrelated radar tracks' entering the UK air defence region.[9] These were identified as Russian 'bears' (intruder planes), but no explanation could be found in the case of an 'unidentified aircraft' that overtook a patrol of RAF Tornadoes above the North Sea on 5 November 1990. This incident was the subject of parliamentary question by the late Martin Redmond, MP, who was informed that 'no firm conclusions were drawn about the nature of the phenomena … but the events were not judged to be of defence significance'.[10] The MoD's definition of 'no defence significance' relates to 'an event that is regarded as presenting no direct military threat against sovereign territory'. If that was the case, was the North Sea UFO a 'friend' rather than a foe?

Nick Pope maintains that during his posting to the MoD's UFO investigation branch Secretariat (Air Staff) 2 from 1991 to 1994 he never once came across a UFO report that was confirmed as a sighting of a 'secret' prototype aircraft. Nor could he accept that such sensitive projects would be test flown above British towns and cities when specially designated ranges existed out at sea, well away from prying eyes.[11]

Nevertheless, on occasion the will to believe in UFOs has provided an effective cover story for covert military testing, including blunders that have resulted in terrifying near misses with civil aircraft. The most disturbing example occurred on 21 April 1991 when an Alitalia jet carrying 57 passengers from Milan to London narrowly avoided colliding with a missile-shaped flying object. This UFO passed within 300 metres of the aircraft at 22,000 feet above Kent and was reportedly tracked by radars at West Drayton ATC.[12]

The MoD subsequently claimed that checks had ruled out a military aircraft or missile and an extensive inquiry by the Civil Aviation Authority failed to provide any explanation. The pilot was simply told: 'The investigation has therefore been closed and the sighting will be listed as an unidentified flying object.'[13]

Secret Knowledge or Ignorance?

'...where secrecy is known to exist one can never be absolutely sure that he knows the complete truth...'

Dr Edward Condon[14]

Until the final decade of the 20th century the extent of the British government's knowledge of and interest in the UFO phenomenon remained a Cold War secret. Before then, evidence for official studies of the subject came exclusively from countries such as the USA and France, whose governments had established studies or, in the case of Spain and Australia, had opened their files to scrutiny by civilian investigators.[15] The US Constitution guaranteed a more open system of government and when the Freedom of Information Act arrived in 1974, a mass of formerly secret documents hidden away during the Cold War suddenly became available for study.

By the late 1980s more than 30,000 UFO-related documents had been released into the public domain. The files included dozens produced by the FBI and CIA, both of which had previously denied any interest in the subject. Furthermore, the US authorities admitted that hundreds of additional documents created by more shadowy bodies such as the Defence Intelligence Agency (DIA) and the National Security Agency (NSA), which specialise in electronic eavesdropping, continued to be withheld on the grounds of national security. This decision simply encouraged accusations that the US government was involved in a cover up of evidence for the ET origin of UFOs.

More perceptive commentators suggested that this said more about the agenda of UFOlogists than it did about the actual content of the missing files. In 1982 a judge at the US District Court was told that a total of 239 documents relating to UFOs existed in NSA files, primarily in the form of 'signal intelligence' and 'communications intelligence' reports. In other words, the 'secret' information did not necessary relate to alien UFOs, but more to the sensitive methods by which intelligence agencies collected their information across the world. The court ruled their release 'could seriously jeopardize the work of the agency and the security of the United States'.[16]

A similar argument has been used by the MoD in response to British MPs who have demanded that UFO files should be released to the public. While claiming there is nothing to hide, the Ministry admits that 90 per cent of its records are destroyed at first review, five years after the closure of files.[17] This system allows potentially sensitive material to be weeded out before it enters the public records system. Furthermore, electronic recordings of the air picture that might contain 'hard' evidence of UFOs are retained for just 30 days and their content remains classified as a NATO secret. Even today, the MoD continues to destroy after five years operational records of aircraft scrambled to intercept UFOs in UK airspace. The policy is justified on the grounds that such records are judged to be of 'transitory interest'. This ensures that no one outside the corridors of Whitehall will ever see any evidence that might contradict the official mantra of 'no defence significance'.

Numerous attempts have been made to persuade the British government to allow public or scientific access to official UFO files. In 1967 UFOlogist Julian Hennessey enlisted MPs in a campaign to obtain copies of the MoD's most impressive cases. Although his demands were rejected, MPs discovered that many files predating 1962 had already been lost.[18] Routine destruction of UFO files was halted and in March 1970 it was decided that records would eventually become available under the terms of the Public Records Act, 30 years after the last action was taken on the file. MPs were assured that 'if a major scientific organisation of high standing had strong reasons for obtaining access' then the application would be considered on its merits.[19] Newly released documents reveal the MoD believed it was unlikely that any scientific institution would take up this offer in the light of the negative conclusions reached by the Colorado University study, which allowed the USAF to close down Project Blue Book. Panic ensued in 1975 when scientists from the Royal Holloway College at the University of London approached Whitehall with a formal request for access to the papers.[20] The college's request resulted in an MoD review of 2,600 files dating back to 1962. An internal assessment concluded:

> '... any examination of the papers in S4 custody could lead an outside body to the conclusion that the reports are given very little investigation or lead to questions about the nature of our investigations – questions which we would not wish to get involved in.'[21]

S4 argued that to allow access to the files:

> '... would lead to allegations that we were covering up information when we always maintain in correspondence that the MoD view on UFOs is quite straightforward and we do not suppress facts.'[22]

Not surprisingly, the college's application was turned down.

Another attempt to gain access to MoD files was launched by UFOlogist Jenny Randles in 1978. Jenny was trying to establish a working co-operation between responsible civilian groups and the MoD, arguing that if studies of the phenomena had found no evidence of a defence threat they should allow independent scientists access to official files. Miss G. J. Jamieson of S4 replied:

> 'If UFO reports were made available to public scrutiny every single piece of paper would have to be edited to remove the

identity of the observers, or their written permission would have to be obtained to divulge the information [they had] provided.'[23]

Such an undertaking was considered too costly to contemplate, especially as the problem would be compounded by the additional editing that would be necessary to remove 'classified information' of the type withheld by the US courts in 1982.

Undeterred, Jenny used the influence of a new study group set up in the wake of the House of Lords UFO debate of 1979 to keep up the pressure.[24] Eventually the MoD relented, saying that a decision had been made to publish some of their reports once these had been carefully edited.[25] Copies of standard report forms were released, but most of the vital information, for example the results of investigations, had been deleted, leaving the material useless for research purposes. Nevertheless, the MoD told *Observer* it was now willing to 'consider providing reports on specific incidents to serious inquirers'.[26]

This limited level of co-operation came to an end in 1983 following the publicity that accompanied the Rendlesham Forest UFO incident. Jenny was told that pressure on defence budgets meant it was deemed too expensive to continue processing UFO reports and that historians would have to wait 30 years until the files were made available at the PRO.[27]

Freedom of Information?

This policy effectively continued until the early 1990s, when major changes in government policy led to a sea change in the tradition of secrecy. The most surprising development was the spirit of *glasnost* that was taking root in Whitehall.

The first cracks in the wall of secrecy began to appear when the senior civil servant Ralph Noyes left his post in 1977 as MoD Under Secretary of State, a rank equivalent to that of air commodore. In retirement Noyes produced a novel based upon the Rendlesham Forest incident[28] and made a number of pro-UFO statements, including his personal belief that UFOs were a form of paraphysical phenomena similar to 'apparitions'.[29] In 1988 he went on record to say that a small number of the reports that reached the air staff in his day 'suggested the existence of transient phenomena which could not be explained either by conventional occurrences of a physical kind or by imagination'.[30]

Ralph Noyes was followed into the public spotlight by another civil servant, Nick Pope, who was equally emphatic in his personal belief that there *was* a 'real' UFO phenomenon. Like Noyes, however, Pope insisted that he had seen no evidence that the government was involved in a 'cover up' of evidence of alien visits.

Both Noyes and Pope have been regarded with suspicion by the conspiracy-minded, who believe they are simply pawns in a government campaign of disinformation. Claims have been made that Pope was a junior civil servant whose level in the MoD hierarchy meant that he was never likely to have been involved in the 'real work' that was conducted into the UFO mystery.

This allegation has been demolished by the testimony of those who were involved at a high level in national security matters throughout the Cold War. Most important of all was the testimony of Lord Peter Hill-Norton, who was Chief of Defence Staff from 1971 to 1973. Like Nick Pope, Hill-Norton became a UFO 'believer' in retirement and has been a persistent critic of the MoD's policy from his position in the House of Lords. In an interview with the BBC, he was asked whether he would have known if information about UFOs was being withheld from the public, given his access to UK's most sensitive defence secrets? His answer was: 'I think I ought to have known, but I certainly didn't, and had I known I would not of course be allowed on an interview like this to say so.'[31]

Cynical commentators point out that if both senior MoD staff such as Hill-Norton and Noyes and juniors such as Nick Pope do not have access to UFO 'secrets', then who does?

For his part, Pope has done much to place the facts behind his former branch's role into the public domain and his statements *are* supported by documentary evidence available at the PRO. During Pope's stint at AS2, all work on the subject was based in one office at Whitehall. Information arrived largely via military signals, post and telephone, and with limited resources there was no time for any in-depth research or visits to witnesses. Investigations were conducted via letters and the telephone, which meant the MoD did not even have access to the information available to civilian UFOlogists. Other MoD branches were consulted only when this was necessary, for example in the analysis of radar film. UFOs were just a small part of AS2's responsibilities, which also included non-operational RAF activities such as providing clearance for military and diplomatic flights abroad and handling complaints about low-flying aircraft.[32] These verifiable facts sit uneasily alongside claims made by pro-ETH and conspiracy authors such as Timothy Good, who quoted one typically anonymous 'MoD scientist' to the effect that in 1978 alone £11 million had been appropriated for official UFO research![33]

Those who find it difficult to accept the MoD's remit could be so limited have claimed that UFO sightings that touched upon national security issues never reached Pope's office but were diverted to the secretive DSI who conducted more in-depth investigations. If this were the case the MoD's stated position that 'to date no UFO report has been judged to be of defence interest' would be a blatant lie.[34]

The Role of Defence Intelligence

The precise role of the Defence Intelligence staff in UFO investigation has until recently remained a closely guarded secret. Much of their work related to scientific and technical espionage, which by its very nature fell under the curtain of Cold War secrets. In 1996 the MoD told Parliament:

'It has been the policy of successive Governments not to provide information on the functions of individual intelligence branches when this discloses the more recent nature of their duties.'[35]

The ending of the Cold War has gradually eroded the policy of silence and in 1987 the MoD, through accident or design, released to UFOlogists a collection of report forms that included DSTI and DI55 on the distribution list. The fact that both DSTI and DI55 received three times more copies of these reports than Nick Pope's branch strongly indicated they were very deeply involved in behind-the-scenes enquiries. Since that time UFOlogists have speculated endlessly upon Defence Intelligence's role in UFO investigations, with one author suggesting that the infamous MIB could in fact be agents of one or other of the DSTI branches![36]

The documentary evidence we have presented demonstrates that DSTI (renamed DIST, or Directorate of Intelligence Scientific and Technical, in 1991) has indeed played a significant role in UFO research and investigation dating back to the first 'flying saucer' waves of the 1950s. As in the case of the CIA, this involvement was a direct result of Cold War fears, which included the desire to conceal the nature of this interest from the public. Initially, the intelligence community was concerned that UFOs could be jet-propelled circular aircraft developed by the Soviets using German designs captured at the end of the war. When this unlikely hypothesis was found wanting, natural phenomena became more and more prominent in official conclusions.

Despite thousands of reports no evidence ever reached the MoD to suggest that UFOs existed in terms of terrestrial or extraterrestrial craft that could pose a threat to the defence of the realm. All that emerged from these studies was incredible stories from credible witnesses and the limited field investigations revealed that even these did not stand up to careful scrutiny. The MoD's intelligence advisors became aware how easily trained observers could be fooled by mundane phenomena and could draw upon many examples to illustrate their argument. With more pressing demands upon defence budgets, advisors demanded that funds should not be spent on further studies. The involvement of psychologists at this stage suggests that officials had begun to accept that UFOs were a cultural, psycho-social phenomenon rather than a real or potential defence threat.

This pragmatic stance reached its logical conclusion in October 2000 when DIST informed the MoD's UFO branch that they had 'decided that [UFO] reports were of no defence interest and should no longer be sent to them'.[37] Since 1950 unusual reports had been routinely copied to Defence Intelligence 'in case they contained any information of value relating to their primary role of analysing the performance and threat of foreign weapons systems, nuclear, chemical and biological weapons programmes and emerging technologies'.[38] With the threat from the Soviet Union at an end, UFO reports, whether from members of the public or service sources, were deemed of no further intelligence value.

This decision brought an end to half a century of intelligence scrutiny of the UFO mystery in Britain. With declining official interest, civil servants such as Nick Pope were allowed to take an increasing dominant role as the MoD moved towards dealing with UFOs as a public relations, rather than a defence problem.

A Shift in Official Policy

During his duties at AS2 Pope came to realise the MoD knew little more about UFOs than did the public or the UFOlogists. Nevertheless, his lack of success in accounting for the small number of 'unexplained' cases encouraged a personal belief that alien craft were visiting Britain. To place this in context, others who preceded him on the MoD's 'UFO desk' had access to the same data but reached a completely different conclusion. Pope's 'conversion' to ET reality came about not as a result of any privileged access to secret evidence denied to the public, but in much the same way as everyone else, via 'a combination of interpretation and belief'.[39]

Under the current 30-year rule governing MoD records, we are unlikely to learn how Nick Pope's superiors regarded his pro-ETH views before 2024. However, after leaving his post but while still working for the MoD, Pope began work on a book based upon his time on the UFO desk. Although advertised as 'the first time a Government UFO expert speaks out', *Open Skies, Closed Minds* began with a note that the views expressed 'should not be construed as representing the official position' of the MoD or any other official agency.[40] The book was a disappointment for UFO believers and sceptics alike, as it did not contain any revelations of deep government knowledge or military encounters that were not already in the public domain. As a serving MoD employee Pope remained a signatory to the Official Secrets Act and had no option but to submit his manuscript for clearance. He claims there was initially some opposition to publication, but this faded when it became obvious that national secrets would not be compromised. From a public relations point of view, suppression of the book could even be viewed as counter-productive, as yet another example of a government 'cover up'.

Despite its shortcomings as a history of the MoD's interest in UFOs, the release of *Open Skies, Closed Minds* in 1996 marked a seismic shift in official policy on UFOs in Britain. The scornful dismissal of reports that had characterised the Cold War years was replaced with a more open-minded stance. The new policy of official openness had been made possible as a result of profound changes that had occurred in the culture of official secrecy. This can be traced to the world-changing events that began with the fall of the Berlin Wall and ended with the disintegration of the Soviet empire.

The end of the Cold War meant an easing of the paranoia that had in the past prevented the release of information that, it was claimed, might prove useful to an enemy. How justified this policy of concealment had ever been can be judged by the experiences of journalist Paul Lashmar. He noted how ironic it was that despite the ending of the Cold War, the deeply secretive British Establishment continued to withhold material for reasons that made a nonsense of the 'national security' argument used in the past:

> 'Why is this material being withheld? It cannot be because of the Soviets. They knew at the time. It is the British people who are being deprived of their history... British history is now being written from the American point of view or, more remarkably, from the viewpoint of our former enemies. It is now much easier to get pertinent documents and eye-witnesses to many Cold War issues in the former Soviet Union than it is in Britain.'[11]

While Lashmar's comments were made in the context of his attempts to obtain access to files detailing the British role in American spy flights above Soviet territory, his comments are equally applicable to the MoD's involvement in UFO investigations.

Open Government

Since 1992, when Prime Minister John Major's administration introduced a programme of 'Open Government', the MoD has slowly and reluctantly accepted that the culture of secrecy must soon end. Open Government established in law the right of the public to request the release of files retained under the Public Records Act. As subjects of the Crown rather than citizens with rights enshrined in a written constitution as in the USA, Britons have never enjoyed an automatic right of access to official records. The Code of Practice for Access to Government Information meant that for the first time historians could apply for access to closed records, though files could still be censored or be deemed exempt from release if their contents were 'considered to be sensitive'.[42]

Meanwhile, at the PRO an ever-increasing volume of official papers have been released following pressure from MPs and the press. Even the 30-year rule covering UFO files was successfully challenged in 1999 when UFOlogist Dr Colin Ridyard used new appeal procedures to challenge a decision by the MoD. Ridyard had properly applied for copies of UFO reports filed by pilots and radar stations during 1998–99. The MoD rejected his request on the grounds that a search for data would be too expensive and 'would require unreasonable diversion of resources'. Ridyard's MP took his case to the Parliamentary Ombudsman, whose intervention led the MoD to agree to provide the information as 'a one-off exercise'. In his assessment Ombudsman Michael Buckley welcomed the MoD's decision, but accepted the Code 'recognises that there are limits to the resources that a body can reasonably devote to answering requests for information'.[43]

While the Code of Practice gave only limited right of access to closed files, it was the first step in the hard-fought campaign for a genuine FOIA. A British FOIA was a Labour Party election manifesto pledge in 1997 and a 'watered down' version of the Act was eventually published as a White Paper. Full implementation is now expected to be underway by 2004 and although critics have attacked the proposed FOIA as a toothless version of the more comprehensive right of access originally promised, the results have already been seen in an increasingly open response to requests for information. This book would never have been written without the influence of the impending FOIA and the co-operation of the MoD, which has responded to all our requests for specific files and patiently answered our lists of questions. In doing so, officials have provided us with a picture of a government that has been forced since 1950 by the pressure of public opinion to take notice of a elusive aerial phenomenon that could never be captured and, in the words of the late Ralph Noyes, 'had as much "reality" – as well as the absence of solidity – as any rainbow'.[44]

The Ultimate Secret?

The public wants to know the truth about a baffling subject and because the government is involved it is assumed that it must know the answer. From the standpoint of believers in extraterrestrial visitations, all that has to be done is to force the government to release 'the truth' and UFO reality could be established once and for all.

Unfortunately, to use the words of Daniel Webster, 'There is nothing so powerful as the truth and often nothing as strange.' When information is not forthcoming, or when it is released but does not establish the existence of alien visitors, a deeper cover up is suspected and so the argument becomes a circular one. The idea of an official cover up is belief-driven and can never be disproved, only proved. Meanwhile rumours and allegations of conspiracies, crashed saucers and secret studies will continue to circulate.

We suggest that when all the layers of belief are stripped away and the evidence presented in this book is examined objectively, we are left with a clear picture of a government which is as confused as the public it serves. If any cover up does exist, it is a cover up of ignorance.

From the earliest official studies it was concluded that the vast majority of UFO sightings were due to the misperception of natural phenomena. Even those reports that initially appeared to be backed by the evidence of military radar evaporated when the problems of interpretation were taken into account. As the effectiveness of radar cover has improved, so the reports of radar UFOs have disappeared. None of the official documents uncovered to date have provided any evidence to support the claims of those who continue to believe the US government retrieved an alien spacecraft at Roswell in 1947. In the words of the late Dr J. Allen Hynek, extraordinary claims require extraordinary evidence. Unfortunately, all we have are the claims, for the 'evidence' presented is of the same type as found elsewhere in contemporary legend and folklore – hearsay and rumour.

In the absence of 'hard evidence' the few remaining unexplained UFO cases have been interpreted by successive governments and defence scientists in much the same way as by UFOlogists and members of the public. This has varied from outright belief in alien visitors, as was the case with Lord Mountbatten and Hugh Dowding in the 1950s, to the ultra-scepticism of more rational scientific advisors such as R. V. Jones. As Jones himself predicted, none of the official conclusions will ever be accepted by those who believe in alien visitors, as governments face the impossible task of proving a completely negative case.

At the dawn of the 21st century, Britain, in its pivotal role in NATO, has access to the most highly advanced air defence technology in the world, including phased-array radar and satellite early warning systems that constantly scan Earth's atmosphere for evidence of enemy attack. If we believe the MoD, there is no evidence that Britain's airspace has ever been compromised by what it calls 'unauthorised air activity'. Here is the Ministry's final word on the subject:

'The Ministry does not question the
existence, or otherwise, of extraterrestrial
life forms, about which it remains open
minded. To date we are, however, unaware of
any evidence which proves that these
phenomena exist.'[45]

Figure 31 (*opposite*): **Number of UFO sightings reported to the MoD 1959–2000**
(Copyright: MoD)

The authors would be delighted to hear from anyone who has
knowledge of any UFO incident related to the subjects covered in
this book. We can be contacted by writing to:
30 Clifton Common, Clifton, Brighouse, West Yorkshire HD6 1QW
or via email: aj.roberts@blueyonder.co.uk

NUMBERS OF "UNEXPLAINED" AERIAL SIGHTINGS REPORTED
TO THE MINISTRY OF DEFENCE

1959 - 22		1981 - 600
1960 - 31		1982 - 250
1961 - 71		1983 - 390
1962 - 46		1984 - 214
1963 - 51		1985 - 177
1964 - 74		1986 - 120
1965 - 56		1987 - 150
1966 - 95		1988 - 397
1967 - 362		1989 - 258
1968 - 280		1990 - 209
1969 - 228		1991 - 117
1970 - 181		1992 - 147
1971 - 379		1993 - 258
1972 - 201		1994 - 250
1973 - 233		1995 - 373
1974 - 177		1996 - 609
1975 - 208		1997 - 425
1976 - 200		1998 - 193
1977 - 435		1999 - 229
1978 - 750		2000 - 210
1979 - 550		
1980 - 350		

Figures from before 1959 are not available.

NB. The above figures relate to the number of reports, received
by the Ministry of Defence, of aerial activity which was not
immediately identifiable to the witness. They should not be taken
to reflect sightings of "UFO/flying saucers".

References

PRO class references:

AF/AIR: Records created by Air Ministry and RAF (MoD)

AVIA: Records created by the Ministry of Aviation Supply

BJ: Records created by the Meteorological Office

CAB: Records created by the Cabinet Office

DEFE: Records created by the Defence Intelligence Staff (MoD)

FO: Records created by the Foreign Office

HO: Records created by the Home Office

PREM: Prime Minister's personal correspondence

WO: Records created by the War Office

Introduction: UFOs: A Saucerful of Secrets

1. The earliest official record of British government investigations dates from October 1912, when an 'unidentified aircraft' was sighted above Sheerness dockyard in Kent. In this case the 'UFO' was rumoured to have been a German Zeppelin airship. Winston Churchill, as First Lord of the Admiralty, answered questions in Parliament. He said that the identity of the 'aircraft' had not been established. *See* Hansard, 18, 21, 27 November 1912, and AIR 2/2456. Many similar reports were made during World War I.

2. Bartholomew, Bob, 'The Martian Invasion Panic' in *Little Green Men, Meowing Nuns and Head-hunting Panics*, McFarland, London, 2001, pp.217–23

3. Lashmar, Paul, *Spy Flights of the Cold War*, Sutton Publishing, Stroud, 1996

4. Lashmar, Paul, 'Britain's Secret History', *Violations of Rights in Britain*, series 2, no. 19, www.charter88.org.uk/pubs/violatio ns/lasmar.html

Chapter 1: Where There's Foo, There's Fire

1. Bernard Dye, personal communication, 26 May 1987

2. http://www.project1947. com/foo.htm

3. P. V. Wells, personal communication, 16 August 1987

4. Haines, Gerald K., 'A die-hard issue: CIA's study of UFOs, 1947–90', *Studies in Intelligence*, vol. 1, no. 1, 1997

5. Smith, Warren, *UFO Trek*, Sphere, London, 1974, p.19

6. Air Historical Branch, personal communication, 2 February 1988

7. Quoted in Randles, Jenny, and Hough, Peter, *The Complete Book of UFOs*, Piatkus Books, London, 1994, p.47

8. http://foofig.narod.ru/eng/ foo_fighters_of_wwii.htm

9. AIR14/2076: A Note on Recent Enemy Pyrotechnic Activity over Germany

10. AIR14/2076: Enemy Defences – Phenomena, 1942–44

11. AIR14/2076: Report by crew of 61 Squadron

12. Ibid.

13. AIR14/2076: Extract from raid report M/463

14. AIR14/2076: Rocket Phenomena

15 Arthur Horton, personal communication, 19 May 1987

16 Ibid.

17. Bernard Dye, personal communication, 26 May 1987

18. AIR14/2800: No. 115 Squadron News Sheet, 'Bang On', 31 December 1943

19 Ibid.

20 Ibid.

21. Caidin, Martin, *Black Thursday*, Dell, New York, 1960, p.189

22. AIR 40: Annex to Intelligence Report Mission Schweinfurt, 16 October 1943

23. Quoted in Rickard, Bob, 'The F.T. Interview', *Fortean Times*, no. 64, Aug/Sept 1992

24. Quoted in Randles, Jenny, and Hough, Peter, *The Complete Book of UFOs*, Piatkus Books, London, 1994, p.47

25. AIR14/2076: Rocket Phenomena, 8 February 1944

26. Ibid.

27. Ibid.

28. Edwards, Frank, *Flying Saucers Here and Now!*, Lyle Stuart, New York, 1960, p.77

29. Letter from Air Marshal Sir Victor Goddard, *Flying Saucer Review*, vol. 24, no. 1, 1978, 30–31

30. Churchill Archives Centre, R. V. Jones Papers, RVJO D145: Letter from R. V. Jones to Hadrian Jeffs, 22 January 1996

Chapter 2: Ghost Rockets from Erehwon

1. Comment made in a speech at CIA Headquarters on 26 October 1993 http://www.cia.gov/csi/studies/95unc lass/Jones.html

2. DEFE 44/119: DSI/JTIC Report No. 7: Unidentified Flying Objects, 1951

3. Jones, R. V., *Most Secret War*, Hamish Hamilton, London, 1978

4. FO371/56951: Memo from War Office, 6 July 1946

5. 'Ghost Rockets over Sweden', *Daily Telegraph*, London, 12 July 1946

6. FO371/56988: Memo from C. B. Jerram (Stockholm) to Foreign Office, 13 July 1946

7. Ibid.

8. Ibid.

9. Ibid.

10. FO371/56988: Memo from C. B. Jerram (Stockholm) to Foreign Office, 19 July 1946

11. FO371/56951: Reports on Suspected V-Weapons over the Baltic

12. Ibid.

13. Ibid.

14. FO371/56951: Memo from British Legation (Helsinki) to Foreign Office, 22 July 1946

15. Ibid.

16. FO371/56951: Memo from Mr Henderson (Stockholm) to Foreign Office, 27 July 1946

17. Anders Liljegren, 'General Doolittle and the Ghost Rockets' in *UFO 1947–1997*, eds Hilary Evans and Dennis Stacey, John Brown Publishing Ltd, London, 1997, pp.35–42

18. Quoted ibid.

19. FO371/56951: Memo from R. Hankey (Foreign Office) to Stockholm, 3 August 1946

20. FO371/56951: Memo from Air Attaché (Stockholm), 22 August 1946

21. Ibid.

22. 'Sweden denies asking for radar experts', *Scotsman*, 23 August 1946

23. FO371/56951: Memo from Mr Henderson (Stockholm), 26

August, handwritten note with undecipherable signature added 30 August 1946

24. FO371/56951: Memo from Air Attaché (Stockholm), 22 August 1946

25. FO371/56951: Memo from J. Henderson (Stockholm) to Rt. Hon. Clement Atlee, 26 August 1946

26. Clifford, Alexander, 'Spook bombs over Sweden', *Daily Mail*, London, 3 September 1946

27. Ibid.

28. Ibid.

29. Ibid.

30. Quoted in 'Ghost rockets "slander" – Soviet denial', *Daily Telegraph*, London, 4 September 1946

31. 'Investigation of Missile Activity over Scandinavia' (Science) AI2(g), 9 September 1946. Almost certainly authored by R. V. Jones.

32. 'Mystery rocket over Sweden', *Daily Telegraph*, London, 6 September 1946

33. DEFE10/493: DSI/JTIC Alleged Flights of Missiles over Scandinavia, 1946

34. Jones, R. V., *Most Secret War*, Hamish Hamilton, London, 1978, pp.510–13

35. Ibid.

36. Ibid.

37. Ibid.

38. FO371/56951: Memo from Cabinet Offices, 16 September 1946

39. Ibid.

40. Quoted in Liljegren, Anders, and Svahn, Clas, 'Ghost Rockets and Phantom Aircraft' in *Phenomenon: Forty Years of Flying Saucers*, McDonald, London, 1988

41. Liljegren, A., and Svahn, C., 'Sweden's Ghost Rocket Delusion of 1946' in *UFOs and Alien Contact*, eds R. Bartholemew and G. Howard, Prometheus, New York, 1988

42. Ibid.

Chapter 3: The Coming of the Saucers

1. Ayto, John, *20th Century Words*, Oxford University Press, Oxford, 1999, p.275

2. Latham, Colin, *An ABC of Radar*, Marconi Radar, Chelmsford, 1983

3. 'Ghost plane over coast, RAF spot it – can't catch it', *Daily Mail*, London, 29 April 1947

4. David Richards, personal communication, 22 January 2001

5. Ibid.

6. AIR 29/1370: ORBs, Eastern Sector Fighter HQ, 1947

7. Air Ministry memo, 8 August 1947, copied to FBI (Project Blue Book files, National Archives, Washington DC)

8. AIR 29/1597: ORBs, RAF Trimley Heath, 1947

9. Air Ministry memo, op. cit.

10. David Richards, op. cit., 19 February 2001

11. Ibid., 22 January 2001

12. Air Ministry memo, op. cit.

13. AIR 29/1369: ORBs, RAF Neatishead, 1947

14. AIR 29/1930: ORBs, Northern Signals HQ, 1947

15. Ibid.

16. AIR 29/1370 and AIR 29/1369

17 Group Captain W. Kent, personal communication, 24 June 2001

18. AIR 29/1370

19. Mike Hall, personal communication, 1 October 2000, quoting from Edward J. Ruppelt's personal papers

20. AIR 29/1369

21. *Daily Telegraph*, London, 2 May 1947

22. *Yorkshire Post*, Leeds, 30 April 1947

23. Ibid.

24. Ibid.

25. Arnold, Kenneth, 'What Happened on June 24, 1947?' in *UFO*

1947–1997, eds Hilary Evans and Dennis Stacy, John Brown Publishing Ltd, London, 1997, pp.28–35

26. *Times-News*, Twin Falls, Idaho, 27 June 1947

27. Durant, Robert, 'Public Opinion Polls and UFOs' in Evans and Stacy, op. cit., pp.230–40

28. Quoted in Devereux, P., and Brookesmith, P., *UFOs and Ufology*, Blandford Press, London, 1997, p.25

29. 'Flying saucers ablaze in sky', *Daily Express*, London, 4 July 1947

30. *Yorkshire Post*, Leeds, 9 July 1947

31. *Daily Express*, London, 14 July 1947; *Buenos Aires Herald*, Buenos Aires, 22 July 1947

32. Clark, J., *UFO Encyclopedia*, vol. II, Omnigraphics, Detroit, 1998, p.747

33. Ruppelt, Edward J., *The Report on UFOs*, Gollancz, London, 1956, pp.54–55

34. Ibid.

35. DEFE 44/119: DSI/JTIC Report No. 7: Unidentified Flying Objects, 1951, p.2

36. Clark, op. cit., pp.603–607

37. Ruppelt, op. cit., pp.61–62

38. Ibid.

39. Ibid., p.62

40. Randle, K., *The UFO Casebook*, Warner Books, New York, 1989

41. *Daily Express, Daily Telegraph, The Times, Hong Kong Telegraph*, 9 July 1947

42. Berlitz, Charles, and Moore, William, *The Roswell Incident*, Grosset & Dunlap, New York, 1980

43. 'The Roswell Incident', US National Archives and Records Administration, USAF Fact Sheet: www.nara.gov/foia/bluebk.html

44. Ruppelt, op. cit., p.122

45. DEFE 41/117: Unorthodox Aircraft 1949–50; DEFE 41/118: Unorthodox Aircraft 1950–52

46. Keyhoe, Donald, *The Flying Saucers are Real*, Fawcett Publications, New York, 1950

47. Scully, Frank, *Behind the Flying Saucers*, Henry Holt, New York, 1950

48. Heard, Gerald, *The Riddle of the Flying Saucers: Is another world watching?*, Carroll & Nicholson, London, 1950

49. *See* Redfern, Nick, *The FBI Files*, Simon & Schuster, London, 1998, p.225

50. Keyhoe, pp.188–89

51. DEFE 41/117

52. *Sunday Dispatch*, London, 14 April 1957

53. *News Chronicle*, London, 31 October 1950

54. FO 371/81093: Flying Saucers over Asmara Airport, Ethiopia

55. AIR 20/7390: Unidentified Aircraft/Objects

56. Ibid.

57. Ibid.

Chapter 4: Flying Saucers: By Royal Appointment

1. *Sunday Dispatch*, London, 1 October 1950

2. Ziegler, Phillip, *Mountbatten: The Official Biography*, BCA, London, 1985, p.38

3. Broadlands Archive BAI 172: Letter from Mountbatten to Charles Eade, 26 March 1950

4. Ibid.

5. Ibid.

6. Ibid.

7. Ibid.

8. *Sunday Dispatch*, op. cit.

9. Broadlands Archive: BAI 172: Statement by Mountbatten dated 23 February 1955

10. Leslie, Desmond, 'Did Flying Saucers Land at Broadlands?', *FSR* 26/5 (September/October 1981), 4

11. BAI 172: Letter from Captain R. V. Brockman, The Admiralty, to Margaret Church, 15 April 1955

12. BAI 172: Letter from Mountbatten to J. Leslie Otley, 19 July 1961

13. Creighton, Gordon, 'The "Monty Python Foot" ', *FSR* 41/3 (Autumn 1996), 24

14. Creighton, Gordon, 'An Early British Naval Sighting', *FSR* 28/3 (May/June 1983), 21–22

15. *Los Angeles Examiner*, Los Angeles, 22 May 1955, quoted in *FSR* 1/3 (July/August 1955), 6

16. Ibid.

17. Creighton, 'The "Monty Python Foot",' op. cit., 25

18. Redfern, Nick, *Cosmic Crashes*, Simon & Schuster, London, 1999, pp.23–28

19. Brunvand, Jan Harold, *The Choking Doberman and Other New 'Urban' Legends*, W. W. Norton & Co., London, 1994, pp.198–99

20. Bruni, Georgina, *You Can't Tell the People*, Sidgwick & Jackson, London, 2000, pp.2–4

21. BAI 172: Letter from Captain R. V. Brockman, The Admiralty, to Ted Bloecher, 25 March 1959

22. *Wall Street Journal*, New York, 28 August 1989

23. *See* Randles, Jenny, and Fuller, Paul, *Crop Circles: A mystery solved*, Robert Hale, London, 1993, p.93

24. *Sun*, London, 26 March 1969, quoted in *Spacelink* 6/1 (July 1969), 8

25. Horsley, Peter, *Sounds from Another Room*, Leo Cooper, London, 1997, pp.177–78

26. *Sunday Express*, London, 17 July 1955

27. Good, Timothy, *Above Top Secret*, Sidgwick & Jackson, London, 1987, p.37

28. Creighton, Gordon, 'The "Monty Python Foot" ', *FSR* 41/3 (Autumn 1996), 23–24

29. Horsley, op. cit., pp.172–73

30. Interview with Sir Peter Horsley, 11 November 2000

31. Horsley, op. cit., pp.174–76

32. Geoffrey Smythe, personal communication, 2 March 2001

33. *Sunday Dispatch*, London, 28 March 1954

34. Horsley, op. cit., p.179

35. Ibid.

36. Ibid.

37. Ibid., p.180

38. *Sunday Dispatch*, London, 11 July 1954

39. Ibid.

40. Interview with Sir Peter Horsley, 11 November 2000

41. Horsley, Peter, *Sounds from Another Room*, Leo Cooper, London, 1997, pp.181–95

42. Quoted in the *Adelaide Advertiser*, Adelaide, 16 July 1997

43. Geoffrey Smythe, personal communication, 2 March 2001

44. *The Times*, London, 21 May 1959

Chapter 5: Britain's Flying Saucer Study

1. Quoted in the *Sunday Dispatch*, London, 2 July 1950

2. Barfield, Norman, 'Tim Woodman: Deadly in the darkness' (Obituary), *Guardian*, London, 27 July 1996

3. Woodman, R. G., 'Those god-damn flying saucers', unpublished article submitted to *Flight*, 1 March 1967, credit: Clive Williams

4. Squadron Leader R. G. Woodman, personal communication, 7 September 1987

5. Woodman, 'Those god-damn flying saucers', op. cit.

6. Ibid.

7. DEFE 41/74: Minutes of DSI/JTIC 10th Joint Meeting, 15 August 1950

8. *Daily Herald*, London, 7 June 1950

9. *Daily Mail*, London, 7 June 1950

10. DEFE 41/74: DSI/JTIC Minutes 1950–51

11. Ibid.

12. DEFE 41/74: Top Secret Annexe to minutes of DSI/JTIC 14th Joint Meeting, 10 October 1950

13. Juliet Formby, personal communication, 20 April 2001

14. DEFE 10/496

15. WO 279/690

16. DEFE 44/1: Letter from Hugo Young to Sir Henry Tizard, 10 October 1950

17. DEFE 41/75: Minutes of DSI/JTIC 11th Joint Meeting, 19 June 1951

18. DEFE 41/76 and DEFE 44/1: List and register of DSI/JTIC joint reports

19. I. D. Goode, Defence Records, personal communication, 6 November 2000

20. Ibid., 29 May 2001

21. DEFE 44/119: DSI/JTIC Report No. 7: Unidentified Flying Objects, 1951

22. Ibid.

23. Ibid.

24. Ibid., p.2

25. Juliet Formby, personal communication, 20 April 2001

26. DSI/JTIC Report No. 7, op. cit., p.2

27. Ibid., p.3

28. Ibid.

29. Ibid.

30. Wing Commander S. J. Hubbard, personal communication, 2 July 2001

31. Ibid.

32. Ibid.

33. Ibid.

34. DSI/JTIC Report No. 7, op. cit., p.3

35. Ibid.

36. Hubbard, op. cit.

37. DEFE 44/119: DSI/JTIC Report

No. 7: Unidentified Flying Objects, 1951, p.3

38. Hubbard, op. cit.

39. Wing Commander Frank Jolliffe, personal communication, 1 July 2001

40. Ibid.

41. Wing Commander S. J. Hubbard, personal communication, 2 July 2001

42. DSI/JTIC Report No. 7, op. cit., p.3

43. Ibid.

44. Ibid.

45. Ibid.

46. Ibid., p.6

47. Ibid.

48. Hubbard, op. cit.

49. Jolliffe, op. cit.

50. DEFE 44/119: DSI/JTIC Report No. 7: Unidentified Flying Objects, 1951, p.4

51. Ibid.

52. Ibid.

53. DEFE 41/75: Minutes of DSI/JTIC 11th Joint Meeting, 19 June 1951

54. Ibid.

55. DEFE 44/1: Letter from B. K. Blount to Sir Henry Tizard, 26 June 1951

Chapter 6:
The UFO Invasion

1. Joel Carpenter, posting on Project 1947 newsgroup, 22 January 2001

2. *The Times*, London, 30 July 1952

3. Connors, Wendy, and Hall, Michael, *Summer of the Saucers 1952*, Rose Press, Albuquerque, 2000, pp.267–81. *See also* Gilgoff, Dan, 'Saucers full of secrets', *Washington City Paper*, 14–20 December 2001

4. Carpenter, ibid.

5. Menzel, Donald, and Boyd, Lyle, *The World of Flying Saucers*, Doubleday and Co., New York,

1963, pp.155–63. For British reports *see* WO 95/14802 and AIR 2/18654.

6. Interview with M. J. E. Swiney, OBE, 28 April 2001

7. Horsley, Peter, *Sounds from Another Room*, Leo Cooper, London, 1997, p.174

8. Interview with M. J. E. Swiney, op. cit,

9. Ibid.

10. Horsley, op. cit., p.178

11. Swiney, op. cit.

12. AIR 20/9994: HQ No. 11 Group, 'Reports on Aerial Phenomena', 16 December 1956.

13. Swiney, op. cit.

14. AIR 29/2310: Operational Records Book, Central Flying School, 1952.

15. PREM 11/855: Memo from Winston Churchill to the Secretary of State for Air, 28 July 1952

16. PREM 11/855: Reply from the Secretary of State, 9 August 1952

17. PREM 11/855: Reply from Lord Cherwell, 14 August 1952

18. Sir Anthony Montague-Browne, personal communication, 26 November 2000

19. Ibid., December 2000

20. Ruppelt, Edward, *The Report on Unidentified Flying Objects*, Gollancz, London, 1956, p.257

21. US Philosophical Society: Condon Papers, file V3: Letter from B. V. Wilson, Royal Navy, to Dr Edward Condon, 18 March 1967

22. Noyes, Ralph, 'The magical mystery tour', *Magonia* 29 (April 1988), 3–5

23. AIR 20/7390: Signal to Air Ministry, 20 September 1952

24. *Sunday Dispatch*, London, 21 September 1952

25. Ibid.

26. Ibid.

27. Quoted ibid.

28. AIR 16/1199: Report by Flt. Lt.

J.W. Kilburn to AOC Topcliffe, 19 September 1952

29. Quoted in the *Sunday Dispatch*, London, 21 September 1952

30. Quoted in the *Sunday Pictorial*, London, 21 September 1952

31. Sir Peter Horsley, personal communication, 23 October 2000

32. Interview with Sir Peter Horsley, 11 November 2000

33. Noyes, 'The magical mystery tour,' p.4; Memorandum for the Record, USAF Special Study Group, 29 April 1952, credit: Jan Aldrich

34. Quoted in *News Chronicle*, London, 17 June 1952

35. Churchill Archives Centre, R. V. Jones Papers RVJO D137: Letter from R. V. Jones to Dr I. Gratton-Guinness, 15 May 1978

36. Chadwell, H. Marshall, 'British Activity in the Field of UFOs', CIA memorandum for the record, 18 December 1952 (released 13 July 2001)

37. Ibid.

38. AIR 40/2756: Air Intelligence organisation. *See also* Pitt, John, 'Tell us please, Mr Birch!', *FSR* 2/5 (September/October 1956), 11

39. Myles Formby, personal communication, 23 April 2001

40. William Owen Farrior, personal communication, 22 May 2001

41. Ruppelt, Edward, *The Report on Unidentified Flying Objects*, Gollancz, London, 1956, p.175

42. *Sunday Graphic*, London, 21 September 1952; Memo from Brigadier-General William Garland to Brigadier General Millard Lewis, ACS US Air Force in Europe, 12 May 1952, credit: Jan Aldrich

43. *Sunday Dispatch*, London, 28 September 1952

44. Ibid., 7 December 1952

45. Letter from I. D. Goode, Defence Records, MoD, 3 September 2001

46. AIR 2/16918

47. AIR 2/18117; Hansard, 2 February 1959

48. Australian National Archives: RAAF memo to Rt Hon A. G. Casey, Minister for External Affairs, 23 February 1954, credit: Bill Chalker

49. Australian National Archives: Memo from L. R. McIntyre to Rt. Hon A. G. Casey, 12 January 1955, credit: Bill Chalker

50. Ibid.

51. Haines, Gerald, 'A die-hard issue: CIA's role in the study of UFOs 1947–90', *Studies in Intelligence*, vol. 1, no. 1, 1997, 71

52. Fawcett, Lawrence, and Greenwood, Barry J., *Clear Intent*, Prentice-Hall, Englewood Cliffs, NJ, 1984, p.123, quoting memo from H. Marshall Chadwell to CIA Director Walter Smith, 24 September 1952

53. Ibid.

54. Haines, op. cit., p.71

55. Stacy, Dennis, 'UFOs and the CIA: the early years', *FSR* 31/4 (July/August 1985), 16

56. Gillmor, Daniel S. (ed.), *Scientific Study of Unidentified Flying Objects*, Vision, London, 1969, p.918

57. *See* Jones, R. V., *Most Secret War*, Hamish Hamilton, London, 1978, pp.378–79. In a letter dated 6 November 2000 the MoD informed us that the file relating to Jones' 1953 visit to the US, DEFE 40/27, 'remains sensitive and should continue to be retained in department .... [however] the file contains no references to UFOs'.

58. Jones, R. V., 'The natural philosophy of flying saucers', *Physics Bulletin* 19 (July 1968), 228

59. Ibid.

60. Air Commodore Peter Cribb, personal communication, 28 June 2001

61. Group Captain Harold Collins, personal communication, 17 April 2001

62. Aldrich, Jan, 'Origin of the CIRVIS Reporting System', unpublished MS, 2001

63. T. Johnson, personal communication, 11 December 2000; *Kent Messenger*, Maidstone, 13 November 1953

64. Geoffrey Smythe, personal communication, 5 December 2000

65. Ibid.

66. Ibid.

67. Quoted in the *Daily Express*, London, 19 November 1953

68. Ibid., 20 November 1953

69. *The Times*, London, 25 November 1953.

70. Geoffrey Smythe, op. cit.

71. AIR 20/9994

72. Ibid.

73. Christian Peterson, *Sunday Dispatch*, London, 24 April 1955

74. PREM 11/855: Minute from Anthony Montague-Browne to Duncan Sandys, MP, 14 March 1955

75. AIR 22/93: Air Ministry Secret Intelligence Summary 10/3 (March 1955): 'Flying Saucers ... an object was reported...'

76. Hansard (House of Commons), 4 May 1955, question by Major Sir Patrick Wall, 'Flying Saucers'

77. AIR 2/16918: Letter from Julian Ridsdale, MP, to Patrick Wall, MP, 3 August 1962

Chapter 7: Intercept UFO!

1. Personal communication, July 2001

2. Memo from H. Marshall Chadwell to Deputy Director (Intelligence), CIA, 11 September 1952, subject 'Flying Saucers'

3. *Montreal Gazette*, Montreal, 23 December 1960

4. Quoted in the *Guardian*, London, 30 November 1960

5. *Sunday Express*, London, 20 April 1958

6. Sir Edward Fennessy CBE, personal communication, 28 November 2001

7. Ibid.

8. AVIA 7/3783: Eastwood, E., Bell, J. D., Phelp, N. R., 'Ring angels over SE England', *Nature* 4677, 20 June 1959, 1,759–61

9. Gough, Jack, *Watching the Skies: The history of ground radar in the air defence of the UK*, HMSO, London, 1993, pp.139–40

10. DEFE 31/119; *see also* Hendry, Allan, *The UFO Handbook*, Sphere, London, 1979, pp.237–41

11. DEFE 31/118: HQ Fighter Command Air Staff Instruction No. F/1: Reporting of Unusual Aircraft or Aerial Phenomena, 10 October 1963

12. Ibid.

13. Hansard (House of Commons), 5 November 1996: Reply from Nicholas Soames to Martin Redmond, MP: 'Unidentified Flying Craft'

14. DEFE 31/118

15. Ibid.

16. John Bowden, personal communication, 8 August 2001

17. Ibid.

18. Quoted in RAF Air Defence Radar Museum *Newsletter* 28 (July 2001), 7

19. AIR 2/18564: Jones, R. F., 'Radar Echoes from Atmospheric Inhomogeneities', Air Ministry Meteorological Research Committee, 13 August 1952

20. DEFE 31/118: Air Ministry Secret Intelligence Summary 10/3 (March 1955); WO 195/14802: Spurious Echoes on Radar, 1959

21. Quoted in Hardy, Kenneth, 'Unusual Radar Echoes' in *UFOs: A scientific debate*, eds Carl Sagan and Thornton Page, Cornell University Press, Ithaca and London, 1972, pp.188–89

22. Ibid.

23. Quoted in the *Sunday Dispatch*, London, 17 November 1954

24. Ibid.

25. Creighton, Gordon, 'Friends or foes?: Those invisible squadrons overhead', *FSR* 29/4 (July/August 1984), 26–27

26. Wightman, David, 'Flying saucers on radar – mystery solved?', *Uranus* 5/2 (September/October 1958), 27

27. AIR 2/18564 and AIR 20/9320

28. Gillmor, Daniel S. (ed.), *The Scientific Study of Unidentified Flying Objects*, Vision, London, 1969, pp.163–64, 248–56; Hynek, Dr J. Allen, *The Hynek UFO Report*, Sphere, London, 1978, pp.129–34

29. National Archives, Washington: Project Blue Book: Air Intelligence Information Report IR-1-56, compiled by Captain Edward L. Holt, 31 August 1956

30. Ibid.

31. Grahame Schofield, personal communication, 16 May 2001. The Venom's tip tanks were recovered from a cornfield outside the Cambridge city boundary. The story never reached the local press.

32. Project Blue Book: Report from Captain George Gregory, ATIC to Washington, DC, September 1956

33. Project Blue Book: Teletype BOI-485 from Lakenheath to Colorado Springs, ATIC (Wright-Patterson AFB), Director of Intelligence (Washington, DC), 16 August 1956

34. Condon archive: Letter from Forrest Perkins to University of Colorado, received 13 February 1968

35. Ibid.

36. Interview with F. H. C. Wimbledon, 25 March 2001

37. AIR 29/1369; AIR 29/2631; Dennis Walmsley, personal communication, September 2001

38. AIR 20/12056: Letter from L. W. Ackhurst, S4 (MoD) to P. R. Smith, 31 March 1969

39. Project Blue Book: USAF teletype,

BOI-485, Lakenheath to Washington, 16 August 1956.

40. Wimbledon, op. cit.; R. G. Grocott, personal communication, 28 July 2001

41. Quoted in *The Sunday Times*, London, 9 April 1978

42. Perkins, op. cit.

43. Ibid.

44. BOI-485

45. Wimbledon, op. cit..

46. Ivan Logan, personal communication, 23 October 2000

47. Letter from F. H. C. Wimbledon to Gordon Thayer, 23 September 1978, credit: Martin Shough, quoted in *The Encyclopedia of UFOs*, ed. Ronald D. Story, Doubleday & Co., New York, 1980, p.201

48. Interview with F. H. C. Wimbledon, 25 March 2001

49. Interview with Ivan Logan, 12 November 2000

50. Grahame Schofield, personal communication, 16 May 2001

51. Interview with John Brady, 11 February 2001

52. Ibid.

53. Logan, op. cit., 23 October 2000

54. Brady, op. cit.

55. C. C. Smith, personal communication, 17 March 2001

56. Brady, op. cit.

57. 23 Squadron archive, RAF Waddington: 23 Squadron Diary: Monday, 13 August 1956, credit: Flt Lt Chris Hann

58. Gillmor, Daniel S. (ed.), *Scientific Study of Unidentified Flying Objects*, Vision, London, 1969, p.164

59. Menzel, Donald, and Taves, Ernest H., *The UFO Enigma: The definitive explanation of the UFO phenomenon*, Doubleday & Co., New York, 1977, p.92. Forrest Perkins, in a letter to Stanton Friedman dated 14 March 1975, claims the rotation of the radar antennae was increased to one revolution every nine seconds

during the incident. Credit: Martin Shough.

60. WO 195/14802: Spurious Echoes on Radar, 1959.

61. Clark, Jerome, *The UFO Encyclopedia*, vol. II, 2nd edition, Omnigraphics, Detroit, 1998, p.570

62. Project Blue Book: Report from Captain George Gregory, ATIC to Washington, DC, September 1956

63. Paul Fuller, personal communication, 17 April 2001; Meteorological Office archive, Bracknell

64. AIR 2/18564: Jones, R. F., 'Radar Echoes from Atmospheric Inhomogeneities', Air Ministry Meteorological Research Committee, 13 August 1952

65. Thayer, Gordon David, 'Lakenheath Bentwaters (England) Radar/Visual Sightings' in *The Encyclopedia of UFOs*, ed. Ronald D. Story, Doubleday & Co., New York, 1980, p.200

66. AIR 2/18564: Briefing from A. Giffen Peacock, DDI (Tech), Air Ministry, to S6, 11 April 1957

67. Ibid.

68. Air Vice Marshal Charles Moore, personal communication, 24 June 2001

69. Interview with F. H. C. Wimbledon, 25 March 2001

70. Ibid.

71. AF/S4f(Air)/422: UFOs: BBC Radio Oxford Programme, 1971–2

72. Letter from Janet Turner, DAS 4 (MoD), 26 October 2001

Chapter 8: Phantom Echoes

1. WO 195/14802: Radar and Signals Advisory Board: Spurious Echoes on Radar, 1959

2. AIR 20/9320: PQ: Stan Awbery, MP, 17 April 1957

3. AIR 2/18564: PQ: Patrick Wall MP: 4 May 1955

4. AIR 20/9320: PQ: Stan Awbery, op. cit.

5. AIR 20/9321: PQ: Patrick Wall, MP: 15 May 1957

6. AIR 2/18564: Briefing from DDI (Tech), Air Ministry, to US of S (RAF), 8 May 1957

7. *Air Pictorial*, January 2002, 70–71; Duncan Curtis, personal communication, December 2001

8. Ibid.

9. Ibid.

10. AIR 20/9994: Reports on Aerial Phenomena, December 1956

11. Personal communication, July 2001

12. Jenny Randles interview with Ralph Noyes, November 1995, credit: Jenny Randles

13. Ibid.

14. Ibid.

15. BJ 5/311: UFOs: Meteorological Aspects 1968–70

16. Quoted in Redfern, Nick, *A Covert Agenda*, Simon & Schuster, London, 1997, pp.54–55

17. Hansard (House of Lords), 4 March 1982

18. Ken England, personal communication, 7 August 2001

19. AIR 2/19564: Letter from Wing Commander W. P. Whitworth to S4 (MoD), 6 July 1971

20. Ibid.

21. Ibid.

22. AIR 20/9320

23. Ibid.

24. Morgan, Roger J., 'British government UFO files in the Public Record Office', *Magonia* 30 (August 1988), p.15

25. Quoted in the *Evening News*, London, 6 April 1957

26. AIR 2/18564: Letter from S4 (MoD) to W. P. Whitworth, 9 September 1971

27. AIR 2/18564: Memo from Wing Commander R. C. Skelton, DDI (Security), Air Ministry, to CO, RAF West Freugh, 18 June 1957

28. *Evening Standard*, London, 6 April 1957

29. *Sunday Graphic*, London, 7 April 1957

30. John Heptonstall, personal communication, 2000

31. Haines, Gerald K., 'A die-hard issue: CIA's study of UFOs, 1947–90', *Studies in Intelligence*, vol. 1, no. 1, 1997, p.73

32. Pendlow, G. W., and Welzenbach, D. E., 'The CIA and the U-2 Program, 1954–74', US Navy Fact Sheet 1998

33. AIR 2/18564; AIR 20/9320

34. Ibid.

35. Interview with Ralph Noyes, 1989: *UFO Brigantia* 48 (May 1991), 12

36. CAB 157/27: JIC 38th Meeting: Aerial Phenomena, 11 April 1957

37. JIC Weekly Intelligence Briefing (Red Book) 49, 12–17 April 1957, credit: Nick Redfern

38. *Reynolds News*, London, 17 June 1957

39. Pitt, John, 'Tell us please, Mr Birch!', *FSR* 2/5 (September/October 1956), 11

40. Letter from M. Lamb, Air Ministry to Major Donald Keyhoe (NICAP), 11 September 1957, credit: Richard Hall

41. Ibid.

42. AIR 2/18564: Memo from MO16 (Harrow) to AI (Tech) 5b, Air Ministry, 5 April 1960; Letter from Janet Turner, DAS (MoD), 26 October 2001

43. Ralph Noyes, 1989, op. cit.

44. DEFE 31/118: UFO Policy 1954–63: Memo from Flight Lieutenant Sheppard to Inf 2 (Air Ministry), 30 July 1958

45. Ibid.

46. DEFE 31/118: Memo from D. A. J. West, S6 (Air Ministry) to DDI (Tech), 26 August 1958

47. Letter from Ralph Noyes to Jenny

Randles, 11 April 1984, credit:
Jenny Randles

48. A. Bardsley, personal communication, 8 May 2001

49. Interview with Alex Birch, 6 November 1998

50. AIR 2/16918

51. Quoted in *FSR* 9/2 (March/April 1963), 7

52. Interview with David Brownlow, 3 December 1998

53. AIR 2/17527: Minute from A. Bardsley, AI 5b (MoD) to S4, 27 November 1964

54. DEFE 31/118: Minute from D. A. J. West, S6 (Air Ministry) to S4, 19 August 1958

55. *The Times*, London, 6 March 1959; *Guardian*, Manchester, 7 March 1959

56. CAB 159/31: JIC Meeting 18 March 1959, 'Aerial Phenomena'

57. Letter from Alan Glennie, Historical and Records Section, Cabinet Office, 9 April 2001

Chapter 9:
The Year of the Flying Cross

1. AIR 2/18117

2. Quoted in *The Times, Daily Express*, London, 25 October 1967

3. Quoted in the *Exeter Express & Echo*, Exeter, 24 October 1967

4. Ibid.

5. Quoted in the *Sun*, London, 25 October 1967

6. AF/S4f(Air)U/506: Statistical Analysis of UFOs

7. DEFE 31/119: Briefing, 2 November 1967: 'Causes of UFO Reports'

8. Ibid.

9. DEFE 31/119: Briefing 12 December 1967: 'Analysis of Reports from Service Sources'

10. AIR 20/11888

11. AIR 20/11887

12. AIR 20/11612

13. AIR 20/11612: Briefing, 26 October 1967

14. Quoted in the *Daily Express, Evening Standard*, London, 25 October 1967

15. AIR 20/11889

16. AIR 20/11889: Minute from W. P. Cassell, S4 (MoD), to US of S (RAF), 17 May 1968

17. Quoted in *The Times*, London, 9 November 1967

18. AIR 20/11612; AIR 2/18117

19. AIR 20/11612: Minute from Private Secretary for S of S (Air) to S4, 9 November 1967

20. Alex Cassie, personal communication, 15 May 2001

21. AIR 20/11612: Minute from J. E. Carruthers, S4 (MoD), to US of S (Air), 26 October 1967

22. AIR 20/11890: Report of visit by J. Dickison, DI 55, to Exeter Police Station (undated)

23. AIR 20/11612: Minute from W. P. Cassell to US of S (RAF), 19 December 1967

24. Ibid.

25. AIR 2/18115–7; AIR 20/11612; AIR 20/11887–92; DEFE 31/119

26. DEFE 31/119: Briefing, 2 November 1967: 'Causes of UFO Reports.'

27. Ibid.

28. Ibid.

29. Ibid.

30. Ibid.

31. DEFE 31/119: Minute from W. P. Cassell, S4 (MoD), to DSTI and RAF (Ops), 8 November 1967; AF/3459/75: UFO Policy 1970–75

32. DEFE 31/119: Policy document

33. AIR 20/11612; AIR 2/18117

34. DEFE 31/119: Briefing, 12 December 1967: 'Annexe B – US Air Force Studies'

35. AIR 20/11612: Minute from L. W. Ackhurst, S4 (MoD), to US of S (RAF), 13 January 1967

36. Ibid.

37. DEFE 31/119: Briefing by Wing Commander S. E. Munns, DI 61 (Air), to DSTI, 9 February 1967

38. Ibid.

39. DEFE 31/119: Minute from Group Captain F. V. Armstrong, Tech Int (Air) to DSTI, 9 February 1967

40. DEFE 31/119: Minute from A. O. Hunter, ADI/DI55, to A. Potts, DSTI, 13 June 1967

41. Ibid.

42. Ibid.

43. DEFE 31/119: Secret minute from Squadron Leader Eric Humpston, DI55b, to DSTI, 7 June 1967

44. DEFE 31/119: Minute from A. Potts, DSTI, to DGI Sir Alfred Earle, 19 June 1967

45. DEFE 31/19: Confidential minute from Air Commodore J. A. C. Aiken (Intelligence) to DGI Sir Alfred Earle, 27 June 1967

46. Ibid.

47. DEFE 31/119: Confidential minute from DGI Earle to DSTI, 29 June 1967

48. DEFE 31/119: Minute from D. Hanson, S4 (MoD), to DI55, 17 July 1967

49. Ibid.

50. AIR 20/18117

51. Ibid.

52. AIR 2/16117: Letter from L. W. Ackhurst, S4 (MoD), to R. G. Woodman, 14 December 1967

53. *The Times*, 15 November 1967; DEFE 31/119: Briefing from J. E. Carruthers, S4 (MoD), to DSTI and RAF: 'UFOs: Co-operation with the Americans and Russians', 20 November 1967

54. DEFE 31/119: Briefing from W. P. Cassell, S4 (MoD), to US of S (RAF): 'USAF Studies', 12 December 1967

55. DEFE 31/119: Letter from A. Potts, DSTI, to Air Commodore C. T. Nance, British Embassy, Washington, 17 August 1967

56. Condon papers: Letter from C. T. Nance, RAF, to Robert Low, University of Colorado, 25 October 1968

57. DEFE 31/119: Letter from A. Potts, DSTI, to Robert Low, 28 September 1967

58. DEFE 31/119: Confidential minute from A. Potts, DSTI, to DGI Sir Alfred Earle, 10 November 1967

59. DEFE 31/119: Minute from A. Potts, DSTI, to J. E. Carruthers, S4 (MoD), 7 November 1967

60. Jones, R. V., 'The Natural Philosophy of Flying Saucers', *see* Gillmor, Daniel S. (ed), *The Scientific Study of Unidentified Flying Objects*, Vision, London, 1969, p.230

61. Gillmor, op. cit., pp.922–33

62. Jones, op. cit., p.230

63. Ibid.

64. DEFE 31/119: Letter from A. Potts, DSTI, to R. V. Jones, University of Aberdeen, 6 November 1967

65. Churchill Archives Centre, R. V. Jones papers RVJO: D129: Letter from J. E. Carruthers, S4 (MoD), to R. V. Jones, 19 January 1968

Chapter 10:
They Knew Too Much...

1. Quoted in Spencer, John and Anne, *Fifty Years of UFOs*, [t/c], p.149

2. AIR 2/17983: UFOs, 1966

3. *See* Randles, Jenny, *MIB*, Piatkus, London, 1997, for the most recent summary of the MIB mythology.

4. *Rochdale Observer*, Rochdale, 23 February 1957

5. Ibid., 2 March 1957

6. Ibid., 23 March 1957

7. Hansard (House of Commons), 20

march 1957. 'Airborne Object, Wardle.' Reply by Mr. C.L. Orr-Ewing, Secretary of State for Air to Mr Leavey.

8. Quoted in the *Heywood Observer*, Heywood (Lancashire), 1 June 1989

9. Thornton, Clifford, 'The Wardle Mystery', *Flying Saucer Review* 3/3 (May–June 1957), 4

10. Quoted in the *Daily Herald*, London, 27 May 1957

11. Norris, Geoffrey, 'Something in the air', *RAF Flying Review*, vol. 12/11 (July 1957), 15

12. AIR 20/9320. The 'missing' file is referred to as PQ 121/57.

13. Good, op. cit., pp.45–46; Redfern, Nick, *A Covert Agenda*, Simon & Schuster, London, 1997, pp.61–62

14. *See* 'History of the D-Notice System', www.dnotice.org.uk/history.htm; Ayre, Richard, 'D for discredited', *UK Press Gazette*, 10 November 2000, 15

15. Good, Timothy, 'Are UFO reports subject in Britain to the D-Notice system and the Official Secrets Act?', *Flying Saucer Review* 28/3 (May–June 1983), 4–5

16. Ibid.

17. *See* Good, *Above Top Secret*, op. cit., pp.120–23; Redfern, *A Covert Agenda*, op. cit., pp.209–26; Redfern, Nick, *Cosmic Crashes*, Simon & Schuster, London, 1999, pp.222–54, 263–4, 267–70

18. Letter from Janet Turner, DAS 4 (MoD), 25 July 2001

19. Interview with Jim Templeton, 9 July 2001

20. Ibid. *See also Cumberland News*, 12 June 1964

21. Ibid.

22. Randles, Jenny, *MIB*, Piatkus, London, 1997, pp.83–88

23. AIR 2/17526; AF/7463/72 Pt 1 (Imperial War Museum)

24. Quoted in *Cumberland News*, 4 September 1964

25. Callaghan, Russell, 'The Cumbrian spaceman', *UFO Magazine* (UK), May–June 1997, 38–41

26. Interview with Nick Pope, 12 April 2001

27. AIR 20/12062: UFO Reports, August 1969

28. AIR 20/12055: UFO reports, January 1969

29. AIR 20/12055: Letter from L. W. Ackhurst, S4 (MoD), to Northumbria Police, 17 January 1969

30. AIR 20/12055: Statement by D. W. D. Robson to Northumbria Police, 23 January 1969

31. Ibid.

32. See Good, Timothy, *Above Top Secret*, Sidgwick & Jackson, London, 1987, pp.118–19, 226–27; Redfern, Nick, *Cosmic Crashes*, Simon & Schuster, London, 1999, pp.188–91

33. Air Commodore Peter Cribb, personal communication, 28 June 2001

34. AIR 20/12384: Memo from M.D. Ling, DI 55 to L.W. Ackhurst, S4 (MoD), 8 September 1971

35. Redfern, Nick, *The FBI Files*, Simon & Schuster, London, 1998, pp.289–317

36. 'Spies like us', *Guardian G2*, 11 September 2001

37. Memo: Director, Psychological Strategy Board, from Walter B. Smith, CIA Director, Subject: Flying Saucers, 1952

38. Moore, William L., 'The Crown of St Stephen and crashed UFOs', *Far Out Magazine* 1 (1992), 32–3

39. Tully, Andrew, *The Super Spies: A history of the CIA and the DIA*, Arthur Baker, London, 1969, p.78

40. *Independent*, London, 1 June 2001

Chapter 11:
Closer Encounters

1. AIR 2/17527: Letter from R. A. Langton, S4 (MoD), to Lt John Spaulding, USAF, 24 June 1965

2. Durant, Robert, 'Public opinion polls and UFOs', *UFO 1947–97*, John Brown Publishing, London, 1997, pp.230–39

3. Major Sir Patrick Wall, the Conservative MP for Humberside, asked a number of parliamentary questions on UFOs during his 30 years in the Commons. During the Cold War he was a military advisor to NATO but claimed he had no special knowledge of UFOs not available to the public. He later became the President of the British UFO Research Association (BUFORA).

4. BJ 5/311: 'Procedure for Investigating Unidentified Flying Objects', January 1968

5. Ibid.

6. AIR 20/11890

7. Brooks, Angus, 'Remarkable sighting near Dorset coast', *FSR* 13/6 (November/December 1967), 3–5

8. AIR 20/11890: L. W. Ackhurst, S4 (MoD): 'Note on the meeting with Mr Brooks of Overmoigne, Dorset', 14 March 1968

9. AIR 20/11890: Minute from Alex Cassie, Science 4 (RAF), 'UFO seen by Mr Angus Brooks', 5 April 1968

10. Ibid.

11. AIR 20/11890: Memo from Dr John Dickison, DI 55, 4 March 1968

12. AIR 20/11890: Letter from L. W. Ackhurst, S4 (MoD), to Angus Brooks, 5 April 1968

13. Ibid.

14. AIR 20/11890: Minute from M. D. Hobkirk, S4 (MoD), to US of S (Air), 13 May 1968

15. Spencer, John and Anne, *Fifty Years of UFOs*, Boxtree, London, 1997, pp.63 –67

16. AIR 20/11894

17. AIR 2/18117

18. AIR 20/12061

19. Ibid.

20. Ibid.

21. Interview with Nick Pope, 13 April 2001

22. Gillmor, Daniel S. (ed.), *The Scientific Study of Unidentified Flying Objects*, Vision, London, 1969, pp.1–6

23. AF/3459/75

24. AF/S4f(Air)/422: UFOs: BBC Radio Oxford Programme

25. Ibid.

26. AF/419: *Man Alive* Programme: UFOs; see also AIR 20/12377-12388: UFO Reports January-December 1971

27. BBC 2 *Man Alive: UFOs*, 2 February 1972; Producer: David Filkin

28. AF/419: Minute from DPR to US of S (RAF), 22 December 1971

29. AF/419: Minute from Air Commodore A. Davis, S4 (MoD) to DUS (Air), 6 January 1972

30. Ibid.

31. *Hull Daily Mail*, Hull, 22/23 October 1992; 'Captain Shaeffer's Last Flight', *FSR* 39/1 (Spring 1994), 16–21

32. Jennings, Michael, *RAF Coltishall: Fighter Station*, Station history (undated), 86–87. This account claims that Lightnings from QRA squadrons at Leuchars, Binbrook and Coltishall were involved in the hunt for the UFO. The ORB for 11 Squadron at Leuchars,(AIR 27/3018) lists four scrambles during September 1970 to intercept Russian 'badgers' but no activity on 8 September.

33. Dodd, Tony, *Alien Investigator*, Headline, London, 1999, pp.183–98

34. Ibid, 190–91

35. Bowman, Martin W., *English Electric Lightning*, Crowood Press, Marlborough, 1997, 148–50

36. Ibid, p.150; Interview with Nick Pope, 2001

37. Letter from M. L. Hatch, Air Historical Branch (RAF), 14 April 1999

38. Clarke, David, and Roberts, Andy, *Phantoms of the Sky*, Robert Hale, London, 1990, pp.55–62

39. *Daily Mirror*, London, 15 January 1974

40. Quoted in the *Daily Mail*, London, 29 January 1974

41. HO 371/74/94 'Alleged unauthorised helicopter flights in Derbyshire and Cheshire', March 1974; Letter from Andrew Brown, Metropolitan Police Records Branch, 8 March 2001

42. HO 371/74/94: Special Branch memo, 20 March 1974

43. HO 372/74/94: Special Branch memo, 22 March 1974

44. Redfern, Nick, *A Covert Agenda*, Simon & Schuster, London, 1997, pp.111–24; Redfern, Nick, *Cosmic Crashes*, Simon & Schuster, London, 1999, pp.124–45.

45. Roberts, Andy, 'Fire on the Mountain' in Randles, Jenny, Roberts, Andy, and Clarke, David, *The UFOs That Never Were*, London House, London, 2000, pp.144–64

46. AF/584: UFO Reports, January 1974

47. *The Times; Guardian*, London, 25 January 1974

Chapter 12:
Lights Through the Trees

1. D/Sec(AS)12/2/1 Part A: Letter from P. D. Watkins, DS8 (MoD), to Squadron Leader Donald Moreland, RAF Woodbridge, 9 November 1982

2. Randles, Jenny, 'Military contact alleged at air base', *FSR* 26/6 (November/December 1981

3. Butler, B., Street, D., and Randles, J., *Sky Crash*, Grafton, London, 1986, pp.12–16

4. Roberts, A., 'An Interview with Ralph Noyes', 1989; *UFO Brigantia* 41 (May 1991), 12–14

5. *World-Herald*, Omaha, Nebraska, 11 June 1979

6. Randles, Jenny, 'Impact – and after', *The Unexplained* 9/106 (1982), 2, 101–105

7. Watkins to Moreland, op. cit.

8. D/Sec(AS)12/2/1 Part A: Letter from Pam Titchmarsh, DS8 (MoD), to Jenny Randles, 13 April 1983

9. *News of the World*, London, 2 October 1983

10. Fawcett, Lawrence, and Greenwood, Barry J., *Clear Intent: The Government Coverup of the UFO Experience*, Prentice-Hall, Englewood Cliffs, NJ, 1984, pp.217–18

11. Randles, Jenny, *UFO Crash Landing?*, Blandford, London 1998, pp.96–124

12. D/DS8/10/209 Part A: Letter from Squadron Leader Donald Moreland to DS8 (MoD), 15 January 1981

13. Warren, Larry, and Robbins, Peter, *Left at East Gate*, Michael O'Mara, London, 1997; *see also Daily Express*, London, 28 December 2000

14. Randles, Jenny, *UFO Crash Landing?*, Blandford Press, London, 1998

15. Bruni, Georgina, *You Can't Tell the People*, Sidgwick & Jackson, London, 2000

16. Ridpath, Ian, 'The Rendlesham Forest UFO Case', www.debunker.com/texts/RidpathRendlesham1.html

17. Easton, James, 'Rendlesham revealed', *Fortean Times* 152 (November 2001), 28–31; www.rendlesham.com

18. Hansard (House of Commons), 24 October 1983: 'RAF Woodbridge (Alleged Incident)'

19. D/Sec(AS)12/2/1 Part A: 'UFO Sightings in Rendlesham Forest'

20. Interview with Nick Pope, 13 April 2001

21. D/Sec(AS)12/2/1 Part A: Letter from Ralph Noyes to Brian Webster, DS8 (MoD), 7 November 1984

22. Interview with Ralph Noyes, 1989: *UFO Brigantia* 41 (May 1991), 14

23. D/Sec(AS)12/2/1 Part A: 'UFOs: Report of sighting, Rendlesham Forest, December 1980'

24. Michael J. Tonnison, Director of Information Exploitation, MoD, personal communication, 2 October 2001

25. Interview with Nick Pope, 13 April 2001; Jenny Randles interview with Nick Pope, December 1995; Nick Redfern interview with Nick Pope, 1994; credit: Jenny Randles and Nick Redfern

26. Pope, Nick, 'The Rendlesham files revisited', *UFO Magazine* (October 2001), 48–52

27. D/Sec(AS)12/2/1 Part A: 'Defensive Press Briefing', 3 October 1983

28. D/DS8/10/209 Part A: Minute from C. P. Comper, DI 55 (MoD), to Ops(GE) RAF, 2 March 1981

29. D/DS8/10/209 Part A: Minute from R. Moorscroft ADI/DI52 to DI 55, 23 February 1981

30. D/Sec(AS)12/2/1 Part A: Handwritten note by Nick Pope, 15 April 1994

31. Quoted in Ridpath, Ian, 'Rendlesham Follow-up: Were the Radiation Readings Significant?' www.debunker.com/texts/RidpathRendlesham1.html

32. Ibid.

33. Pope, Nick, *Open Skies, Closed Minds*, Simon & Schuster, London, 1996, p.148

34. Interview with Nick Pope, 13 April 2001

35. Ridpath, op. cit.

36. Ibid.

37. Birdsall, M. I., and Olbison, V., 'Interview with Nick Pope, British MoD UFO office', *International UFO Reporter* 2/3 (Fall 1996), 21

38. Pope, 13 April 2001, op. cit.

39. D/Sec(AS)12/2/1 Part A: '*News of the World* article on UFOs', 3 October 1983

40. Butler, B., Street, D., and Randles, J., *Sky Crash*, Grafton, London, 1986, p.195

41. D. J. Coumbe, personal communication, 10 June 2001

42. Rayl, A. J. S., 'Baffled at Bentwaters', *OMNI* (April 1994), quoted in James Easton, 'Rendlesham Unravelled', www.rendlesham.com.

43. Good, Timothy, *Above Top Secret*, Sidgwick & Jackson, 1987, p.95

44. Butler, Street and Randles, op. cit., pp.32–34

45. Bruni, Georgina, *You Can't Tell the People*, Sidgwick & Jackson, London, 2000, pp.39–40; Interview with Nick Pope, 13 April 2001

46. Quoted in Redfern, Nick, *A Covert Agenda*, Simon & Schuster, 1997, p.148

47. D. J. Coumbe, personal communication, 10 June 2001

48. D/Sec(AS)12/2/1 Part A: Minute from Squadron Leader D. J. Coumbe, Eastern Radar, to MoD Ops (GE) RAF, 26 February 1981

49. D/Sec(AS)12/2/1 Part A: Minute from Squadron Leader J. D. Badcock, Ops (GE) RAF, to DS8 (MoD), 21 March 1983

50. D/Sec(AS)12/2/1 Part A: Letter from Ian Ridpath to Pam Titchmarsh, DS8 (MoD), 14 November 1983

51. Letter from Chief Constable, Suffolk Constabulary, to Ian Ridpath, 23 November 1983, credit: Ian Ridpath

52. D/Sec(AS)12/2/1 Part A: Letter from Squadron Leader Donald Moreland, RAF Woodbridge to Pam Titchmarsh, DS8 (MoD), 25 November 1983

53. Randles, Jenny, *UFO Crash Landing?*, Blandford, 1998, pp.103–15; Bruni, op. cit., pp.229–38, 279–80

54. D/Sec(AS)12/2/1 Part A: Minute from Badcock to DS8, 21 March 1983

55. Quoted in Easton, James, 'Rendlesham Unravelled', www.rendlesham.com

56. D/Sec(AS)12/2/1 Part A: Minute from Badcock to DS8, 21 March 1983

57. Ridpath, Ian, 'Rendlesham Follow-up: Were the Radiation Readings Significant?', www.debunker.com/texts/RidpathRendlesham1.html

58. Easton, op. cit.

59. Ridpath, op. cit.

60. DEFE 31/119: Briefing by J. E. Carruthers, S4 (MoD), to DSTI and RAF, 1 November 1967: 'Causes of UFO Reports'

61. Easton, James, 'The Chris Armold Interview', www.rendlesham.com

62. Mason, John, and Miles, Howard, 'Re-entry of Cosmos 749 Rocket on 1980, December 25', *Journal of the British Astronomical Association* 91/6 (1981), 564–66

63. Easton, op. cit.

64. Statement of Edward N. Cabansag, A1C USAF 81st Security Police Squadron, December 1980?

65. John Burroughs, personal communication to James Easton, 2001; credit: James Easton

66. Statement by John Burroughs, AIC USAF 81st SPS, January 1981

67. Bruni, Georgina, *You Can't Tell the People*, Sidgwick & Jackson, London, 2000, pp.187–97

68. Ibid., p.175

69. Statement by Flt Lt. Fred Buran, 81st SPS, RAF Bentwaters, 2 January 1981

70. Easton, James, www.rendlesham.com

71. Bruni, op. cit., pp.178–82

72. Easton, op. cit.

73. Interview with Ralph Noyes, 1989: *UFO Brigantia* 41 (May 1991), 14

Chapter 13: UFOs: No Defence Significance?

1. *The Times*, London, 23 April 2001

2. *Daily Express*, London, 29 July 1954

3. Memorandum for Record, USAF Special Study Group, 29 April 1952; credit: Jan Aldrich

4. Brookesmith, Peter, *UFO: The government files*, Blandford Press, London, 1996, p.166

5. Haines, Gerald K., 'A die-hard issue: CIA's role in the study of UFOs, 1947–90', *Studies in Intelligence* 1, 1997, 3

6. *Daily Express*, London, 12 January 1999

7. Ibid., 24 April 2001

8. Sheffield, Derek, *UFO: A deadly concealment*, Blandford Press, London, 1996; Pope, Nick, *Open Skies, Closed Minds*, Simon & Schuster, London, 1996, pp.130–35

9. Hansard (House of Commons), 24 July 1996: 'Uncorrelated Radar Tracks (Investigations)'

10. Ibid., 'Unidentified Craft'

11. Interview with Nick Pope, 13 April 2001

12. *The Sunday Times* (London), 5 May 1991

13. Svahn, Clas, and Liljegren, Anders, 'Close Encounters with Unknown Missiles', paper produced by UFO Sweden, 2000

14. Quoted in Gillmor, Daniel S. (ed.), *The Scientific Study of Unidentified Flying Objects*, Vision, London, 1969, p.520

15. Randles, Jenny, *The UFO Conspiracy*, Grafton, London, 1997, pp.200–204 (USA), 180–85 (France), 106–10 (Spain), 171–76 (Australia)

16. Fawcett, Lawrence, and Greenwood, Barry J., *Clear Intent: The government coverup of the UFO experience*, Prentice-Hall, Englewood Cliffs, NJ, 1984, p.xvi

17. Letter from I. D. Goode, Defence Records, MoD, 3 September 2001

18. AIR 2/18117

19. BJ 5/311: Minute to US of S (RAF) from G. W. Owens, S4, 24 March 1970

20. AF/3459/75: Letter from Royal Holloway College to S4, 10 April 1975

21. AF/3459/75: Internal briefing by G. J. Jamieson, S4, 2 June 1975

22. Ibid.

23. Randles, Jenny, 'The Ministry of Defence approach', *FSR* 24/3 (May/June 1978), 27–28

24. Coates, Tim (ed.), *UFOs in the House of Lords 1979*, The Stationery Office, London, 2000

25. Randles, *The UFO Conspiracy*, op. cit., pp.189–99

26. *Observer*, London, 4 March 1984

27. Randles, *The UFO Conspiracy*, op. cit., pp.197–98

28. Noyes, Ralph, *A Secret Property*, Quartet, London, 1985

29. Similar views were expressed by Air Vice Marshal Sir Victor Goddard at a public meeting in 1969. *See* Bowen, Charles, 'UFOs and psychic phenomena', *FSR* 15/4 (July/August 1969), 22–24

30. Letter to *Magonia* online magazine, April 1988

31. Quoted in Good, Timothy, 'The BBC TV interview with Lord Hill-Norton', *FSR* 28/4 (July/August 1983), 2–3

32. Letter from Gaynor South of AS2 to James Easton, 29 September 1999; credit: James Easton

33. Good, Timothy, *Alien Liaison*, Arrow, London, 1991, p.18

34. Letter from Janet Turner, DAS 4, MoD, 26 October 2001

35. Written answer from Nicholas Soames, MP, Ministry of Defence, to Martin Redmond, MP, 28 October 1996; credit: House of Commons Library

36. Randles, Jenny, *MIB: The Men In Black phenomenon*, Piatkus Books, London, 1997, p.209

37. Letter from Janet Turner, 26 October 2001

38. Ibid.

39. Spencer, John and Anne, *Fifty Years of UFOs*, p.150

40. Pope, Nick, *Open Skies, Closed Minds*, Simon & Schuster, London, 1996, 'author's note'

41. Lashmar, Paul, 'Britain's Secret History', *Violations of Rights in Britain*, series 2, no. 19, www.charter88.org.uk/pubs/violations/lasmar.html

42. *Guardian*, 26 October 2001

43. Parliamentary Ombudsman Case No. A.7/00 (1st Report Session 1998–99): Refusal to release information about incidents involving UFOs. *See also Observer*, 4 June 2000

44. Ralph Noyes, Letter to *Magonia* online magazine

45. Letter from DAS (MoD), 22 March 2001.

Glossary

AFOR	Air Force Operations Room
AI5/AI3	Air Intelligence 5b/3 (the Defence Intelligence branch responsible for UFO analysis *c.*1958–64)
AMES	Air Ministry experimental station (WWII term for RAF radar)
angels	Blips on early radar equipment caused by birds and insects
AP	Anomalous propagation (distortions to radar picture caused by meteorological phenomena)
AS2	*See* Sec(AS)2
ATC	Air traffic control (civilian radar)
ATIC	Air Technical Intelligence Center, Wright-Patterson Air Force Base, Ohio (base for USAF Projects Sign and Grudge, 1948–52)
blips	Unknown targets on air defence radar
BMEWS	Ballistic missile early warning system
CH	Chain Home
CHL	Chain Home Low
CIA	Central Intelligence Agency
contactee	Someone who claims to have been in direct physical contact with aliens. Usually refers to 1950s/60s encounters with tall 'Venusian'-type aliens.
DAS4	Department Air Staff 4, the MoD branch responsible for UFO issues 2001–present
DDI (Tech)	Deputy Directorate of Intelligence (Technical), Air Ministry branch responsible for UFO analysis, 1952–1964
DI55	Defence Intelligence 55 (DSTI branch responsible for UFO analysis, 1967–2000)
DIST	Defence Intelligence (Scientific and Technical), MoD, 1991–present.
DS8	Defence Secretariat 8, MoD branch responsible for UFO issues: 1972–85
DSI	Directorate of Scientific Intelligence MoD 1950–64
DSTI	Directorate of Scientific and Technical Intelligence, MoD, 1964–1991
ECM	Electronic counter-measures (radar jamming)
FBI	Federal Bureau of Investigation
flap	Series of UFO sightings witnessed in a localised area, usually within a short space of time
FOIA	Freedom of Information Act
foo-fighter	Term used by USAF for UFOs seen during WWII. Known to RAF as 'the thing' or 'the light'
FSR	*Flying Saucer Review*. Britain's oldest UFO magazine. Leans heavily toward the extraterrestrial hypothesis as the origin of UFO phenomena.

GCA	Ground-controlled approach (airport radar)
GCHQ	Government Communications Headquarters, Cheltenham
GCI	Ground-controlled interception radar system
ghost rockets	UFOs seen primarily over Scandinavia during 1946. Also known as 'mystery projectiles' and 'spook bombs'.
IFF	Identification friend or foe (civil aircraft transponder code)
JIC	Joint Intelligence Committee
JTIC	Joint Technical Intelligence Committee, MoD, 1950–54
MI5	Military Intelligence 5
MIB	Men in black
MoD	Ministry of Defence
MTI	Moving target indicator (radar technique used to eliminate stationary echoes, for example 'ground clutter')
NATO	North Atlantic Treaty Organisation
NORAD	North American Aerospace Defence Command
NSA	National Security Agency – USA electronic eavesdropping agency
ORB	Operations record books (RAF log books)
OSA	Official Secrets Act
PPI	Plan position pndicator (circular radar screen display)
PQ	Parliamentary question
PRO	Public Record Office
QRA	Quick reaction alert (term for RAF squadrons at readiness 24 hours to react to breaches of UK air defences)
RAF	Royal Air Force
S4/S6 (Air)	Air Ministry Secretariats responsible for UFO issues 1958–72
Sec(AS)2	Secretariat (Air Staff) 2A, MoD branch responsible for UFO issues, 1985–2000
Secret	MoD designation for papers that could endanger national security in unfriendly hands
SIS	Secret Intelligence Service (MI6)
specials	Term used by RAF radar personnel to denote overflights of secret or non-conventional aircraft (for example. U-2, Stealth)
Top Secret	MoD designation applied to papers which could cause exceptionally grave damage to the nation in the wrong hands
UFOlogist	Someone who is interested in or studies the subject of UFOs
UFOlogy	The study of reports of UFOs and flying saucers
USAAF	United States Army Air Force
USAF	United States Air Force
wave	Series of UFO sightings witnessed across a large geographical area, usually within a short space of time

Select Bibliography

Books

Brookesmith, Peter, *UFO: The government files*, Blandford Press, London, 1996

Clark, Jerome (ed.), *The UFO Encyclopedia* (2 volumes), second edition, Omnigraphics, Detroit, 1998

Clarke, David, and Roberts, Andy, *Phantoms of the Sky: UFOs, a modern myth?*, Robert Hale, London, 1990

Clarke, David, Randles, Jenny, and Roberts, Andy, *The UFOs That Never Were*, London House, London, 2000

Coates, Tim (ed.), *UFOs in the House of Lords 1979*, The Stationery Office, London, 2000

Connors, Wendy, and Hall, Mike, *Edward J. Ruppelt, Summer of the Saucers: 1952*, Rose Press, Albuquerque, 2000

Evans, Hilary, and Stacy, Dennis (eds), *UFO 1947–97*, John Brown Publishing Ltd, London, 1997

Fawcett, Lawrence, and Greenwood, Barry J., *Clear Intent: The government coverup of the UFO experience*, Prentice-Hall, Englewood Cliffs, NJ, 1984

Fowler, S., Elliott, P., Conyers Nesbit, R., and Goulter, C., *RAF Records in the PRO*, PRO Publications, London, 1994

Gillmor, Daniel S. (ed.), *The Scientific Study of Unidentified Flying Objects*, Vision, London, 1969

Good, Timothy, *Above Top Secret*, Sidgwick & Jackson, London, 1987

Gough, Jack, *Watching the Skies: The history of ground radar in the air defence of the United Kingdom*, HMSO, London, 1993

Hendry, Allan, *The UFO Handbook*, Sphere, London, 1979

Jones, R.V., *Most Secret War*, Hamish Hamilton, London, 1978

Lashmar, Paul, *Spy Flights of the Cold War*, Sutton Publishing, Stroud, 1996

Pope, Nick, *Open Skies, Closed Minds*, Simon & Schuster, London, 1996

Randles, Jenny, *The UFO Conspiracy*, Blandford Press, London, 1987

— *MIB: Investigating the truth behind the Men In Black phenomenon*, Piatkus Books, London, 1997

— *Something in the Air*, Robert Hale, London, 1998
  UFO Crash Landing?, Blandford Press, London, 1998

Redfern, Nick, *A Covert Agenda*, Simon & Schuster, London, 1997

— *The FBI Files*, Simon & Schuster, London, 1998

— *Cosmic Crashes*, Simon & Schuster, London, 1999

Ruppelt, Edward J., *The Report on Unidentified Flying Objects*, Gollancz, London, 1956

Articles

Haines, Gerald K., 'A die-hard issue: CIA's role in the study of UFOs, 1947–90', *Studies in Intelligence: Semiannual Unclassified Edition* 1 (1997), 67–84

Jones, R.V., 'The natural philosophy of flying saucers', *Physics Bulletin* 19 (July 1968), 225–30

Morgan, Roger J., 'British government UFO files in the Public Records Office', *Magonia* 30 (August 1988), 12–15

Index